Undermining Rural Development with Cheap Credit

Westview Special Studies in Social, Political, and Economic Development

Undermining Rural Development with Cheap Credit

edited by Dale W Adams, Douglas H. Graham, and J. D. Von Pischke

In the past several decades large amounts of money have gone into agricultural credit programs in low-income countries. The results of these efforts have often been disappointing: Serious loan-recovery problems persist, the rich get most of the cheap loans, low interest rates discourage local savings deposits, political intrusions are common, and many financial institutions in low-income countries are floundering. The contributors to this book cite ubiquitous low-interest-rate policies and improper use of financial markets as principal reasons for these problems, recommending that higher and more flexible interest-rate policies be allowed and that little or no attention be given to specifically targeted loans. They also argue that informal lenders provide more valuable services than is generally thought and that voluntary savings capacities in rural areas may be substantial. Less emphasis on discouraging the informal lender, more emphasis on voluntary savings mobilization, and more access to formal loans by nonfarm rural firms are other policy changes recommended in this comprehensive survey. The authors conclude that many traditional agricultural credit programs in fact undermine efficient, equitable rural development, whereas attractive product and input prices, along with higher yields, would be much more powerful ways of stimulating rural development.

Dale W Adams, a former staff economist with AID, is currently professor of agricultural economics at Ohio State University. **Douglas H. Graham** is professor of agricultural economics and director of the Latin American Studies Program at Ohio State University. **J. D. Von Pischke** is senior financial analyst in the Economics and Policy Division of the Agriculture and Rural Development Department of the World Bank.

Undermining Rural Development with Cheap Credit

edited by Dale W Adams,
Douglas H. Graham,
and J. D. Von Pischke

Routledge
Taylor & Francis Group
NEW YORK AND LONDON

First published 1984 by Westview Press, Inc.

Published 2021 by Routledge
605 Third Avenue, New York, NY 10017
2 Park Square, Milton Park, Abingdon, Oxon OX14 4RN

Routledge is an imprint of the Taylor & Francis Group, an informa business

Library of Congress Cataloging in Publication Data
Main entry under title:
Undermining rural development with cheap credit.
(Westview special studies in social, political, and economic development)
Includes index.
1. Agricultural credit—Developing countries.
2. Rural development—Developing countries—Finance.
3. Saving and investment—Developing countries
I. Adams, Dale W. II. Graham, Douglas H. III. Von Pischke, J. D. IV. Series.
HD1440.D44U53 1984 332.7′1′091724 83-26074
ISBN 0-86531-768-2

ISBN 13: 978-0-3672-1268-1 (hbk)
ISBN 13: 978-0-3672-1549-1 (pbk)

We dedicate this book to the hundreds of millions of rural poor in low-income countries who get neither cheap credit nor decent returns on their savings and do not understand why; to the thousands of employees of agricultural banks and cooperatives who give their best to credit programs that work poorly, for reasons beyond their control; and to the hundreds of policymakers who try to help the rural poor, but can think of no better way to do so than through cheap credit.

Contents

Part 4
New Directions for Rural Financial Markets

Tables and Figures

Tables

Figures

Preface

Numerous people and organizations contributed to this book. Graduate students labored with mounds of data, donor-agency employees supported the research that led to the conclusions reported here, and large numbers of policymakers, technicians, and academicians in low-income countries shared their views and time with the chapter authors. Many of the presentations included here were sharpened through seminars, conferences, and workshops held over the past dozen years in Bangladesh, Bolivia, Brazil, Canada, Costa Rica, the Dominican Republic, Ecuador, England, Ghana, Guyana, Jamaica, Kenya, Nepal, Panama, the Philippines, Thailand, Tunisia, Turkey, and the United States. More than 2,000 people participated in these meetings; their insights and experiences added a great deal to our thinking about rural financial markets policy.

The 23 chapters in this book also draw heavily on research and consulting work done by the authors in about four-dozen countries. Two organizations have been particularly helpful in these efforts. The first is the U.S. Agency for International Development (AID), which has supported research on rural financial markets for almost 20 years. The patience of its staff in allowing academicians time and money to work through complicated issues is remarkable, given political pressures for quick results. We want to especially thank the AID employees who were monitors or supporters of our various research projects. They include Gary Adams, Clifton Barton, David Bathrick, Ralph Battles, Charles Blankstein, Albert Brown, Roberto Castro, Douglas Caton, Lewis Clark, Harlan Davis, William Douglass, Robert Firestine, Jerry French, Paul Fritz, Lawrence Harrison, Harlan Hopgood, John Hyslop, Donor Lion, Erven Long, Robert Meehan, Thomas Mehen, E. B. Rice, William Rodgers, Frank Sheppard, Douglas Tinsler, Don Wadley, Raymond White, and Stephen Wingert. They took care of country clearances, wrote project proposals, made travel arrangements, processed expense accounts, and set up meetings that made our work possible.

The second organization we'd like to single out is the Economic Development Institute of the World Bank. For a number of years it has taken the lead, through project courses, in bringing new thinking about development problems into practice. Institute staff members were particularly helpful in setting up a Colloquium on Rural Finance in Low-Income Countries in September 1981 in Washington, D.C., at which many of the papers in this volume were presented. J. Price Gittinger, Walter Schaefer-Kehnert, Jean Martin, and Vanessa Ward were largely responsible for the arrangements for the colloquium, and we thank them for their efforts.

The views presented in this book should not be attributed to AID or the World Bank, to individuals acting on their behalf, or to organizations affiliated with or receiving support from these agencies. The editors and authors contributing to this volume have done so exclusively in their personal capacities. The usual disclaimers apply.

Dale W Adams
Douglas H. Graham
J. D. Von Pischke

Introduction

Cheap and abundant credit is often regarded as essential for rural development. This assumption has led donor agencies and governments in developing countries to aggressively promote loans to farmers. Their efforts have resulted in large increases in the volume of loans made and the creation of new agricultural credit agencies and rural credit projects. The intent of these activities was to help the poor increase agricultural production by encouraging them to use new technologies and by compensating farmers for government price and investment policies that damaged their interests. Among others, Brazil, India, Jamaica, Mexico, the Philippines, and Thailand have used agricultural credit programs as a main component of their rural development strategies.

Despite the optimistic expectations of their sponsors, the results of these programs have been disappointing. Loan-default problems are often serious. Most poor farmers are still unable to obtain formal loans, and those who succeed in using such credit are often unnecessarily and inequitably subsidized. Many agricultural banks and other specialized formal lenders serving rural areas are floundering, and as a result they often severely limit the range of services they provide. Few aggressively offer savings-deposit facilities, for example. Their medium- and long-term loan portfolios are supported almost entirely by resources provided by government and development assistance agencies rather than by resources mobilized directly from savers and investors.

These problems persist after three decades of development assistance. They endure in spite of the fact that some governments have nationalized their banks in efforts to expand credit access, while others have piled regulation on regulation in an attempt to improve the performance of rural financial markets. Despite institutional and cultural diversity, similar problems fester in a large number of countries. Credit programs tend to self-destruct, and policymakers are largely resigned to recurring institutional problems and poor financial results from rural credit programs. A few of these problems can be attributed to unique factors, but the common symptoms imply universal explanations and raise serious questions about the effectiveness of treatments traditionally prescribed to overcome the problems.

Recent Research and Evaluation

The increase in rural financial market activity by governments and donors has created a parallel expansion in research and evaluation. The U.S. Agency for International Development (AID) has taken the lead in funding research on agricultural credit, rural savings, rural capital formation, and rural financial markets in developing countries. Ohio State, Arizona State, Michigan State, and Syracuse universities have been the main U.S. institutions participating in these research efforts, in cooperation with universities and research institutions in other countries. In 1972–1973, AID sponsored an extensive survey of credit programs in developing countries, called the Spring Review of Small Farmer Credit. The review, led by E. B. Rice, resulted in the publication of 20 Spring Review volumes plus a book by Gordon Donald entitled *Credit for Small Farmers in Developing Countries.* The Spring Review synthesized the results of research on agricultural credit and described the extent of the problems found in rural financial markets. Later conferences by the Food and Agriculture Organization (FAO) of the United Nations and studies sponsored by the World Bank further explored the problems.

A sampling of some 50 articles on rural finance practices and efforts to find more satisfactory ways of delivering rural financial services can be found in *Rural Financial Markets in Developing Countries: Their Use and Abuse,* edited by J. D. Von Pischke, Dale W Adams, and Gordon Donald. That volume was prepared under the auspices of the Economic Development Institute (EDI) and published for the World Bank in 1983. The collection of articles for that volume was undertaken to provide a comprehensive description and analysis of financial program performance and originated through curriculum development efforts for the EDI rural credit projects training courses. This task stimulated support for a forum in which research results and policy prescriptions could be presented to, and discussed with, practitioners in development assistance agencies. Accordingly, a Colloquium on Rural Finance in Low-Income Countries was sponsored by EDI, AID, and The Ohio State University in Washington, D.C., on September 1–3, 1981. Papers presented at the colloquium make up the bulk of the book before you. Discussion in the colloquium was oriented toward diagnosis of rural financial market performance in developing countries and proposed remedies for existing problems.

The Major Arguments

The arguments presented in colloquium papers were controversial: They challenged traditional thinking about agricultural credit and rural savings. The authors of these arguments questioned the way credit projects are designed and evaluated and advocated a major overhaul in the way financial markets are manipulated by governments and donors to support development. Five points were stressed. First, the view that credit is an input was criticized because it supports policies and projects that are detrimental to rural financial market performance. Second, traditional assumptions about agricultural credit were challenged. Third, cheap-credit policies were pinpointed as the most important factor causing agricultural credit programs to miscarry. Fourth, it was argued that political considerations often block rural financial market reform. And, fifth, it was concluded that the results of recent research and evaluation could contribute to the improvement of rural financial market performance.

The Nature of Credit. Viewing credit as an input, like fertilizer, causes people to conclude that farmers have specific credit needs that can be met by delivering predetermined amounts of loans to farmers. This approach leads policymakers and sponsors to measure the impact of additional loans in terms of how many hectares of rice were financed, how many tons of fertilizer were used, how many additional sacks of potatoes were produced, and how borrowers' incomes were affected by the loans. This has resulted in credit-impact studies that were fruitless, because the underlying assumption that credit is an input—rather than part of the financial intermediation process—ignored the essential property of financial instruments, their fungibility.

Farm inputs are specialized by function. Seeds produce plants, fertilizer stimulates plant growth, and diesel fuel powers engines. A loan is not an input, because its fungibility gives the borrower command over any good or service that can be purchased. A loan provides additional liquidity or purchasing power for use in any of the borrower's production, investment, or consumption activities. Most farmers in developing countries have several farm enterprises, engage in multiple occupations, and have a number of potential uses for additional liquidity. Measurement of the impact of a loan requires the collection of costly information on all changes in these sources and uses of liquidity that are contemporary with loan receipt and then a comparison of the "with" and "without" loan situations. Because the "without-loan" case can be specified only through assumption and conjecture, loan impact can never be determined with certainty.

It is much more appropriate to view credit as a product of financial intermediation. Acceptance of this view results in fewer attempts to measure the impact of loans on borrowers and more attention to the behavior of savers and financial intermediaries and to the overall performance of financial systems. It also directs more attention toward measurement of the costs of using and providing financial services and highlights the effects of policies and of technological change on financial markets.

The Traditional Assumptions. Another major theme of the colloquium was that commonly accepted assumptions about rural financial markets, savings behavior in rural areas, and agricultural credit were weak, untested by appropriate research, or wrong. A thorough airing of assumptions that underlie agricultural credit activities in developing countries is a necessary reform ingredient. Some of the most important assumptions challenged at the colloquium were: (1) borrowers are highly sensitive to interest rates, whereas lenders are not; (2) rural households will not or cannot save in financial form, making it useless for financial institutions to try to mobilize voluntary savings in rural areas; (3) lender behavior can be closely controlled by nationalizing banks or by means of adminstrative directives; (4) the informal financial system in rural areas does not provide socially useful services; and (5) cheap credit can be effectively used to help the poor and to offset the adverse effects on farmers of certain economic policies. Challenges to these assumptions clearly threaten policies built on the assumptions.

Popular Policies. The agricultural credit policy most widely applied by governments is concessionary interest rates that are often lower than the rate of inflation. Cheap credit was the object of much criticism during the colloquium. Although low rates have often been defended as helping the poor, strong arguments were made that the rich are the main beneficiaries because they are the largest borrowers. It was further argued that cheap credit causes inefficient resource allocation, undermines lending institutions, and politicizes financial markets. Colloquium speakers concluded that cheap-credit policies seriously restrict the contribution that financial markets make to development and that more flexible nominal interest rates are required to improve performance.

The Powerful Political Inertia of the Status Quo. A frequent observation by colloquium speakers was that reforms in financial market policies are more often blocked by political obstacles than by economic forces, so that political economy becomes important in explaining events in financial markets. Many political leaders find that intrusions into financial markets are irresistible. It is easy to announce a major increase in the amount of cheap credit to accompany programs directed toward self-sufficiency in a major food crop, to spur the introduction of a new technology, to respond to a rural disaster, or to reward or enlarge groups that support the government. Political opponents of the regime or others concerned about this use of financial markets find it very difficult to attack such efforts; attacks on cheap credit are often regarded as criticism of the activity for which credit is ostensibly provided or of the intended recipients of the loans. The social and economic costs of interest rates kept low by government directive are so poorly understood, and generally hidden, that cheap credit often appears to be an exception to the economic law that there is no free lunch. The highly concentrated benefits, but widely diffused costs, of cheap credit make it an ideal form of political patronage.

No formula was presented in the colloquium for handling these political problems. It was argued, however, that some damaging policies were sustained by incomplete understanding of their adverse effects. Where good intentions produce unanticipated, perverse results, more careful documentation of the performance of financial markets may lead to appropriate reforms.

On the other hand, where financial markets are an overtly important way of allocating political patronage, there is much less chance for reform. Groups in society with power to extract and maintain access to subsidies through cheap credit often also obtain privileged use of other politically created protection through trade concessions, product and factor price controls, fiscal incentives, and access to social services. With lines of power so firmly drawn, politicians and development planners often have little latitude to use other policy changes to buy off opposition to financial market reform. Those who currently receive cheap credit have already effectively mined these other policy options. Under these circumstances, advocates of reform can expose the economic and social results of cheap-credit policies so that the allocation of patronage through financial markets cannot be so easily hidden behind slogans of equity, efficiency, or economic nationalism. Experience suggests that even in these cases liberalization may become a more attractive option in periods of economic stagnation or deterioration. Efforts at reform may thus produce meaningful policy changes only once every 5 or 10 years.

Research Results and Reform Proposals. Traditional ideas about rural financial markets in developing countries die very hard. Stereotypes and conventional wisdom strongly influence the way government and development planners use and abuse rural financial markets. The central theme of this volume is that this traditional thinking often leads to costly and sometimes counterproductive policies and that financial markets would make a much more positive contribution to rural development if appropriate policy changes were adopted. These changes would require a major reorientation toward financial markets. For example, agricultural credit is not an input, and a financial system is more than a set of channels for disbursing loans. Instead, agricultural credit results from processes of financial intermediation in which many very innovative decision makers participate. Further, claims on resources that move through financial markets are fungible at all levels, and it is costly and difficult—some would say impossible—to target their end use effectively. Attempts to redistribute income in favor of the poor through manipulation of financial markets increase, rather than lessen, income concentration.

Maintaining positive real rates of interest on both credit and savings instruments is the most important element in improving rural financial market performance. Where administered rates are kept low, higher rates of interest would allow formal financial intermediaries to mobilize larger amounts of voluntary savings in rural areas. This would benefit many people whose opportunities to hold savings in high-return, secure forms are presently limited.

Accumulation of rural savings in financial form would also diminish or erase the patronal relationships that currently exist between rural borrowers, rural financial intermediaries, central banks or other authorities funding rural credit projects, and—in some cases—donor agencies. Weakening rural dependence by increasing incentives for accumulation of financial assets by rural households would, in turn, reduce the scope for politicalization of rural financial markets and would increase intermediaries' incentives to respond more dynamically to the interests of their depositors rather than to the whims of politicians and planners. The lessening of lenders' dependence on soft sources of funds would encourage them to seek new business and to place more emphasis on creditworthiness and its creation. Broadening and deepening of formal financial intermediation would also increase competition among formal and informal lenders and reduce any monopoly profits that exist in these markets.

The changes in policies suggested by the authors in this book would require reorientation of much agricultural credit research and evaluation. Trying to measure credit need and impact at the farm level would no longer be a major concern. Instead, attention would be focused on explaining the behavior of rural financial intermediaries, an effort that would include documenting the costs and returns associated with various financial services, such as mobilizing rural savings, lending to small borrowers versus lending to large borrowers, and accommodating the seasonality of liquidity flows in agricultural areas. This emphasis would result in a better understanding of the elements required to build rural financial institutions. More attention would be directed toward measuring the performance of the entire rural financial market, with greater sensitivity to and understanding of those features of informal intermediaries that enable them to outperform the formal market in providing certain types of service to the poor.

A Challenge To Readers

The 23 chapters that follow report on research done in more than 25 countries. Most of the authors draw on their experiences in several countries to identify common problems, causes, and treatments, moving beyond the single-project, one-country perspectives that have so often characterized analysis of agricultural credit. Several papers not presented at the colloquium have been included to improve the flow of the presentation and to elaborate on the general theme of the book.

Some readers may strongly object to arguments presented in this book—or to reject them out of hand—because the points made appear counterintuitive or are contrary to many widely held "truths." We firmly believe that readers with the patience to take in the whole discussion will be rewarded with a clearer understanding of those factors that undermine the developmental impact of rural financial markets and will then see more clearly the types of policy changes that could alter the tendency of rural credit portfolios to degrade.

Part 1

Problems in Rural Finance

1
Effects of Finance on Rural Development

Dale W Adams

Suspicions and value judgments have permeated reports on financial activities since man began to record history. The motives and morals of lenders are regularly questioned, and many feel that it is difficult, if not impossible, for financial intermediaries to enjoy a pleasant afterlife. Such negative thinking can obscure the substantial advantages that finance brings to a modern economy—changes that dissolve barter and induce a rapid increase in financial intermediation, resulting in economic growth. Suspicion also nurtures the regulation of financial markets, especially in rural areas, and clouds understanding of the effects that finance has on development. Because policymakers and development technicians poorly understand the basic functions of finance, they often institute policies that damage or limit finance's contribution to development.

It is easy to overlook the importance of financial markets because financial intermediation is a diffused, subtle process that involves a large number of actors and takes place in bits and pieces. Only parts of these activities leave tracks on accounting systems; loans among friends and relatives, activities in rotating credit-savings associations, and merchant credits are typically not recorded. It is also difficult to nail down cause and effect in financial markets because of the fungibility of financial instruments. Illusions of control have reinforced fuzzy thinking by policymakers about the operations of financial markets. Controls, however, are often neutralized because lenders and borrowers can appear to be responding to the intent of regulations, while in fact they are doing something quite different. This appearance of control and compliance lulls policymakers into concentrating their attention on other areas where performance problems are more readily apparent. Governments and donor agencies have felt unreasonably comfortable, as a result, in rapidly expanding the amount of agricultural credit available in many low-income countries. They evidently believe that this supply-led strategy of finance stimulates production, causes more new technology to be adopted, and helps the poor.

In the past two decades some observers have begun to challenge those traditional assumptions and the policies that surround financial intermediation, especially in rural areas (Adams and Graham 1981). Early work by Goldsmith (1969) has documented the growth in financial activities that occurs with overall growth in an economy. Other work by Gurley and Shaw (1960) and Patrick (1966) clarified some of the contributions that finance makes to development. Shaw's work was particularly useful in stimulating others to dig more deeply into how regulations affect financial intermediation. He helped set aside the notion that financial intermediation was only a thin veil that lightly connected consumers and producers in an economy, bringing into focus the true nature of firms in the financial sector and the fact that these firms produced goods and services that were very useful. In this volume, Vogel in Chapter 11 and Gonzalez-Vega in Chapter 10 place particular emphasis on how rural financial markets affect income distributions as well as resource allocation. As is pointed out in other chapters in this volume, a number of people have come to feel that rural financial markets in low-income countries are performing poorly and that this is due to incorrect thinking, wrong assumptions, and resulting faulty policies.

In the discussion that follows, the main effects that financial intermediation have on rural development are outlined. I start by pointing out the ways finance benefits individual firms and households and then move to a discussion of how finance affects rural service organizations. The next topic treated is how finance influences the distribution of resources among groups and sectors in an economy. This is followed by a brief discussion of how financial and political systems relate. The final section of this chapter presents suggestions on improving the contributions of finance to rural development.

Finance and the Firm or Household

It has been common to overlook the benefits that firms and households realize from finance. Long-held biases against being in debt have been reinforced by the pain suffered by some who lose their property through loan default. Nothing is more odious than a moneylender taking the collateral of a financially pressed borrower. The fact that economic misfortune forces some people to go into debt also tends to couple debt with adversity.

It is curious that the discomforts caused by a few people going into debt and not being able to repay tend to dominate general views held about financial intermediation. The use of extreme cases to make general points is refined to an advanced art form in discussions about financial markets. Stories about poor farmers who lose their land to evil moneylenders are retold until people think that most loans go to default and that all lenders of money regularly take away loan collateral. These biases ignore the much, much larger number of borrowers and savers who greatly benefit from financial intermediation.

If all firms and households were alike, there would be little need for financial intermediation. As Meyer and Alicbusan point out in Chapter 2, rural household heterogeneity provides a fertile environment for financial intermediation. Individuals or firms may decide to use the services of a financial intermediary for a number of reasons. One is that financial instruments allow the user to reduce the costs of exchanging real resources. A rural family, for example, can buy a draft from a local bank to pay school fees for a child studying in the capital city. This is less expensive than taking farm produce by bus to the city to exchange with the headmaster of the school. Generating and transferring these claims on resources is an important service provided by financial intermediaries.

A second and more important advantage of financial intermediation is the achievement of more efficient resource allocation. Because of the heterogeneity that exists in rural areas, households and firms may have very different investment and consumption alternatives. At the same time they may experience excesses or shortages of liquidity to respond to these opportunities. A simple example using three widely dispersed corn farmers in a low-income country may help to illustrate this important point. Farmer A, who is elderly, lives on a very productive farm 10 kilometers north of the nearest town, Pueblo Viejo. He expects to receive very low rates of return at the margin, nevertheless, on any additional investments he makes, such as using more fertilizer on his corn. He is satisfied with his current consumption, is trying to put away something for his old age, and is holding a good deal of cash. But he is worried about keeping the cash in the house because of theft and wants to keep the money out of sight so that relatives do not ask for loans. He would also like to get a return from his funds.

Farmer B lives on his farm located 10 kilometers east of Pueblo Viejo. A good farmer, he is middle-aged. He and his family want to buy a television set for family entertainment, but because unusual flooding reduced the corn yields substantially during the past six months, they do not have sufficient liquidity to make the purchase.

Farmer C is a young man who lives on his farm located about 10 kilometers south of Pueblo Viejo. He recently inherited a parcel of land that was covered with brush. He has cleared most of the land and knows that he can get a high corn yield if he can apply moderate amounts of chemical fertilizer. Unfortunately, he has only enough cash to cover costs of seed purchases and family consumption until harvest.

Distance and lack of information preclude Farmers A, B, and C from making face-to-face exchanges in claims on resources. Without financial intermediation, Farmer A will remain unsatisfied because of holding a significant part of his savings in cash, Farmer B and his family will not be able to enjoy watching television, and Farmer C will be unable to buy the fertilizer that would substantially increase his corn yield and income. Substantial gains would occur to all involved if a financial intermediary were to set up shop in Pueblo Viejo, accept deposits from Farmer A and others, and extend loans to Farmers B and C, who are both willing to pay a premium to the intermediary for this service. They expect to receive considerable additional satisfaction or income from the things they buy with the borrowed claims on resources. Farmer A (and other savers) would be pleased with the arrangement because it would provide a safer place to keep money. The intermediary also would be pleased because he or she is rewarded for services by the difference between what is paid to Farmer A for his savings and what is received from the borrowers in interest payments. Society is also better off because output of corn has been increased through the more efficient allocation of resources resulting from exchanges of claims on resources through financial intermediation.

A third advantage of financial intermediation comes through gains in risk management. Rural households and firms are typically subject to large variations in income and expenditures. Agricultural production is heavily dependent on the vagaries of weather, and price variations on agricultural products are often substantial. The rhythm of production in agriculture also contributes to this problem. Production expenses may be heavy during planting periods, and incomes are largely realized with harvest. These variations and instability in sources and uses of liquidity force rural firms and households to be very concerned with risk management.

A number of traditional ways exist for individuals to manage risk. Complex land-tenure arrangements, multiple parcels of land and enterprises, diversified sources of income, and extended family relationships are some common techniques. Households also may manage risks through holding various kinds of assets, through labor-exchange arrangements, and through loans. This includes not only the occasional use of loans but also the maintenance of unutilized credit reserves that can be called on in emergencies. Loans and savings deposits can be important and relatively inexpensive ways for many of the rural households to manage part of their risks.

A fourth advantage of financial intermediation is that it facilitates the acquisition of large investments or large consumer durables. A loan may allow a farmer to buy a tractor years before being able to save enough to buy one with cash. The tractor may help the farmer to generate more than enough additional income to repay the loan. Systematic saving in deposit accounts may also allow a household to accumulate enough funds to buy the same tractor or some large consumer durable. The intermediary can benefit large numbers of households by accepting their short-term deposits and providing a few borrowers with term loans. The scale of an intermediary's operations allows the transformation of the term of these claims on resources to the benefit of both savers and borrowers. The saver does not have to sacrifice liquidity to get a return on savings, and the intermediary can rely on large numbers of depositors for a steady flow of short-term deposits to provide the claims necessary to meet long-run borrowing requests. Again, savers, borrowers, and intermediaries all gain from the transformation of term structures that takes place through intermediation. Lending directly by savers to borrowers or even lending by informal moneylenders cannot provide the liquidity that savers often want and the term transformation that many borrowers require.

Life cycles are a fifth reason for using financial intermediation. The ability to generate income may be poorly synchronized with an individual's or family's needs. In traditional societies this problem is handled by extended families. Members who are in their most productive years are expected to sustain the young and the old in the family. The young "borrow" from their elders until they are old enough to contribute to the family's sustenance, and those of productive age "lend" to the young and repay obligations to the old. Borrowing and lending within extended families begin to break down with geographic dispersion of the family members and the individual independence that emerges in commercialized economies. It becomes more common for the young to borrow through financial intermediaries in order to cover some of their educational expenses, to purchase houses and cars, and to get a start in farming. It also becomes more common for those in middle age to save in financial form for retirement purposes. Where attractive and stable forms of financial saving are available, it is also common for the elderly to rely heavily on financial savings to sustain themselves. With people living longer, handling these intergenerational transfers of claims on what is produced would be virtually impossible without financial intermediation in market economies.

The rapid growth in financial services that accompanies economic advances in a country is a clear indication that there is a demand for these services. People are generally not forced to take a loan or to make a deposit. The fact that the demand expands very rapidly strongly suggests that most people in a society realize substantial benefits from these services.

Finance and Rural Service Organizations

It is common for both private and public organizations to be involved in providing financial services. In most cases informal financial arrangements exclude savings-deposit facilities, because it is difficult for informal intermediaries to offer the liquidity, privacy, and security that attract individuals' savings. In rural areas many individuals and businesses do provide short-term loans to relatives, friends, neighbors, or clients. Some loans are made because the lenders hope to gain from providing the borrower with liquidity, but in most cases the lender extends credit to reinforce or complement some social tie or to encourage the purchase of goods or service. Given a choice, most merchants in low-income countries would rather make cash sales than trouble with credit. Likewise, one may not enjoy lending to one's brother-in-law, but feel compelled to do so to keep peace in the family.

Along with banks, postal savings, credit unions, and savings and loan associations, a number of other agricultural service organizations often provide financial intermediation. In most countries rural cooperatives provide loans to members and in some cases provide deposit services. Agrarian reform agencies, area development programs, crop promotion efforts, and input supply organizations also get involved in granting credit. Provision of loans may also be a major ingredient used to entice formation of rural groups. In many cases such credit activities are supported with funds provided by donor agencies or governments. The aims of the funds may be to help the poor, to promote agricultural production, or to help build the service organization itself. Many of these organizations also view cheap credit as a major tool for helping the rural poor.

As with the local merchant, offering loans allows a service organization to build up the number of clients: Offering cheap credit is a way of enticing people to do business with an organization. Even though carrying some benefits for the organization, extension of financial services may result in some unanticipated costs. If large amounts of funds are available for lending, the credit operations may swamp the other activities of the organization. An agrarian-reform institution may become primarily a supervised credit agency, a multipurpose cooperative may evolve into largely a lending agency, and the staff of extension programs may end up doing mostly loan collection. If the organization experiences serious loan-collection problems, as many do, a large part of the management talent may be tied up in trying to recoup loans at the expense of other activities in the organization.

Ideally, financial intermediation should return a surplus to the organization. This has been true in Taiwan where the credit-savings activities in the very successful farmers associations generate economic surpluses that underwrite many of the other activities of these organizations. This is not common in most countries, however. Organizations usually are forced to extend loans at interest rates that do not cover their costs of lending. If they offer savings-deposit services, the interest rates paid do not provide enough incentive for savers to deposit substantial amounts. This may result in a large number of accounts with small deposits that are costly to service. In addition, the agency may experience serious loan-recovery problems. These costs of lending, costs of deposits, and defaults can undermine the financial integrity of the organization.

Although a government or an outside donor may be willing to temporarily subsidize an agency to cover some of these costs, at some time the agency will be called upon to stand on its own. When this occurs the organization implodes. This is usually associated with accusations of mismanagement or dishonesty and a change in management. The organization may be renamed, disappear, be combined with some other organization, or exist for a time as a virtual empty shell. Like victims of radiation, the members of the organization may never know what sapped the organization's financial vitality. They may not see clearly that it lost money on its financial intermediation activities and that its poor performance in handling savings and credit led to a loss in support at higher levels.

The provision of cheap credit affects organizations in other unanticipated ways. As Gonzalez-Vega points out later in Chapter 7, there is generally excess demand for cheap credit, a situation that forces the lender to ration the credit through nonmarket means. The net result of this rationing process is that the well-to-do and the influential colonize the credit activities, and only a few of the potential clients or members of the organization receive loans. This, in turn, weakens the involvement of the clients who do not get loans. This has the opposite effect of sales, which are used by some merchants to increase the volume of traffic moving through their facilities in the hopes of selling the customer something in addition to the good that is sale priced. Cheap credit, on the other hand, results in fewer people coming to organizations providing this service.

Any organization, or individual for that matter, is beholden to those who provide support. The government or central bank may look to outside donors to provide funds to sustain or expand the amount of agricultural credit. This foreign aid carries obvious obligations beyond repaying the foreign loan. Likewise, banks or cooperatives that draw money from the central bank for on-lending to farmers subject themselves to increased central-bank control, and the farmer who borrows is open to intrusions by the lenders. Banks and agricultural service agencies may become addicted to the cheap funds provided by central banks, especially if they mobilize few local savings. This addiction makes these organizations vulnerable to political intrusions that may evolve into a virtual patronal relationship from top to bottom in the financial system.

Finance and Groups in the Economy

All too often it is overlooked that the operations of financial markets can have a powerful differential impact on various groups. Finance may have a substantial effect on the amount of resources available to various sectors in an economy as well as on income distributions. Because of the diffused nature of finance, these effects are usually not readily apparent. In some cases the operations of financial markets yield results that are diametrically opposed to publicly stated goals.

As allocators and mobilizers of claims on resources, financial markets play a major role in the movement of resources from one sector to another. If a financial system, for example, mobilizes more deposits in an area than it extends in loans, some of the claims on resources mobilized are moved out through the financial system to other areas or sectors. These transferred claims allow borrowers in other areas or sectors to call on resources located in the areas where deposits were mobilized. It is not uncommon for financial markets to mobilize more money in deposits in rural areas and poor urban areas than is extended in formal loans. In some cases the volume of savings transferred out of rural areas and poor urban areas may exceed the amount of government assistance directed at easing problems in these areas. At least in the Japanese case, the transfers of resources through financial markets were substantial, as is documented by Kato (1966).

Where negative real rates of interest are in force, where widespread defaults on loans are tolerated, and where large agricultural credit portfolios are involved, the operations of financial markets can also transfer large amounts of income to borrowers. This may cause a further skewing of the income distribution, because the subsidy is always proportional to the size of the loan. Large borrowers get large subsidies, small borrowers get small subsidies, and nonborrowers get no subsidy. In addition, negative real rates of interest on deposits transfer purchasing power from savers to borrowers. If borrowers are generally richer than savers, this will further skew income distributions.

Finance and Politics

In most countries there is a close relationship between political and financial systems. Governments feel obligated to regulate financial markets. This may include the granting of authority through charters to open up shop as an intermediary, interest-rate controls, reserve requirements, and limitations on the range of activities that the intermediary can undertake. Typically, government controls on the financial system are more comprehensive than are controls on any other marketing system in the country. It is also common, especially in low-income countries, for governments to manipulate financial markets. The government may even go to the extent of nationalizing much or all of the banking system in order to "gain control" over its operations.

It is also very common for governments to use credit to promote a particular industry or enterprise. Cheap credit may be used to support local industries that are part of an import-substitution program, for example, or to try to promote the production of a particular crop such as rice. Credit programs also may be used as a form of disaster relief. Droughts, wars, frosts, typhoons, floods, and hail may all be used as excuses for initiating a new concessionary credit program. Governments commonly try to promote long-term investments, such as irrigation facilities, tree crops, or livestock, by offering long-term loans. In some countries these credit activities make up a large part of all of the efforts aimed at rural development. As might be expected, donor agencies are involved in activities that reinforce government priorities. As a result, agricultural credit projects have made up a large part of the agricultural portfolio of the World Bank, the Inter-American Development Bank, and the Agency for International Development.

At times, some of the economic considerations involved in manipulation of financial markets can be swamped by political considerations. Because of the normal use-value of loans, the potential for default transfers, and the income transfer involved in negative real rates of interest on loans, credit can become a potent tool for allocating political patronage. The beauty of this tool is that it is very flexible, its results are generally well masked, the benefits can be effectively targeted, and the costs of the patronage are diffused throughout the economy (Olson 1982).

Improving the Contribution of Finance

Few careful observers of formal rural financial markets in low-income countries are satisfied with their recent performance. These markets are highly fragmented, provide little or no service to many rural residents, and are riddled with politics, and official lenders are often on the edge of bankruptcy. These problems are compounded by the very low expectations that most policymakers have regarding agricultural credit programs. They have come to expect that loans will not be repaid, that rural people will not save in financial form, and that credit agencies cannot pay their own way. In all too many cases they assure these results by adopting policies that force lenders and borrowers to conform to these low expectations. Such expectations and policies seriously limit the overall contribution of financial intermediation to rural development. Financial markets that are stunted do not adequately support the development process.

Improvements in the performance of rural financial markets will require major changes in how these markets are used and a much clearer understanding by policymakers of the important contributions these markets make to economic development. Because of the diffused and subtle nature of the rural financial markets, much of their contributions must be taken on faith. Some additional research, however, could help clarify the extent and nature of these contributions. Once policymakers more clearly understand financial markets, they may come to understand the limitations of policies aimed at altering market performance. Frequently the policies are responsible for poor performance.

In all too many cases agricultural credit programs are initiated because they are easy to start or expand and because their ultimate effects are diffused and masked. These cheap agricultural credit activities divert attention and resources from more important problems in rural areas: paying producers decent prices for their output, improving technology so that farmers get higher yields, and investing in other services that will make rural areas more pleasant places in which to live.

The operations of financial markets are difficult to understand. It is even more difficult to comprehend the effects that these markets have on economic development. Traditional suspicions, assumptions, and biases undermine this understanding. It is past time for more positive views to emerge about the contribution and importance of rural financial markets.

References

Adams, Dale W, and Douglas H. Graham. "A Critique of Traditional Agricultural Credit Projects and Policies." *Journal of Development Economics* 8(1981):347–366.

Goldsmith, Raymond W. *Financial Structure and Development.* New Haven, Conn.: Yale University Press, 1969.

Gurley, John G., and Edward S. Shaw. *Money in a Theory of Finance.* Washington, D.C.: Brookings Institution, 1960.

Kato, Yuzuru. "Mechanisms for the Outflow of Funds from Agriculture into Industry in Japan." *Rural Economic Problems* 3(1966):1–20.

Long, Millard. "A Note on Financial Theory and Economic Development." In *Rural Financial Markets in Developing Countries: Their Use and Abuse,* edited by J. D. Von Pischke, Dale W Adams, and Gordon Donald. Baltimore: Johns Hopkins University Press, 1983.

Olson, Mancur. *The Rise and Decline of Nations.* New Haven, Conn.: Yale University Press, 1982.

Patrick, Hugh T. "Financial Development and Economic Growth in Underdeveloped Countries." *Economic Development and Cultural Change* 14(1966):174–189.

Shaw, Edward S. *Financial Deepening in Economic Development.* New York: Oxford University Press, 1973.

2
Farm-Household Heterogeneity and Rural Financial Markets: Insights from Thailand

Richard L. Meyer
Adelaida P. Alicbusan

Until recently policymakers have viewed rural finance largely as a process of channeling cheap credit to farmers. Attention has been focused almost exclusively on farm enterprises with little concern for financing nonfarm enterprises in rural areas. However, a new perspective on the role of finance in development appears warranted from evidence that the finances of farm households in low-income countries are much more complex than previously assumed.

Two types of heterogeneity facilitate rural financial intermediation. The first concerns the broad range of firms and households found in rural areas. Some of these units can benefit primarily from a ready source of credit that is appropriately priced relative to the cost and risk of the loan desired. At the same time, other units have surplus funds and can benefit from a safe, reliable way to hold savings. The second type of heterogeneity stems from the changing financial situation of firms and households over time. At one time, a firm may choose to borrow; at another time, it may choose to hold savings. This heterogeneity across firms and within firms over time provides scope for financial intermediation. When such heterogeneity is recognized and appropriate financial intermediaries and instruments are made available, development is accelerated. When the heterogeneity is ignored and the financial market impeded or fragmented, development is retarded.

The objective of this chapter is to discuss the complexity of farm-household finance in low-income countries and the implication of that complexity for rural financial intermediation. Data from Thailand are presented to illustrate the heterogeneity that exists among farms.

Data are not available to make the same argument for rural nonfarm firms. The paper by Kilby, Liedholm, and Meyer (Chapter 21), however, suggests that there may be a number of similarities between farm and nonfarm firms in this respect.

Financial Intermediation and the Rural Household

There is surprisingly little information in the literature on the role of financial intermediation in rural households. (Exceptions are Lee 1983 and Baker 1973.) Intermediation occurs because not all firms and households want to borrow or save at the same time: Some want to borrow at exactly the time others want to save. This heterogeneity provides an opportunity for an intermediary to bring the interests of borrowers and savers together. The resulting transaction—representing an exchange of resources and financial claims through the intermediary—allows both borrowers and savers to reach greater income levels. Through the transaction, resources are channeled to the highest bidder who expects the greatest economic returns. Thus, financial intermediation causes increased efficiency through resource allocation from savers to borrowers and among borrowers to those willing and able to pay the highest interest rate.

Heterogeneity of economic activities among firms and households gives rise to their financial heterogeneity. Various types of heterogeneity in rural areas influence financial markets. A first type concerns the wide range of firms and households that exist. A typology of activities found in the rural sector is presented in Chapter 21 by Kilby, Liedholm, and Meyer. Farm households range from poor, landless laborers to rich, complex agricultural estates and plantations. The rural sector also includes small towns with farm and nonfarm households, processing plants, input supply dealers, repair and service centers, and retailers. These nonfarm firms and households have forward and backward linkages with farm households that are often overlooked in statistics and policy analysis (Chuta and Liedholm 1979). Their financing is also usually overlooked, and they are often excluded from credit programs.

A second type of heterogeneity is the focus of this chapter. It concerns the differences among farm households and how this gives rise to opportunities for financial intermediation. Like nonfarm firms, farm households are heterogeneous. Some have access to irrigation and practice double and triple cropping. Others lack sufficient water and are limited to one crop per year. Some households specialize in only one farm enterprise, while others engage in several and are also involved in nonfarm enterprises during slack labor periods. Some households are rich and operate large farms. Others are poor and landless, and many exist on meager incomes. These differences in income levels, asset ownership, and farm organization give rise to differences in demand for financial services.

A third type of financial heterogeneity concerns the changes that occur in households over time. Within a year a household may experience shortfalls in cash inflow during several weeks or months. Desired expenditures may exceed household income. At other times income exceeds expenditures. During some periods the household prefers to be a net borrower; at other times it prefers to be a net saver. If all households simultaneously faced the same financial situation there would be little scope for financial intermediation. During one period there would not be enough funds to satisfy everyone. At another period funds would be overabundant, and there would be too few borrowers to utilize these funds.

An important role of financial intermediation is to help households smooth seasonal cash flows and synchronize income and expenditures. Unevenness in cash inflow and outflow is inherent in most biological processes of crops and livestock. Inputs for a crop are required months before harvest and sale, and most livestock and poultry enterprises involve an even longer lag between investments and returns. A regular pattern of cash inflow and outflow can be anticipated for some enterprises and for household expenses. Consumption expenditures, school expenses, and some ceremonial obligations, for example, can be anticipated. The household must also consider such unpredictable events as crop failure, market failure, and sickness.

The selection of production and marketing alternatives affects the synchronization of cash inflow and outflow. For example, a diversified combination of enterprises may be selected to produce a marketable surplus several times during the year. Nonfarm enterprises, such as weaving, blacksmithing, tailoring, and handicraft manufacture, play an important role in many countries in generating income for farm households during the dry season (Chuta and Liedholm 1979). Forward contracting of production with advance partial payment can be used, in some cases, to finance inputs. Frequently, households will store commodities for home consumption in the dry season (to avoid cash outlays), for future use in barter, or for sale to obtain cash.

Adjustments in the timing and magnitude of consumption expenditures can help synchronize inflows and outflows. Cash outlays can be held to a minimum during periods of low income; the purchase of clothing and durable goods, and some traditional religious and ceremonial activities, can be deferred until harvest time or whenever major sales are made.

There are limits, however, to the household's ability to manage cash flow through production, sales, and consumption strategies. The household's cash position may vary substantially month by month. Given this variation, there are several ways that financial intermediation can help in the household's liquidity management. One way is through the management of savings or temporary surpluses. Some savings are always required to finance expenditures that exceed income for some period (Von Pischke 1979). In the absence of reliable financial institutions, households in low-income countries frequently hold their savings in the form of nonfinancial liquid assets: crop inventories, livestock and poultry, and gold ornaments. But holding these assets can be both unproductive and risky and causes inefficiencies in resource allocation. A more productive, less risky alternative consists of selling unproductive assets and holding the receipts in interest-bearing financial instruments until cash is needed.

Besides providing savings alternatives, another way financial markets can be helpful is in the obvious role of providing loans. There are some households that during some periods want to spend more cash than they have. Borrowing provides an alternative to liquidating physical assets during these periods. To engage in borrowing, the household must perceive that the cost and risk of the loan are preferable to disposing of assets.

Still another way management assistance comes from financial markets is through provision to the household of credit reserves. Baker (1973) defines these reserves as the ability to borrow. This reserve acts as a substitute for cash. With a reliable source of loans, a household can utilize cash holdings for productive purposes knowing that the credit reserve can be drawn upon when cash requirements are greater than cash holdings and savings.

A fourth way that financial heterogeneity arises is through differences in family life cycles. Over time households typically go through an expansion, maintenance, and contraction cycle. In the early years of a family, demands for cash often exceed supply. Child rearing, establishing a home, acquiring desired durables, and beginning farming all require more funds than a young family can easily obtain from annual income. As time passes, household income rises until it eventually matches and finally surpasses desired expenditures. The household may shift from being a net borrower to being a net saver. In low-income countries, young families frequently live with parents and in-laws so the older generation can subsidize or lend to the younger family members. The amount of funds may not be sufficient in this internal transfer, however, so a financial intermediary can provide a service by linking savers with borrowers who do not know each other, cannot easily establish personal relationships, and may even be separated by great distances.

Diverse investment opportunities are a fifth type of heterogeneity that creates opportunities for financial intermediaries. These opportunities arise because of actual or perceived differences among households for making profitable investments. Some households have, or perceive they have, few opportunities to profitably invest in their current farm and nonfarm enterprises. They have exhausted all alternatives with acceptable levels of income and risk. They lack information on investment opportunities in urban areas. Their best option may be to invest their liquid resources in a financial instrument. Simultaneously, another household that perceives an opportunity to increase income by using improved seeds, applying more fertilizer, buying machinery, or starting a new enterprise lacks finance to take advantage of these opportunities. The liquid household would gain by decreasing current consumption and providing resources to the borrower household, while the deficit household would gain by increasing current consumption and repaying a loan out of future income. Both households benefit from a financial institution that mobilizes the savings of one and lends to the other when they are not able to meet face to face and make a direct loan one to the other.

The finances of households are much more complex than normally assumed in agricultural credit programs. Although it is true that some households may productively use short- or long-term loans, many other households may need to hold short- and long-term savings in attractive and safe ways. If *all* farm households could productively borrow at the same time, then channeling large supplies of central-bank or donor credit to rural lenders—ignoring savings mobilization and the diversity of rural economic activity—might be appropriate. But with heterogeneous objectives and patterns of activities, savings ought to be mobilized in rural areas for simultaneous lending to local borrowers.

Cash-Flow Analysis of Thai Farm Households

Few studies collect enough data to adequately analyze the heterogeneity of farm-household finance. An exception is the recent Rural Off-Farm Employment Assessment Study in Thailand. A description of this project is found in Onchan and others (1979). The objective was to analyze the potential for increasing rural nonfarm employment. The prevailing wisdom was that rural people were poor in large part because they were underemployed (Fuhs and Vingerhoets 1972), but little information was available to support this argument or to assess the possibility of expanding rural employment.

The project set out to analyze employment for a full year on a sample of Thai farm households. A preliminary survey was conducted to determine the distribution of rural enterprises. A total of 20 villages was selected in four provinces to represent typical farm situations. Over 400 households were selected at random in the villages. Local teachers collected data weekly and monthly from households in their respective villages beginning March 1980 and ending February 1981. The data were edited and processed at Kasetsart University. A major component of the project concerned a financial analysis of the farm households interviewed: Detailed cash-flow data were collected during the year to show how financial situations changed over time and how the households managed their financial resources.

In the mid-1970s, Thailand had embarked on an aggressive expansion of formal agricultural credit (Meyer and others 1979). Commercial banks were required to lend a portion of their loan portfolios to agriculture or deposit an equivalent amount of funds in the Central Bank. The Bank of Agriculture and Agricultural Cooperatives was provided with funds for a major expansioin in its agricultural lending. At the same time, savings mobilization was largely limited to urban areas. It was expected that the impact of these credit programs would show up in the financial information of the sample households.

Tables 2.1 and 2.2 report cash-flow data for two sets of households (the data represent average values for the variables reported for the households included in each group). These households were located in two widely separated villages in Khon Kaen Province in Northeast Thailand, representing farms with wet-season irrigated rice production and a large amount of upland sugarcane, cassava, and kenaf. Compared to other areas in the province, the farms were cropped fairly intensively. Other areas with access to good irrigation water were cropped even more intensively in the dry season.

These households are a subset drawn from the larger sample. They were selected because the data were complete enough for the required analysis, they represented small farms of fewer than 20 rai (about 8 acres), and they had both farm and nonfarm enterprises. Since the farms were small and incomes were low, it was expected that cash-management problems would be pronounced and borrowing would be common. The households were divided into a borrower group and a nonborrower group. The criterion for the division was that a household borrowed from all sources a total of at least 500 baht (about US$25) in new loans during the year. Surprisingly, in spite of their small size and low income, only 5 of the 19 households

Table 2.1 Cash Flow Statement for Borrower Households in Thailand[a]

	Month												
Item	March	April	May	June	July	August	Sept.	Oct.	Nov.	Dec.	Jan.	Feb.	Total
Farm Cash Receipts	60	82	56	198	50		90	8	812	6	2,694	1,436	5,492
Operating Expenses	19	98	36	118	58	46	60	496	52	266	34		1,283
Net Cash Farm Income	41	(16)	20	80	(8)	(46)	30	(488)	760	(260)	2,660	1,436	4,209
Net Cash Nonfarm Income	195	594	432	773	418	613	464	777	418	1,496	1,298	546	8,024
Net Capital Sales	(580)										1,700		1,120
Other Cash Receipts	50	110	50	20	40	80	260	410	250	51	50	50	1,421
Family Living Expenditures	1,344	3,507	473	605	333	504	768	549	1,848	660	1,015	718	12,324
Other Cash Expenses	494	1,805	208	73	49	43	45	16	111	14	121	518	3,497
Net Borrowing	1,660	400	200	100	100					(100)	(500)	(2,300)	(440)
Surplus (Deficit)	(472)	(4,224)	21	295	168	100	(59)	134	(531)	513	4,072	(1,504)	(1,487)

[a]All values reported in Baht. U.S. $1.00 approximately equal to 20 Baht.

Note: Parentheses indicate negative values.

Table 2.2 Cash Flow Statement for Nonborrower Households in Thailand[a]

Item	Month												
	March	April	May	June	July	August	Sept.	Oct.	Nov.	Dec.	Jan.	Feb.	Total
Farm Cash Receipts	364	753	30	533	383	1,312	2,286	329	363	1,061	1,955	748	10,117
Operating Expenses	215	359	327	68	36		21	156	32	30	111	14	1,369
Net Cash Farm Income	149	394	(297)	465	347	1,312	2,265	173	331	1,031	1,844	734	8,748
Net Cash Nonfarm Income	1,987	455	501	1,339	536	1,044	760	772	562	1,639	1,268	1,222	12,085
Net Capital Sales	(419)	(38)		(8)	(40)	(62)	(63)	(6)		(13)	(2)	(357)	(1,008)
Other Cash Receipts	151	152	59	168	304	143	157	397	143	229	270	157	2,330
Family Living Expenditures	1,096	901	577	556	388	479	611	479	412	542	642	877	7,560
Other Cash Expenses	1,345	91	258	293	155	191	424	196	112	463	88	18	3,634
Net Borrowing		(7)			(16)	14	(25)						(34)
Surplus (Deficit)	(573)	(36)	(572)	1,115	588	1,781	2,059	661	512	1,881	2,650	861	10,927

[a]All values reported in Baht. U.S. $1.00 approximately equal to 20 Baht.

Note: Parentheses indicate negative values.

reported borrowing at least 500 baht. This low level of borrowing was also found with the households in the rest of the sample, in spite of the recent major emphasis on expanding the supplies of agricultural credit.

The main rice-growing season in these villages runs from planting in June-July to harvest in November-December. Thus the data in the tables cover the end of the 1979-1980 dry season, the entire 1980 wet season, and the beginning of the 1980-1981 dry season. Household cash receipts were subdivided into net cash farm income, net cash nonfarm income (including net income from nonfarm enterprises and off-farm work), net capital sales, and other miscellaneous cash receipts. Household expenditures were classified as family living expenses (e.g., food, clothing, and education) and other cash expenses. Net borrowing refers to the difference between value of new loans received from all sources and repayments on old loans. The differences between total cash inflow and total cash outflow were reported as cash surpluses or deficits for the month. These amounts represent the potential that exists for financial intermediation in the form of loans or savings.

These two groups of households are similar in that both earned more income from nonfarm than from farm sources. This is a result of small farm size and the widespread existence of nonfarm enterprises in rural Thailand. The borrower households in Table 2.1 had a cash-flow pattern typically assumed by agricultural credit planners. Farm cash receipts were concentrated in certain times of the year: 75 percent were received from rice and kenaf during the postharvest months of January and February. About 60 percent of the operating expenses occurred in the two months of October and December. Net cash farm income was negative in five months. Nonfarm income was substantial every month, but the largest amounts were earned in December and January because of the employment available in harvesting. Thus total net cash income from all sources was much higher in the period November through February than in any other period.

Over 50 percent of the living expenses for the entire year occurred in the four dry-season months of January through April. This is the period when major religious festivals are held and is also the period just after rice harvest when households have the most cash.

Borrowing occurred in the preplanting and planting months of March through July; repayments were concentrated in the postharvest months of December through February. This is the classic cash-flow pattern expected in typical agricultural credit projects: Households borrow during the planting period when they experience cash deficits and repay after harvest when they have cash surpluses. Total cash outflow roughly equaled total cash inflow during the months May through December. Outflow greatly exceeded inflow in April, and inflow strongly exceeded outflow in January. The cash balances that were accumulated in January financed the cash deficits in February, March, and April.

Although the data on the cash flow of the nonborrower households (Table 2.2) show some similarities with the borrower group, they also exhibit some major differences. Total net cash farm income was higher and more evenly spread throughout the year for nonborrowers. Nonborrowers had a more complex combination of enterprises, including cassava and sugarcane, that generated income more frequently during the year. Nonborowers also earned more nonfarm income.

Surprisingly, in spite of their higher income, nonborrowers had lower total family living expenses than borrowers, and these expenses were somewhat less concentrated in the postharvest months. These households made payments on loans received in previous years during months other than postharvest.

In March through May, the nonborrower households experienced a cash-deficit period when cash outflow exceeded inflow. However, for the rest of the year they saved. It is not clear where and how these savings were held. Given the absence of attractive and readily accessible rural financial savings opportunities, it is expected that they were held in cash or converted to unreported assets. Compared to the borrower group, nonborrowers could have benefited from a safe, convenient way to hold their savings. Simultaneously, intermediaries could have mobilized these resources rather than relying mainly on Central Bank funds.

Results from Other Studies

How representative are these households of others in Thailand or of households in other low-income countries? We have not located any other studies with analysis similar enough to permit exact comparison, but what we have found is supportive. Using data from this same Thailand project, Priebprom (1982) analyzed the income of households on both irrigated and rainfed farms in the Khon Kaen sample. His analysis showed, as expected, that the proportion of total household income earned from nonfarm and off-farm sources declined as farm size increased. Further, the importance of these sources of income was less on irrigated farms than on rainfed farms. Even so, households on large irrigated farms reported about 15 percent of total income from nonfarm and off-farm sources compared to 73 percent for small rainfed farms. This large amount of nonfarm income should have reduced the sharp seasonality of farm cash inflow and outflow, as we noted for the farms analyzed above.

Laguna Province in the Philippines was selected for detailed small-scale surveys in a rice-growing culture similar to Thailand. Hayami (1978) analyzed the data collected from mid-1975 to mid-1976 for a daily record-keeping project with 11 households in a Laguna village. Few nonfarm enterprises existed in the village, but on the average the households earned 28 percent of their income off the farm, principally by working on neighboring farms. Monthly cash income and expense were highly uneven, as in the Thailand case. There were three periods totaling several months of the year when monthly consumption expenditures exceeded income. On the other hand, there were two periods when rice was sold, and income far exceeded expenditures. Monthly cash receipts ranged from a low of US$48 to a high of $176; monthly cash payments ranged from $53 to $211. Financial assets as a percent of total assets ranged from a low of 2 percent to a high of 14 percent depending on the type of household and time of year. Even though Laguna Province is favored with considerable social services, only about a third of the loans came from institutional sources. The balance came from moneylenders or in the form of time purchases.

Also in the Philippines, Ledesma (1980) collected daily records from 16 households in Iloilo Province from September 1977 to March 1978. Sources of income were similar to those in the Hayami study. The data for 1 landless family showed weekly expenses exceeded income for a total of 18 out of 26 weeks during six different periods of time. The longest period was 6 weeks. Two weeks with large rice sales produced income far above expenses. Off-farm work and sales from livestock enterprises helped even out household cash flow during the period.

Ledesma conducted a particularly interesting analysis of the complex borrowing and lending behavior of these households. All 16 households borrowed cash and/or rice in kind. Landless-worker households tended to borrow frequently and in small amounts. Many households borrowed more than 20 different times during the 26 weeks. Many of these loans were small. At the same time, 13 households lent cash and/or rice to an average of 4 other households during this same period. The households tended to hold their savings in the form of rice that was lent to other households.

Another relevant survey was conducted by Matlon (1977) of 140 households during a 12-month period in three villages of Kano State, Nigeria, in 1974-1975. These households reported almost 30 percent of total income earned off-farm from a variety of sources. This income represented over half of the total cash income of the households. A surprising finding was that farm sources of income declined as household income rose. Work in nonfarm activities was highest during slack farm periods. Even though hourly returns were low for this work, the income earned helped stabilize household cash flow. Over half of the households borrowed during the year, but the total value of the cash loans equaled only 7 percent of all expenditures. The timing of loans was consistent with the reported purpose. Loans for farming expenses were reported mostly in preplanting and planting periods, whereas consumption loans tended to be reported during holiday and ceremony periods.

Implications

Farm households are financially heterogeneous. They vary because of differences in enterprise combination, production and marketing techniques, family life cycle, investment opportunities, management efficiency, consumption preferences, and a variety of other factors. The financial management of the typical farm household is far more complex than is assumed by many designers of agricultural credit programs, who tend to set up rigid, one-sided systems in low-income countries, such as Thailand. Loans are provided while savings opportunities for households are ignored. The financial market is fragmented and made up largely of specialized institutions: One institution supplies operating loans, another supplies investment funds. Loans are packaged for specific amounts, purposes, and maturities. The borrowing and repayment cycle is assumed to be simple. For production loans, it is often assumed that farmers will borrow once at the beginning of the production period for repayment once at the end. Loans for consumption and nonfarm purposes are usually discouraged or completely denied. Loan application and documentation procedures are complicated, time consuming, and expensive for the borrowers. The system as set up considers the convenience and interests of the lenders more than the borrowers. Therefore, formal credit institutions are not highly valued by the rural community, reach few farmers, poorly serve those that are reached, and must offer low interest rates to induce farmers to borrow.

Flexible, multipurpose financial intermediaries would better serve farm households. These institutions should be one-stop centers that offer both borrowing and savings services. Production, consumption, investments, and nonfarm loans should all be available to borrowers, with the amount and timing based on repayment ability rather than fixed formula or simple packages. Opportunities are needed for households to borrow and repay several times per year to facilitate synchronization with household cash inflow and outflow. Loan procedures must be streamlined to reduce borrower costs, yet comprehensive enough to provide essential information for screening borrowers. Interest rates on loans must be set high enough to cover lender costs and also high enough to attract savers.

These recommendations recognize the heterogeneity of farm households and their complex patterns of financial management. This heterogeneity implies that rural financial markets must do much more than simply channel large amounts of cheap credit if they are to serve farmers effectively.

References

Baker, Chester B. "Role of Credit in the Economic Development of Small Farm Agriculture." In *AID Spring Review of Small Farmer Credit,* vol. 19, edited and published by the Agency for International Development. Washington, D.C., 1973.

Chuta, Enyinna, and Carl Liedholm. "Rural Non-Farm Employment: A Review of the State of the Art." MSU Rural Development Paper no. 4. East Lansing: Michigan State University, 1979.

Donald, Gordon. *Credit for Small Farmers in Developing Countries.* Boulder, Colo.: Westview Press, 1976.

Fuhs, F. W., and J. Vingerhoets. *Rural Manpower, Rural Institutions, and Rural Employment in Thailand.* Bangkok: National Economic Development Board, Government of Thailand, 1972.

Hayami, Yujiro. *Anatomy of a Peasant Economy.* Los Baños, Philippines: International Rice Research Institute, 1978.

Ledesma, Antonio J. "Landless Workers and Rice Farmers: Peasant Subclasses Under Agrarian Reform in Two Philippine Villages." Ph.D. dissertation, University of Wisconsin, 1980.

Lee, Warren F. "The Role of Financial Intermediation in the Activities of Rural Farms and Households." In *Rural Financial Markets in Developing Countries: Their Use and Abuse,* edited by J. D. Von Pischke, Dale W Adams, and Gordon Donald. Baltimore: Johns Hopkins University Press, 1983.

Matlon, Peter J. "The Size Distribution, Structure, and Determinants of Personal Income Among Farmers in the North of Nigeria." Ph.D. dissertation, Cornell University, 1977.

Meyer, Richard L., and others. "Agricultural Credit in Thailand." Research Report no. 6. Bangkok: Center for Applied Economics Research, Kasetsart University, May 1979.

Onchan, Tongroj, and others. "Description of the Rural Off-Farm Employment Assessment Project in Thailand." Unpublished manuscript, Center for Applied Economics Research, Kasetsart University, 1979.

Priebprom, Somsak. "Employment and Income from Farming, Nonfarm Enterprises, and Off-Farm Work on Irrigated and Rainfed Farms, Khon Kaen, Thailand." Ph.D. dissertation, Michigan State University, 1982.

Von Pischke, J. D. "Towards an Operational Approach to Savings for Rural Developers." *Development Digest* 17(1979):3–11.

3
Problems with Specialized Agricultural Lenders

Compton Bourne
Douglas H. Graham

In many low-income countries (LICs), specialized agricultural lenders have been formed in the past several decades to achieve rural development objectives: rapid increases in agricultural production, expansion in rural employment and income, modernization of agricultural technology and practices, domestic self-sufficiency in food production, a favorable agricultural balance of trade, and equity within the rural sector and between rural and urban areas. The results of these programs are not encouraging (Von Pischke 1981). Because of the fungibility, divisibility, and substitutability of money, it is difficult to attribute specific increases in production and income to credit activities (David and Meyer 1980). Also, in some cases, credit expansion has coincided with output decreases and more agricultural imports (Graham and Bourne 1980). Rural inequality appears to have increased as a consequence of agricultural credit policy. Furthermore, many rural credit institutions and programs are not financially viable. The portfolios of some have tended to decline or stagnate rather than to grow in real or nominal terms (Adams 1980).

In our view, the weaknesses of specialized agricultural credit institutions are a consequence of faulty assumptions and, in part, a result of major defects in their design and operation. This chapter critically appraises this strategy and offers recommendations for the reform of rural financial markets.

Specialized Agricultural Lenders

The emphasis on forming specialized agricultural lenders is part of a more general strategy of supply-leading finance. According to Patrick (1966), supply-leading finance is "the creation of financial institutions and the supply of their financial assets, liabilities, and related financial services in advance of demand for them, especially the demand of entrepreneurs in the modern, growth-inducing sectors" (p. 175). Unlike demand-following finance, supply-leading finance "presents an opportunity to induce real growth by financial means . . . [although] as the process of real growth occurs, the supply-leading impetus gradually becomes less important, and the demand-following financial response becomes dominant" (pp. 176–177). Patrick's supply-leading strategy can apply to any part of an economy, but our concern here is only with the agricultural sector.

Various assumptions provide the basis for forming specialized agricultural lenders. Although these assumptions are widely accepted, they are open to serious question. The establishment of financial programs on these weak foundations has contributed to the widespread problems experienced by financial institutions. Efforts at reform usually fail to examine the assumptions underlying supply-led agricultural finance.

One fundamental premise is that credit is an appropriate instrument for promoting agricultural development. Improvements in farming technology are believed to be constrained by lack of farm capital, and loans are expected to encourage expenditures on new and better production activities. The validity of this premise is questionable. It is not always clear that credit is the most binding limitation to agricultural development. Many inputs and technologies are divisible and can be adopted in small amounts. Also, improvements in production technology may raise physical yields, but such changes do not result in corresponding increases in farm revenues unless marketing facilities, input supplies, and prices create incentives to ensure effective use of credit (Schultz 1977; Brown 1978). The production and equity objectives of credit projects are often defeated by marketing conditions and price policies. Credit per se is a weak instrument for promoting agricultural development in the face of these other distortions and constraints.

A second common assumption is that long-term finance is needed by many farmers. Even if a capital constraint does exist, many small- to medium-sized farmers invest in quick payoff items, such as seed drills and spraying equipment, that do not require long-term loans. Moreover, improved inputs such as new seeds, chemicals, and fertilizers are highly divisible and self-liquidating. These inputs require short-term operating credits and not long-term investment loans. This implies that the overall effective demand for credit among the target group of farmers is more short term than long term. Thus, specialization in long-term loans, often prescribed for supply-leading financial institutions, is inappropriate in terms of portfolio balance and results in an unwarranted divergence between the term structure promoted by the lender and that generally desired by many borrowers.

The creation of specialized agricultural credit institutions is also frequently justified by a third assumption, the presumed existence of an unsatisfied demand for credit that can and should be met. It is often noted that commercial banks in LICs do not reach and service many farmers, presumably because producers are not creditworthy or the information needed by banks to determine their creditworthiness is too expensive to collect and interpret. This leads some to argue that specialized institutions or programs (usually with a costly overhead of supervisory credit personnel) are required to reach these potential customers, even if the costs far exceed interest receipts.

Maintaining such a costly program is frequently justified on the grounds that the alleged social benefits outweigh the social costs. Administrators also argue that concessionary interest rates are called for to induce these borrowers to undertake new production techniques. This interest subsidy is also expected to mitigate the start-up costs for long-term investments that will not yield returns for several years. Finally, explicit subsidies to borrowers conveniently reinforce the argument that subsidies are justified for the financial intermediary.

As is argued elsewhere in this volume, much of this reasoning is misleading, inappropriate, or erroneous. First, many farmers obtain liquidity satisfactorily through informal loans (Bouman 1977). Second, to the extent that farmers are reached by these programs, their total borrowing costs are often not very different from the nominal rates of interest charged by informal lenders (Adams and Nehman 1979). Third, the history of high delinquency rates in these programs suggests that either the system is being exploited by the borrowers or the farmers are, in fact, not creditworthy. In this case, subsidized credit cannot be justifed on the grounds that social benefits outweigh social costs. Moreover, there is always a downward bias in the estimates of social costs because the destruction of effective financial intermediation is ignored as one of the costs. Also ignored in these estimates is the probable inequitable trade-off in transferring tax revenues generated from a typically regressive tax structure (or equally regressive inflationary financing) to subsidize relatively well-off borrowers through unviable government credit programs.

A fourth rebuttal is that subsidized interest rates are an inappropriate device to deal with the financial problem of sustaining farming operations while slow-yielding enterprises, such as tree crops, mature. Instead, one should introduce a grace period for amortization payments but still charge realistic interest rates. Fifth, if the rate of return to farming is so low that loan repayments cannot be met, other measures are called for to deal more directly with the factors limiting farming profits. In summary, using scarce resources to treat farm financial problems through credit instruments carries a high opportunity cost.

Operations of Specialized Lenders

Specialized agricultural lenders, especially agricultural development banks, differ substantially from nonspecialized financial institutions. Specialized institutions have distinctive liability structures, a large degree of supervisory and technical involvement in the production activities of their borrowers, a long-run project appraisal approach to granting loans, different performance criteria than commercial banks, and different skill requirements for their staff. These distinctive features contribute to many of the problems they encounter.

The liability structure of supply-leading financial institutions is often characterized by an absence of deposit liabilities and by limited use of bond issues to the private sector.[1] These institutions rely on loans and grants from foreign donors and on equity contributions and quasi-equity loans from local governments and tend to be financial intermediaries only in the very restricted sense of converting public-sector financial contributions into rural loans. Many are incomplete institutions that do not mobilize savings and offer only long-term loans. The absence of deposit facilities means these institutions do not realize potential multiplier effects that arise when borrowers deposit loan proceeds and project income with the lending institution, increasing its supply of loanable funds.

Several explanations have been suggested for the lack of deposit facilities in these institutions. Some argue that deposit facilities are too costly. However, a more convincing reason is that deposit costs require more realistic loan pricing and more careful lending policies. It is relatively easy for managers of supply-leading institutions to obtain cheap funds from governments and international donors and thereby avoid competition with commercial banks for local funds. Typically, governments guarantee the institutions' debts to external agencies and governments; they sometimes also guarantee customers' debts to the agricultural bank. These arrangements considerably reduce the responsibility of financial managers. In contrast, resource mobilization from many depositors introduces powerful pressures for accountability. In addition, the task of pooling deposits and of synchronizing resource inflows with credit transactions makes greater demands on the skills of bank officials.

Close credit supervision is another important feature of specialized financial institutions. Supervision and planning are a natural consequence of long-term loans aimed at increasing output of specific commodities or at transforming farm technology. Credit supervision is justified as a means of preventing credit diversion to nonapproved uses and of educating farmers in the use of new technology. However, the fungibility of finance makes attempts at preventing credit diversion costly and futile. Further, as we shall argue later, it is doubtful whether the high costs resulting from credit supervision can be justified in terms of the actual technical assistance provided by credit officials.

The planning perspective extends to identifying target groups of intended beneficiaries on the basis of enterprise type and of regional and equity considerations. The planning perspective, which leads policymakers to rank planning goals higher than the internal viability of the institution, results in project appraisal and creditworthiness criteria that are at variance with those employed by nonspecialized lenders. What would normally be externalities are internalized; social-cost–social-benefit considerations become integral elements in the decision calculus. Conventional creditworthiness criteria are relaxed as riskier and allegedly more socially beneficial projects are emphasized.

The performance indicators of specialized agricultural lenders are also often based on a planning perspective. Initially, quick loan approval and disbursement and rapid growth in the number and volume of loans to previously identified target groups are the most important yardsticks used to evaluate performance. Much less attention is paid to internal financial performance indicators. Lending costs, loan delinquency, and default are largely ignored until a financial crisis emerges. It is not surprising, therefore, to find that arrears information is handled poorly and that it has little weight in evaluations of bank personnel (Von Pischke 1980, 1981).

All too often individual accountability for program or loan failure is weak in these specialized institutions. This is a consequence of several factors. The loan-approval process is protracted and diffused over so many divisions and levels that all managers are jointly, but none is individually, responsible. Problems in projects that are heavily weighted with long-term loans appear only after three or four years. By this time many of the original credit officers have often been reassigned. The attribution of responsibility is further complicated by the difficulty of distinguishing *post hoc* between weaknesses in project appraisal and monitoring on the one hand and—on the other hand—unanticipated economic difficulties and the impact of governmental policies beyond the control of the credit institution. There is also the pervasive view that high-risk ventures are the business and *raison d'être* of supply-leading financial institutions, so that some loan failures are to be expected. However, this view begs the question of what is the acceptable level of project failures and usually only serves to provide a weak defense for deficient project appraisal and monitoring.

Finally, in sharp contrast to commercial banks, government-owned development banks frequently become political profit centers for the party in power (Ladman and Tinnermeier 1981). They can be used to attract badly needed foreign exchange and to employ political favorites. Cheap credit also can be allocated to pay off critical constituencies or political support groups. Announcement of an increase in the supply of cheap credit meets the needs for the political system to do something when faced with a problem. More often than not this turns out to be some form of reorganization and recapitalization to start the process all over again with similar results later (Von Pischke 1981). Potentially, a development bank is a powerful political weapon that can be used and abused more effectively by political leaders than can a more diffused and decentralized set of financial intermediaries.

Operational Problems

Specialized agricultural lenders have a number of operational problems, which include institutional viability and inefficiencies in credit delivery. A review of these problems shows the negative consequences of supply-leading finance and also provides some guidance as to the kinds of reforms necessary for improved financial-market performance (Bourne and Graham 1981).

The composition of a credit institution's liabilities may adversely affect financial performance in several ways. Consistent with the maxim of "he who pays the piper calls the tune," governments may impose portfolio restrictions that limit the outreach of credit programs by excluding certain potential borrowers on the basis of wealth, farm size, enterprise, and loan maturity. As a result, the scope is reduced for loan-portfolio diversification as a means of risk minimization, revenue maximization, and more even repayment inflows. Foreign funding agencies also have biases in their portfolio preferences, and they have an influence on the lending policies of local lenders. Frequently this influence moves in the same direction as that of local governments.

The influence of external and internal funding agencies usually intrudes into interest-rate policies. In keeping with the premises of supply-leading finance, concessionary interest rates are common. Although sometimes calculated to yield a small operating margin to the credit institutions, fixed interest rates usually do not cover average operating costs. Also, they often are too low to protect the purchasing power of the lender's loan portfolio. In sharp contrast to low single-digit interest rates common in these programs, the limited studies on lending costs in agricultural development banks point out that administrative costs and costs of funds together typically run between 10 and 20 percent of the value of loans outstanding. When delinquency and default are included, this can substantially increase the annual costs of lending in direct proportion to the magnitude of the default rate. Consequently, the real capital position of the financial institutions is eroded as financial reserves (if there are any) and new capital contributions are used to defray operating losses.

As pointed out later in Chapter 7 by Gonzalez-Vega, it is not unusual for credit institutions confronted with unrealistic interest-rate ceilings to attempt to protect their capital resources and to seek financial viability by rationing credit in order to reduce loan administration and default costs. This rationing can take many forms: reducing the number of loans to new borrowers, favoring borrowers who have the most collateral, and making shorter-term loans and loans with lower market and crop risks. This rationing raises the transactions costs per unit of credit to many borrowers, thereby impairing the efficiency of the financial intermediation process. Increases in borrower transactions costs and other rationing devices such as stricter collateral requirements discriminate against small and new borrowers and thus operate contrary to equity objectives.

Other problems are associated with the reliance on official funds. Inflows of funds tend to be discontinuous, peaking at the time of each new injection of international contract funds, government capital, and loan contributions. These discontinuities result in prolonged and repeated periods of excess capacity in these financial institutions. Capacity built to provide peak-period services is maintained during the inevitable downturn in loan activity as credit fund infusions are exhausted. At the same time, loan recoveries are often too small to create significant amounts of revolving funds within the institution. Furthermore, these credit institutions may experience difficulties in sustaining or expanding inflows of loanable funds when the preferences and emphases of governments and foreign-assistance agencies change.

Because of these discontinuities in resource availabilities, actual and potential credit customers might perceive specialized agricultural lenders as transient, undependable institutions; the "quality" of this source of credit is poor. In such situations, loan repayments often suffer as debtors delay payments in the hope that the institution will wither away and as potential borrowers become pessimistic about the future availability of loans. Obtaining additional economies of scale in lending is not possible when the portfolio is stationary or declining. The small volume of loan activity also imposes economic and political limits on asset diversification by decreasing the extent to which the lender can realize "scope" economies (i.e., higher per unit returns through multiproduct operations) and "traditional diversification economies" (i.e., lower risk costs through asset diversification). In such circumstances, borrowing costs would usually have to be increased if break-even loan-pricing policies were implemented.

Another defect in the operations of specialized agricultural lenders is the high cost of supervising loans. This includes emphasis on close and continuous monitoring of loan use. Credit officers make frequent visits for the alleged purpose of encouraging farmers to adopt new practices and follow farm plans. The credit institution accepts the responsibility for providing technical assistance and hires staff accordingly. All these activities add to administrative costs. Loan monitoring for purposes of preventing credit diversion and ensuring loan repayment is often ineffective, and credit supervision ends up being wasteful.

Despite large staffs, long loan-appraisal and disbursement lags are common in these agencies. In an inflationary environment, such lags result in large, unanticipated increases in investment costs that may outweigh explicit and implicit borrowing costs. Project viability and repayment ability can be compromised. Borrowers have even been known to hold the lender responsible for financial difficulties resulting from the untimeliness of disbursements and to develop attitudes inimical to loan repayment.

Specialized financial institutions in agriculture tend to suffer from highly imperfect information. Data are not generally available on the financial activities and financial status of loan customers since these specialized institutions do not hold the demand deposits and savings accounts of their customers. Moreover, these credit institutions are usually deficient in macroeconomic and sector-specific economic intelligence. Consequently, management decisions are often unsound and are revised too late to adjust to ups and downs in the economy. Lending costs are rarely documented. Even essential internal indicators of operational efficiency, such as the arrears ratio, are often constructed on a loans-outstanding basis rather than on an amounts-due basis, a more effective indicator of internal financial performance.

The problems of loan delinquency and default experienced by supply-leading financial institutions are critical. Many credit institutions and programs have become illiquid because of poor loan repayment (Von Pischke 1981). These arrears problems are associated with many of the operational features, characteristics, and problems already discussed.

Possibilities for Reform

The problems of specialized agricultural lenders discussed in this chapter constitute a compelling case for financial reforms. Although the precise nature and timing of any reforms must be time and place specific, it is worthwhile to outline a few guidelines that may be useful for local and donor agencies.

With regard to the range of financial services provided, consideration ought to be given to performing a more complete set of functions, including noncredit services such as financial advice. These institutions should be more than retailers of credit. In particular, deposit facilities and local bond issues should be used to help overcome difficulties that originate from the traditional way specialized agricultural lenders are funded. Furthermore, deposits generate important information for credit institutions when loan customers maintain accounts with the lender. Deposits can thus provide a basis for continuous insight into the financial situation of borrowers, assist in monitoring progress, and allow the institution to offer higher-quality services. However, the success of these resource-mobilization activities will be influenced by whether potential depositors perceive the credit institutions as permanent. This perception is strongly influenced by the degree to which the institution is considered financially viable.

The major objective of interest-rate reforms should be to ensure institutional viability. This implies lending rates that cover costs and are flexible in the face of inflation. Another objective should be to let the cost of credit reflect the scarcity value of capital and to give positive real rates of return to savers. Meaningful interest-rate reform, therefore, will result in higher nominal loan rates of interest. The level, the frequency, and the loan contracts on which interest rates are periodically adjusted are open to discussion. Reforms applied only to new loan contracts might result in very high nominal charges to new customers and involve *ex post* resource transfers from those customers to the beneficiaries of earlier low-cost loans. On the other hand, retroactive increases in loan charges on previous long-term loans, if sizable, might cause further problems of loan delinquency and default and might be considered unfair if retroactivity clauses were not included in the original loan contracts. Thus, both approaches raise issues of equity and propriety. Regardless of how the increased loan charges are apportioned among borrowers, it is possible to ease the burden of adjustment by innovations such as flexible payment schemes that allow most of the repayment in the later years of the contract.

The increase in nominal interest rates, warranted by the goals of viability and positive real rates of interest, depends on the costs of lending and inflation. Lending costs can be reduced through reforms that place greater responsibility on officials in lending institutions. The market discipline imposed by depositors and other private holders of the institutions' liabilities could help to foster better management. Reduction in default and delinquency can also be achieved by more efficient information systems. This calls for a reform of decision criteria as well as for the collection of appropriate statistics on lending costs, arrears rates, agricultural-input and commodity-price movements, and other relevant macroeconomic information.

Although enforcement of sanctions against loan defaulters would also help to lower lending costs, it is important not to underestimate the institutional and political obstacles to more effective implementation of sanctions against defaulters. This is one of the costs of using credit as a political instrument. There are ample opportunities for political interference within the prolonged decision-making process. In some cases there might be strong societal and community opposition to repossession or appropriation of the assets of loan defaulters—for example, because they were recent beneficiaries of agrarian-reform programs.

Financial institutions and their credit customers are vulnerable to national and international economic conditions beyond their control. Financial reforms, although necessary, may not be sufficient for success unless accompanied by complementary reforms in the producing sector and in the entire economy. Policies that reduce the rate of inflation moderate pressures for further upward revisions in nominal interest rates. Realistic output and input prices enhance the profitability of agriculture and remove a major reason for loan delinquency. Interest-rate revisions in the absence of such complementary real-sector policy changes reduce the chances for successful reform of rural financial markets.

Concluding Remarks

It has become increasingly apparent that the performance of many specialized agricultural lending institutions in LICs has deteriorated in the past decade. The initial enthusiasm that policymakers had for specialized agricultural lenders and major increases in the supply of agricultural credit is starting to wane. Serious problems have undermined these efforts. In part, this has resulted from inappropriate pricing and investment policies that eroded the rate of return to farming and weakened the creditworthiness of borrowers. Poor management also has frequently contributed to the demise of some specialized agricultural lenders. Erroneous assumptions about the role of credit and the form that credit must take to reach small farmers and to change farming practices have been another contributing factor.

In too many cases, incomplete and highly vulnerable financial institutions have been developed as mere retailers of credit. At the same time the failure to recognize factors leading to credit diversion and the essential property of finance, its fungibility, meant that the additionality or impact of credit was far less than hoped for (David and Meyer 1980). Elaborate technical farm plans with high administrative costs to both lenders and borrowers were emphasized to the exclusion of relevant information on lending costs, arrears rates, and a realistic evaluation of the risks and returns to farming. Institutional viability was sacrificed or ignored to gain ill-defined and illusory social benefits. Lender rationing behavior and farm-level delinquency, in the face of interest-rate ceilings and rising inflation, have created a more unequal and concentrated pattern of rural income distribution than existed before these efforts.

Attempts to redress this state of affairs are required. Crucial to this reform is the need to build more complete financial institutions that effectively mobilize domestic savings at positive rates of interest and offer credit at realistic and flexible interest rates. Only through this revitalization of financial intermediation can LICs hope to overcome the shrinking supply of international funding. The reliance on a more disciplined and continuing source of domestic savings will require a more balanced portfolio in terms of term structure and farm type; more helpful internal financial indicators of changing lending costs, arrears rates, and risk; and more rigorous standards of staff rewards and accountability. Delinquency rates will very likely decline substantially once these reforms are in place and the source of funding is more widely known to be domestic. Rural residents can appreciate that, although they may not all get loans, a large number of them would receive positive rates of interest on their savings and thus benefit from financial intermediation. More effective support for sanctions against delinquency and default would result.

We conclude that heavy emphasis on forming specialized agricultural lenders is a mistake and that much of the funds currently going into these lenders could be better spent. It is clear that credit cannot be made to do all the things expected of it in the past. The risks and returns to farming cannot be ignored. Pricing policies that penalize agriculture should be changed, and more investments should be aimed at increasing yields and reducing risks in farming. With these broad reforms in place in both the financial and real markets, we can expect to see rural financial markets make a more substantial contribution to rural development.

Notes

We thank the Rural Development and Development Administration Office of the Agency for International Development (AID) and the AID Mission in Jamaica for research support that allowed the authors to assemble the findings reported here.

1. A 1976 survey study by the Inter-American Development Bank (p.14) notes that of the 262 development banks in Latin America in 1974, few have mobilized domestic savings directly through demand and savings deposits.

References

Adams, Dale W "Recent Performance of Rural Financial Markets." In *Borrowers and Lenders: Rural Financial Markets and Institutions in Developing Countries,* edited by John Howell. London: Overseas Development Institute, 1980.

Adams, D. W, and G. I. Nehman. "Borrowing Costs and the Demand for Rural Credit." *Journal of Development Studies* 15(1979):165–176.

Araujo, Paulo F. C., and Richard L. Meyer. "Agricultural Credit Policy in Brazil: Objectives and Results." *American Journal of Agricultural Economics* 59(1977):957-961.

Bhatt, V. V. "Interest Rate, Transactions Costs, and Financial Innovations." *Savings and Development* 3(1979):95–126.

Boakye-Dankwa, K. "A Review of the Farm Repayment Problem in Low-Income Countries." *Savings and Development* 3(1979):235–252.

Bouman, F.J.A. "Indigenous Savings and Credit Societies in the Third World. A Message." *Savings and Development* 1(1977):181–218.

Bourne, Compton, and Douglas H. Graham. "Funding and Viability of Rural Development Banks." *Savings and Development* 4(1980):303–319.

———."Economic Disequilibria and Rural Financial Market Performance in Developing Economies." *Canadian Journal of Agricultural Economics* 31(1983):59–76.

Brown, Gilbert T. "Agricultural Pricing Policies in Developing Countries." In *Distortions of Agricultural Incentives,* edited by Theodore W. Schultz. Bloomington: Indiana University Press, 1978.

David, Cristina C., and Richard L. Meyer. "Measuring the Farm-Level Impact of Agricultural Loans." In *Borrowers and Lenders: Rural Financial Markets and Institutions in Developing Countries,* edited by John Howell. London: Overseas Development Institute, 1980.

Gonzalez-Vega, Claudio. "Interest Rate Restrictions and Income Distribution." *American Journal of Agricultural Economics* 59(1977):973–976.

Graham, Douglas H., and Compton Bourne. "Agricultural Credit and Rural Progress in Jamaica." In *Borrowers and Lenders: Rural Financial Markets and Institutions in Developing Countries,* edited by John Howell. London: Overseas Development Institute, 1980.

Inter-American Development Bank. "The Role of National Development Finance Institutions in the Mobilization of Domestic Resources in Latin America." Unpublished paper, Washington, D.C., 1976.

Ladman, Jerry R., and Ronald L. Tinnermeier. "The Political Economy of Agricultural Credit: The Case of Bolivia." *American Journal of Agricultural Economics* 63(1981):66–72.

Patrick, Hugh T. "Financial Development and Economic Growth in Underdeveloped Countries." *Economic Development and Cultural Change* 14(1966):174–189.

Schultz, Theodore W. "Uneven Prospects for Gains from Agricultural Research Related to Economic Policy." In *Resource Allocation and Productivity,* edited by T. M. Arndt and others. Minneapolis: University of Minnesota Press, 1977.

Von Pischke, J. D. "The Political Economy of Specialized Farm Credit Institutions." In *Borrowers and Lenders: Rural Financial Markets and Institutions in Developing Countries,* edited by John Howell. London: Overseas Development Institute, 1980.

_____. "The Political Economy of Specialized Farm Credit Institutions in Low Income Countries." World Bank Staff Working Paper no. 446, Washington, D.C., April 1981.

World Bank. "The Financial Cost of Agricultural Credit: A Case Study of Indian Experience." World Bank Staff Working Paper no. 296, Washington, D.C., October 1978.

4
Illusion and Reality in Allocating Agricultural Credit: The Example of Colombia

Robert C. Vogel
Donald W. Larson

Like many developing countries, Colombia has followed a policy of setting interest rates for agricultural credit below equilibrium levels in an attempt to promote agricultural production and to subsidize farmers, especially small farmers. These subsidized interest rates have resulted in excess demand for agricultural credit, which in turn has necessitated rationing devices and procedures to allocate this credit. The Colombian government has developed elaborate rationing mechanisms in an attempt to allocate specific amounts of bank credit to various crops and thereby to promote their production. The primary purpose of this chapter is to examine these rationing mechanisms and to evaluate their success in achieving the planned allocation of agricultural credit and in promoting the production of designated crops.

In Colombia two government institutions are responsible for almost all institutional credit allocated to the agricultural sector. The first is the Fondo Financiero Agropecuario (FFAP), a department of the Banco de la Republica (Colombia's central bank), which rediscounts bank loans to the agricultural sector. Resources for these rediscounts are obtained primarily from bonds (which Colombian banks are required to hold), from international lending institutions, and at times directly from the Banco de la Republica. The government's Junta Monetaria establishes the conditions for these agricultural loans and rediscounts and, in fact, for all agricultural credit from the banking system. The second government institution is the Caja Agraria, founded in the 1930s—the largest bank in Colombia. Like other banks in Colombia, the Caja Agraria has access to rediscounts from FFAP, and it makes substantial use of these resources. However, unlike the other banks, the Caja Agraria also makes substantial use of its own resources (obtained primarily from demand deposits and from time and savings deposits) in its agricultural lending. Also, unlike other banks and FFAP, the Caja Agraria is oriented toward serving small farmers, and the majority of Caja credit from its own ordinary resources is, in fact, allocated to small farmers. In the subsequent analysis, Caja loans based on FFAP rediscounts are included in FFAP statistics, whereas Caja statistics refer only to loans from the Caja's ordinary resources.

In the next section we examine agricultural credit policy in Colombia during the 1970s and, in particular, the rationing mechanisms developed by the Colombian government in its attempt to allocate agricultural credit to various seasonal crops. Although essentially the same mechanisms are used in allocating credit for permanent crops, livestock, infrastructure, agricultural equipment, and so forth, the focus here is on the major seasonal crops.[1] The main reason for this focus is that credit policies can be related more directly to price and output in the case of seasonal crops than is true of other agricultural activities.

The third section examines the Colombian government's agricultural price policies for seasonal crops, especially as they relate to the allocation of agricultural credit. The fourth section compares the realized allocation of agricultural credit with the planned allocation and indicates why there is so little relation between the credit program and actual credit use. In the final section we draw some conclusions about the relationship between credit and agricultural production and about the success of credit policies in promoting the production of certain crops and in subsidizing farmers.

Agricultural Credit Policy

In Colombia during the 1970s real rates of interest on most bank loans to the agricultural sector were very low or even negative. Since 1972 the rate of inflation, measured by either the wholesale or consumer price index, has averaged more than 20 percent per year, at times reaching 40 percent. On the other hand, nominal interest rates, which are set by the Junta Monetaria, have generally ranged between 10 and 20 percent per year for bank loans to the agricultural sector. More specifically, nominal interest rates on short-term loans for seasonal crops from the Caja's ordinary resources have ranged from 10 to 18 percent and from 10 to 17 percent on loans rediscounted by FFAP.[2] The resulting low or negative real rates of interest suggest that there should be substantial excess demand for this agricultural credit, especially since borrowers have at times been able to earn up to 26 percent (nominal) interest on certain classes of time deposits and more than 30 percent on short-term and virtually risk-free securities.

In recognition of this excess demand for agricultural credit, the Colombian government has established rationing mechanisms in an attempt to allocate credit to activities that are considered particularly desirable. The Oficina de Planeacion del Sector Agropecuario (OPSA) of the Ministerio de Agricultura has primary responsibility for planning the amounts to be lent for various agricultural activities, especially under FFAP rediscounts. Twice each year, in advance of the planting season, OPSA develops its credit programs for seasonal crops (once each year for permanent crops and other agricultural activities). In developing these credit programs OPSA relies heavily on regional and national committees that are composed of representatives of government institutions concerned with the agricultural sector, financial institutions, producer groups, and sometimes user groups or other interested individuals.

Based on perceptions of national requirements and information on crop yields, these committees recommend the areas to be planted to different crops. Then, based on estimates of production costs per hectare for each crop, recommendations are formulated for the amount of credit to be allocated to each crop. However, not all production costs are financed (land rent and acquisition and some labor costs are ineligible), and not all of the eligible costs are financed. For each production period the percentage of eligible costs to be financed is set, and these percentages vary both over time and among crops, presumably to provide different incentives for the production of different crops. Moreover, as OPSA has admitted in the publication of its agricultural programs, considerable uncertainty surrounds the estimates of production costs. In part this uncertainty is due to differences among regions and technologies for each crop. Just as it is in the interest of producer groups to have high support prices, it is also in their interest to have production costs and the percentages to be financed set as high as possible, in order to obtain more credit at subsidized rates of interest.

The recommendations of the regional committees are reviewed by OPSA in conjunction with national committees for each of the major crops and then submitted to the Junta Monetaria for approval. In determining the final version of the agricultural credit program and, in particular, the amounts to be lent under FFAP rediscounts, the Junta Monetaria takes into account not only the OPSA recommendations but also overall economic and financial conditions such as the rate of inflation, recent patterns of growth in money and credit, and resources available to FFAP from loan repayments and new foreign loans. Although the Junta Monetaria may change the total amount of credit programmed for the agricultural sector based on these considerations, the priorities established by OPSA within the agricultural sector are rarely changed, in part because FFAP officials are in close contact with OPSA and the regional and national committees throughout the planning process.

When using FFAP rediscounts the Caja Agraria is subject to the FFAP credit program, but when lending from its ordinary resources the Caja Agraria follows its own credit program. However, Caja programming closely parallels OPSA programming in two respects: (1) Caja officials participate in most of the regional and national committees, and (2) in its credit programming the Caja Agraria is quite decentralized, in that it relies heavily on information provided by its regional offices. Differences between the Caja and FFAP credit programs thus do not result from differences in approach or information, but rather from Caja's basic objective of serving small farmers. Since small farmers tend to grow traditional crops, the Caja's credit programs emphasize traditional crops such as beans, corn, potatoes, sesame, and wheat, whereas FFAP focuses on commercial crops—such as cotton, rice, sorghum, and soybeans—that are grown by large farmers. In addition, it is argued that even for the same crop production costs per hectare are lower for small farmers using traditional technologies than for large farmers who rely more heavily on purchased inputs. This is said to explain why the Caja Agraria establishes higher percentages of production costs to be financed but for most crops actually lends less per hectare than is lent under FFAP rediscounts.

Agricultural Price Policy

In attempting to influence the level and composition of agricultural output and to subsidize certain producer groups, the Colombian government uses price policies as well as credit policies. The Instituto de Mercadeo Agropecuario (IDEMA) is the main governmental institution responsible for implementing price support and stabilization policies. IDEMA's primary functions are to buy agricultural products at support prices, accumulate buffer stocks, stabilize prices, and import or export products as required. The price supports apply only to some basic products such as rice, corn, beans, sorghum, soybeans, wheat, and sesame, but IDEMA also buys a few other agricultural products.

The influence of support prices on farmers' production decisions depends basically on the level of the support price, the degree of farmer confidence in the declared price, and farmers' ability to sell at the support price. The support price is supposed to cover all production costs plus a reasonable profit margin for the average producer. However, for the reasons previously mentioned, the estimates of production costs that are developed in the credit-planning process may be quite subjective and not representative for a significant number of producers. Moreover, except for rice and wheat, support prices during the 1970s were generally set at levels below the prices actually received by farmers, and these low support prices were reflected in IDEMA purchases averaging less than 5 percent of annual production for products other than rice and wheat. These small purchases by IDEMA have failed to reduce seasonal price fluctuations. The financial problems of IDEMA resulting from large operating losses may have limited purchases and encouraged low support prices and may also have contributed to a lack of farmer confidence in the price-support program.

Farmers frequently are unable to sell their products at the support price because the small number of purchase points (41 permanent locations plus 50 mobile units) restricts farmer access and because IDEMA's quality specifications often result in substantial discounts for products that do not meet IDEMA's inflexible standards. The delay in IDEMA's payments may present a further difficulty. It has been reported that payments by IDEMA to farmers have sometimes been delayed for several months, in contrast to the immediate cash payments offered by private buyers.

Political pressures in urban areas to maintain adequate domestic food supplies at prices favorable to consumers may often result in practices such as controls over retail food prices and marketing margins. Such market interventions tend to reduce profits and create incentives for producers to divert resources into nonfood or nonagricultural production where prices are uncontrolled and rates of return are higher. Price controls over food have been widely applied in Colombia in the past, but, in any case, the worldwide price increases for many primary commodities that occurred during the early 1970s have tended to increase the real gross income per hectare in Colombia for most of the products included in this study. Moreover, Colombian farmers are receiving prices for these products that appear to be quite close to international f.o.b. prices when the comparison is made at the official exchange rate. However, when the official exchange rate is adjusted for the overvaluation implicit in the structure of protection,

Table 4.1 Relation of Amount of Loans Approved to Amount of Credit Programmed, 1971-77

	Range in Ratio of Credit Approved to Credit Programmed		Correlation of Credit Approved With Credit Programmed	
	Fondo Financiero Agropecuario	Caja Agraria	Fondo Financiero Agropecuario	Caja Agraria
Cotton	1.29 - 5.15	.82 - 2.34	.56	.01
Rice (Irrigated)	1.04 - 2.38	1.66 - 5.45	.36	.62
Sorghum	.96 - 4.94	.39 - 1.98	-.06	.14
Soybeans	.54 - 2.06	.64 - 2.39	-.07	.04
Beans	.12 - 2.27	.82 - 2.46	-.10	-.57
Corn	.72 - 1.50	.90 - 2.06	.27	-.07
Potatoes	.82 - 1.56	1.15 - 2.43	.82*	.57
Rice (Dryland)	.86 - 2.88	.27 - 1.25	.47	-.05
Sesame	.43 - 4.18	.79 - 1.60	.01	-.01
Wheat	.09 - 1.60	.62 - 1.13	.42	-.32

Peso amounts used in the calculation for this table were deflated to 1970 prices using the wholesale price index for agricultural products.

* Significant at the 10 percent level.

Source: "El Credito y la Productividad," unpublished material from a Seminar on Productivity sponsored by the Ministerio de Agricultura, Neiva, Colombia, May, 1977; and Ministerio de Agricultura, Cifras del Sector Agropecuario and Programas Agricolas, Bogotá, Colombia, various years.

Colombian farmers are likely to be receiving prices that are well below the international prices for these products.[3]

Planned Versus Realized Allocation

To evaluate the success of government rationing mechanisms in determining the allocation of agricultural credit, the amount of credit programmed by FFAP and the Caja Agraria for each of the main seasonal crops has been compared with the amount of loans actually approved during each Colombian agricultural year from July 1971-June 1972 through July 1976-June 1977. Table 4.1 presents the ranges in the ratio of the amount of loans approved to the amount of credit programmed by FFAP and the Caja Agraria for each of the main seasonal crops during this period. All of the ranges are very wide, indicating that there is no apparent relation between the amount of credit programmed and the amount of loans actually made for any of the seasonal crops. The only pattern that emerges is that commercial crops grown by large farmers (e.g., cotton, irrigated rice, and sorghum) tend to have the highest ratio of loans made to credit programmed. Table 4.1 also presents the correlations between the amount of credit programmed by FFAP and the Caja Agraria in real terms and the amount of loans approved for each of the seasonal crops. There is again no apparent relation between the amount of credit programmed and the amount of loans approved. Only one correlation coefficient is significant at the 10 percent level, and most are not significant at even the 50 percent level.

It thus appears that the credit programs of FFAP and the Caja Agraria have virtually no impact on the actual allocation of credit among the various seasonal crops. Whether this is desirable or not remains to be discussed, but before dealing with this issue it is worthwhile to ask what factors (other than the credit program) may influence the realized allocation of agricultural credit. Price and profit expectations, as discussed in the preceding section, should be significant factors if the allocation of credit is primarily determined by producer demand. Because of the uncertainty surrounding the estimates of production costs, the following analysis focuses mainly on crop prices rather than on profit expectations. When IDEMA support prices for the concurrent period were used to explain the allocation of credit, no statistically significant relation could be found. However, for the reasons indicated in the preceding section, IDEMA prices may have little influence on producer behavior. Average prices paid to the producers of each crop have thus been used as an alternative explanatory variable, but with a lead of six months (e.g., prices for calendar year 1971 related to credit for agricultural year 1971-1972). In this case prices tend to have the expected positive impact on the amount of credit actually allocated to the various seasonal crops relative to the amount of credit programmed.

Because agricultural credit is made available to producers at subsidized rates of interest, the amount of financing that can be obtained per hectare is another factor that might influence the demand for credit. There is some evidence that the amount of credit available per hectare for the various seasonal crops has a positive influence on the ratio of the amount of loans approved to the amount of credit programmed. However, real production costs per hectare have a more statistically significant positive impact on this ratio. Although higher production costs should have a negative influence on profitability, other things being equal, it has previously been suggested that the production cost estimates used in credit programming may not reflect actual production costs, but rather the power of producer groups to influence cost estimates and thereby increase the amount of subsidized credit available to them.

Lending agencies as well as credit users are likely to influence the allocation of credit. For example, the percentage of production costs that can be financed is an *ex ante* variable set as part of the credit program, but the amount actually lent per hectare is an *ex post* variable and depends in part on decisions made by the lender. The Caja Agraria generally sets higher percentages in its programming than FFAP, but actually lends less per hectare. As previously indicated, this anomaly has sometimes been explained by arguing that small farmers have lower production costs than large farmers. However, it may be that small farmers are lent less per hectare because lenders perceive them to be higher-risk borrowers. Thus, factors affecting lender behavior are likely to play a significant role in the divergence of amounts actually lent from the credit program.

Conclusions

The main justification for credit programming is to stimulate the production of designated crops. However, the conclusion of this paper is that the FFAP and Caja credit programs have virtually no impact on the amounts actually lent for the different seasonal crops. Moreover, even if credit allocation actually followed the credit program, there is ample evidence in Colombia that the amounts lent for the different seasonal crops have no close relationship to the area planted or to the production of these crops. The fact that credit programming and crop production are largely unrelated may not be undesirable if credit, and hence resources, are in fact allocated to activities with the highest rates of return.

Should Colombian policymakers attempt to compel the allocation of credit to follow the credit program, even when the program is at variance with borrower and lender assessments of profitability? Because credit is fungible and borrowers and lenders can easily report using credit for the activities preferred by policymakers, it would be costly if not impossible to police effectively the allocation of credit. Both lenders and borrowers could be audited to ensure that the activities designated in the credit program had been undertaken, but such audits would be very costly and could not possibly reach all borrowers, especially if lenders were expected to serve an appreciable number of small farmers. Moreover, such controls cannot influence the allocation of credit when the lender and borrower carry out the designated activities but devote their own resources (which would otherwise have been devoted to the designated activities) to other activities (Von Pischke and Adams 1980).

Credit programming in Colombia is not only unlikely to influence significantly the allocation of credit, and hence resources, but may also have several undesirable side effects. Scarce human resources are largely wasted in the credit programming process, although some benefits may arise from the exchange of information that is useful for other agricultural policies (e.g., price supports). A second undesirable side effect of credit programming, one seldom recognized, is the introduction into the allocation of credit of rigidities that restrict the flow of credit to new crops and new technologies and hence stifle innovation in the agricultural sector. Because of the costs involved in developing the credit program, only the main crops can be included. Moreover, the need to calculate costs of production in arriving at the amount to be lent per hectare for each crop under the credit program makes it very difficult to consider the appropriate range of either areas or technologies for even the main crops.[4]

As indicated in the preceding section, real production costs per hectare have a positive, rather than a negative, impact on the amounts actually lent relative to the amounts of credit programmed for the different seasonal crops. Because this credit is available at subsidized rates of interest, such a positive relationship may reflect the ability of powerful producer groups to increase the estimates of production costs and thereby to increase the amount of subsidized credit available to them. It was also noted in the preceding section that, even for the same crop, less is lent per hectare to small farmers by the Caja Agraria than is lent to large farmers under FFAP. Such findings suggest that the credit programming process in Colombia may be associated with a tendency to concentrate agricultural credit in large loans to large farmers. As pointed out elsewhere in this book, the phenomenon of subsidized interest rates leading to rationing devices that concentrate subsidized credit in large loans to large farmers (and hence make the distribution of income more unequal) has been widely observed in developing countries, so that it would not be surprising to find this same phenomenon in Colombia.

Notes

Earlier versions of this paper were presented at the 17th International Conference of Agricultural Economists held in Banff, Canada, and published in *Savings and Development* 4(1980):52–62. We particularly wish to thank our colleagues in the Rural Finance Workshop at The Ohio State University for helpful comments, but they are not responsible for any remaining errors.

1. The major seasonal crops, which can be planted twice per year in Colombia, are beans, corn, cotton, potatoes, rice (both irrigated and dryland), sesame, sorghum, soybeans, and wheat.

2. Before 1973 FFAP was called the Fondo Financiero Agrario and was limited to the financing of seasonal crops.

3. Studies by Belassa and associates (1971) estimate that in Brazil and Chile the overvaluation was 27 percent and 68 percent, respectively, in the mid-1960s, and the structure of protection in these countries is not appreciably different from that of Colombia.

4. See Vogel (1979) for an argument that limits on amounts lent per hectare are a perverse rationing device that inevitably follows from subsidized interest rates for agricultural credit.

References

Avramovic, Dragoslav, and associates. *Economic Growth of Colombia: Problems and Prospects.* Baltimore: Johns Hopkins University Press, 1972.

Belassa, Bela, and associates. *The Structure of Protection in Developing Countries.* Baltimore: Johns Hopkins University Press, 1971.

"El Credito y la Productividad." Unpublished material from a Seminar on Productivity sponsored by the Ministerio de Agricultura, Neiva, Colombia, May 1977.

"El Sector Agropecuario Colombiano: Problemas Actuales y Perspectivas." *Conjuntura Economica* 15(1977):3–24.

Lora, T. Eduardo. "Mecanismos y efectos del financiamento al sector agropecuario." *Banca y Finanzas: Revista de la Asociacion Bancaria de Colombia* 157(1977):43–87.

Ministerio de Agricultura. *Cifras del Sector Agropecuario.* Bogota, Colombia, various years.

———. *Programas Agricolas.* Bogota, Colombia, various years.

"Ponencia Sobre Mercadeo y Productividad Agricola en Colombia." Unpublished material from a Seminar on Productivity sponsored by the Ministerio de Agricultura, Neiva, Colombia, May 1977.

Vogel, Robert C. "Subsidized Interest Rates and the Rationing of Agricultural Credit in Developing Countries." In *Problems and Issues of Agricultural Credit and Rural Finance,* edited and published by the Bangladesh Bank. Dacca, 1979.

Von Pischke, J. D., and Dale W Adams. "Fungibility and the Design and Evaluation of Agricultural Credit Projects." *American Journal of Agricultural Economics* 62(1980):719–726.

Part 2

Interest-Rate Policies

5
Overview of the Importance of Interest-Rate Policies

Dale W Adams
Douglas H. Graham
J. D. Von Pischke

An astronaut who was also an economist landed on one of the moons of Jupiter where there was a grain shortage. It appeared to the astronaut that producers had no incentive to grow grain, despite the fact that consumers were being forced to queue in long lines for their allotment of grain. Grain merchants were bribed by the rich, who got a large share of the grain, and the government imported and subsidized the price of grain from other moons of Jupiter. After learning that the astronaut was an economist, the inhabitants asked him for advice about their grain problem. The astronaut inquired about the costs of production, the grain prices received by the producers, and the prices paid by consumers and found that the society had price controls on grain. The astronaut suggested that raising price ceilings could stimulate producers to increase output, thus reducing the long lines and the corruption associated with small supplies.

About this time, an astronaut from Mars, who was also an economist, crash-landed on Earth and was confronted with similar questions about the performances of rural financial markets. The inhabitants of many countries pointed out that few individuals produce savings for deposit in financial institutions, that financial intermediaries often force small and inexperienced borrowers to wait in long lines and incur many transaction costs before a few receive loans, and that funds for agricultural credit come largely from the government or aid donors. Like its earthling counterpart on the Jovian moon, the Martian might conclude that interest-rate restrictions caused rural people not to save in financial form, resulted in long queues of people who want cheap credit, allowed rich people to get a disproportionate share of the cheap credit, and induced foreign-aid agencies to provide money to sustain rural credit programs. The Martian might argue that lifting interest-rate restrictions could help ease these ills.

Many policymakers, technicians, and writers on development often do not think of interest rates as incentives or prices, and they fail to recognize the importance of these prices in affecting the behavior of participants in financial markets. The importance of interest rates as incentives is often clouded by religious dogmas and stereotypes about lenders, savers, and borrowers. It is too often overlooked that in most moderately advanced economies interest rates are the second-most important price after the foreign-exchange rate.

Since the mid-1930s much attention has been given to keeping interest rates low to stimulate investment, in the shadow of John Maynard Keynes's *General Theory*. Much of the popular debate on interest rates fails to distinguish between nominal and real rates. The nominal rate of interest is the rate specified in a loan contract; the real rate is the nominal rate adjusted for changes in prices over the period of the loan. In the 1930s most countries experienced declines in overall price levels, so that real rates of interest were much higher than nominal rates. In several of those years prices in the United States, for example, declined by up to 20 percent. Nominal interest rates of only 5 percent resulted in large real rates of interest, often in excess of 20 percent. The price conditions of the 1930s have not held during the past couple of decades, when prices have generally risen. Many countries have had persistent inflation that typically has exceeded the nominal rates of interest paid on formal loans as well as on deposits. As a result, real rates of interest are often close to zero and in many cases are highly negative. Economists are becoming increasingly aware that the influence of real rates of interest on financial-market performance outweighs by far the effect of nominal rates.

Governments have aggressively used cheap credit in attempts to encourage the use of new agricultural technologies, to stimulate agricultural output, or to try to help the rural poor. The chapters in Part 2 show that cheap credit is a major problem, rather than being the solution to many difficulties found in rural financial markets. These chapters also discuss a number of hidden and unanticipated results of cheap-credit policies—results that often are not well recognized because of the complexity of financial markets and the process by which they generate information. They are highly diffused, include large numbers of actual and potential participants, cover broad geographic areas, and trade instruments that are highly fungible.

Policymakers have stressed the importance of interest rates in influencing borrower behavior. Until recently there has been relatively little discussion about how interest rates affect the behavior of financial intermediaries, savers, and politicians as they interact with or through financial markets. Advocacy of cheap credit has even permeated many cooperatives involved in financial intermediation. Credit cooperatives and credit unions have usually been established to provide inexpensive credit to some members. Cheap credit generally forces cooperatives to pay low rates of return to those members whose money is being lent, limiting the ability of these organizations to expand services to members.

The chapters in Part 2 challenge conventional thinking about the need for cheap agricultural credit. Chapter 6 explores eight arguments traditionally used to defend low interest rates, all of which are found to be deficient. This chapter is followed by several others that clarify the major problems caused by low interest rates. These include loan concentration in the hands of relatively few borrowers, inefficient allocation of resources, high loan-transaction costs for some borrowers and lenders, politicization of financial institutions, patronal relationships in the financial system, weak financial intermediaries, taxation of savers, and distortions in income distribution. The chapters all stress that cheap credit worsens income distribution. It appears to be impossible to provide significant amounts of cheap credit to the rural poor under any kind of government or banking system.

The major conclusion of this part of the book is that relatively stable and generally positive real rates of interest are necessary in financial markets for efficiency and equity. Interest-rate reforms will not be an easy task, especially in those countries where large income transfers are taking place under the guise of cheap credit. Some people argue that interest-rate reforms may be desirable, but that it is impossible to make these reforms without changes in other economic policies pertaining to exchange rates, taxes and subsidies, and price controls. There is certainly merit in this argument, but substantial gains could be made in many cases through reforms in rural financial markets alone. Where regulated interest rates in rural financial markets are much lower than those allowed in other segments of the formal financial system, for example, partial reforms that increase interest rates in rural financial markets to the levels allowed in the rest of the economy would not necessarily require reforms in the entire economy.

It appears that low-interest-rate policies are very closely associated with much of the poor performance of rural financial markets in many developing countries and that reform is necessary to substantially improve performance. Donor agencies might be able to play a key role in reform by helping to clarify the damage done by current policies and the benefits of alternative policies. Donors could also help by not supporting interest-rate policies that damage rural financial markets.

6 Are the Arguments for Cheap Agricultural Credit Sound?

Dale W Adams

Rare is the government of a low-income country that does not fix low nominal interest rates on agricultural credit and even lower rates on loans designated for the rural poor. These rates are usually below those charged on other business or industrial loans, lower than the rate of inflation, and often too low for lenders to cover their loan-transaction costs. Nominal interest rates are usually quite inflexible and are not adjusted with changes in nonagricultural interest rates. Because of volatile price changes, however, it is common for real rates of interest to change substantially and for regulated agricultural lending rates to stay generally negative.[1] The ease of initiating or expanding cheap agricultural credit programs makes them attractive to harried policymakers trying to stimulate food production, to compensate farmers for other adverse policies, to help the rural poor, or to provide relief after some rural disaster.

Arguments used to justify low interest rates are intertwined and have religious and political roots that run deep below the surface of the discussion. Widespread confusion over the role of finance in development and the difference between nominal and real rates of interest further complicates discussion. The varied backgrounds of the people involved make it difficult to clarify, let alone resolve, such arguments: Systematic attempts are often met with blank stares, counterarguments not germane to the point under discussion, and citations of horror stories that are several standard deviations away from any mean. Those who argue against cheap agricultural credit are hampered by the difficulties of documenting the subtle, diffused, and complex effects that low interest rates have on rural households, rural nonfarm firms, lenders, and rural financial markets.

Eight common arguments are used to justify cheap agricultural loans. In the discussion that follows I briefly summarize these arguments and evaluate their strengths and weaknesses. I conclude that higher and more flexible nominal interest rates would result in more equitable income distribution, more efficient allocation of resources, more output, and more viable financial institutions.

The Usury Argument

The charging of interest on loans made to a brother is condemned in the Bible, the Talmud, and the Koran. Partly because of these scriptures, many societies sustain strong biases against moneylenders. *Loan shark, usurer,* and *shylock* are all pejorative terms attached to financial intermediaries. These prejudices are due in part to intermediaries often being "outsiders": Examples are Jews in Europe, Indians in East Africa, Chinese in Southeast Asia, and Middle Easterners in Latin America. Both consumers and producers regularly blame economic problems on those who perform these poorly understood intermediary functions.

Reasoned debate rarely overcomes value judgments about the badness of charging interest and the badness of people who informally lend. Value-based views about usury should be weakened, however, by recent research that shows informal lenders do not regularly receive returns that are much beyond their costs. That is, they do not receive monopoly profits. Research by both Singh (1968) and Harriss (1980) in India documented the high returns that informal lenders get for using their funds in their other, nonlending activities; their opportunity costs for informal lending are high. Also, there are seldom barriers to entry in informal lending—anyone with money can become involved. A number of other researchers have shown that the average borrowing cost from informal sources is much less than is widely thought. For the new borrower of small amounts, these informal borrowing costs may be very similar to the total borrowing cost of acquiring formal loans (Adams and Nehman 1979). As Bouman points out in Chapter 19, the widespread use of informal loans and their high repayment rates also show that most informal lenders provide valuable services to borrowers.

Railings against the moneylender may spice literature, massage prejudices, and offer facile explanations for problems experienced by the uninformed. It is much more difficult, if not impossible, to assemble objective information to support these views. Cheap-credit policies based on assumptions about the evils done by moneylenders who exploit borrowers through high interest rates appear to be chasing ghosts.

High-Income Countries Charged Low Rates

A few policymakers argue that cheap agricultural credit is justified in low-income countries because high-income countries charged low rates on government loans to farmers in periods of crisis, especially during the 1930s. The experience of the U.S. Farm Security Administration is commonly cited. During the 1930s most of the loans made by this agency were at nominal interest rates in the 2–7 percent range. Many of the U.S. technicians who helped develop agricultural credit programs in low-income countries in the last three decades were trained by the Farm Security Administration and successor agencies. Low-interest-rate policies were commonly written into supervised credit programs and cooperative credit activities involving these U.S. technicians.

On careful analysis this line of reasoning turns out to be a nonargument. To clarify this, one must focus on real rather than nominal rates of interest. The nominal rate of interest is the price of the loan specified in the loan contract; it is the 5 percent one receives on a savings account and the 18 percent one pays if a charge-card account is not paid in full. Nominal and real rates of interest are the same when no changes occur in overall price levels. Inflation, however, causes real and nominal rates of interest to diverge and reduces the purchasing power of financial instruments through negative real rates of interest. Deflation does just the opposite. In a number of years during the 1930s overall prices in the United States, and especially agricultural prices, went down. In four years agricultural prices declined by 20 percent or more (1930, 1931, 1932, 1938), resulting in real rates of interest on formal agricultural loans that were among the highest charged anywhere in recent history. This contrasts sharply with recent conditions in low-income countries; most have recently experienced rates of inflation well in excess of 10 percent per year, and several have sustained triple-digit inflation. This widespread inflation has resulted in negative real rates of interest being charged on almost all formal agricultural loans made in low-income countries.

Lenders Get Cheap Money

Occasionally, proponents of low interest rates will argue that agricultural lenders ought to charge low interest rates because their cost of funds is low. An agricultural bank, for example, may receive loanable funds from the government, from deposits that require no interest payment, from cheap rediscount windows at the central bank, and from concessionary loans or grants from foreign donors. The reasoning is that if the lender gets inexpensive funds then these benefits ought to be passed on to the farmer borrower.

This turns out to be another nonargument. It ignores the opportunity cost of money, the foreign-exchange risks involved in borrowing foreign currency, loan-default risks, and the real costs for staff and administrators that are involved in financial intermediation. In fact, many formal lenders around the world lose money on their agricultural loans, especially those made to the rural poor.[2]

Lender Viability

Recent discussions of interest-rate reforms in the United States have focused on how deregulated interest rates would affect the viability of financial institutions such as savings and loan associations (S&Ls). Most S&Ls have a significant portion of their assets tied up in long-term mortgages at fixed interest rates below current market rates. If sold in secondary markets these assets would sell at discounts from their face values. Deregulating interest rates on savings instruments would force S&Ls to pay much higher rates of interest to obtain loanable funds and force many into insolvency. In some cases the argument that higher rates would jeopardize institutional solvency is extended to low-income countries.

There are several reasons why this argument against interest-rate reforms in low-income countries is weak or invalid (Vogel 1979). The most important one is that a large proportion of the loans made by agricultural lenders in such countries is for a single crop season, often for less than a year. Medium- and long-term loans make up a small part of many lenders' portfolios. As a result, if interest rates were adjusted upward, only small parts of the lenders' assets would lose value.

A second reason is that many of the lending agencies that do have significant amounts of medium- and long-term loans in their portfolios are government owned, and direct government subsidies could be used to offset reductions in lender's assets caused by interest-rate reforms. Also, there is precedent in some countries for revising interest rates on existing loan contracts by government decree. Some governments may be able to handle this issue by allowing lenders to renegotiate lending rates on loans already outstanding.

A more relevant viability question is: Do formal lenders receive enough revenues to cover their costs? Agricultural lending is one of the most costly things that formal financial markets do because of geographic dispersion, collateral problems, the small size of loans made, and the risks inherent in farming. Even well-managed lenders who recover a large part of their loans incur lending costs equal to 10 to 20 percent of the value of the loans extended (e.g., see Datey 1978). In many countries, interest-rate ceilings make it virtually impossible for formal lenders to realize enough revenue to cover these costs, especially if the lender is serving many rural poor. Increasing the interest rates that these lenders are allowed to charge would strengthen rather than undermine their financial viability.

Farmer Behavior

A more common argument for low interest rates is that they are necessary to induce farmers to make productive investments and to use new technology and that this is a way for governments to share risks of adopting new techniques. Cheap credit to influence entrepreneurial behavior is a simple extension of the Keynesian views on interest rates formed during the 1930s when real rates of interest were generally very high. Although the extremely high real rates of interest during the 1930s undoubtedly discouraged investments, it is much less certain that negative real rates of interest, currently widely found in low-income countries, are necessary to induce socially desirable investments.

There are other problems with this argument. For example, it assumes that many farmers are irrational when it comes to making borrowing decisions. That is, a bribe is necessary to convince farmers to do something that is profitable. Schultz (1964) and others have effectively shown that most farmers in low-income countries make efficient and rational production decisions. It is surprising that this line of thinking has not been extended more rapidly to views about farmers' financial activities. If farmers allocate their own resources efficiently, including their own funds, why should they not allocate borrowed funds in the same manner? The concern with cheap loans may mask the fact that the expected rates of return available to many farmers are low.

Another problem with this argument is that cheap loans may not be inexpensive for some borrowers (Pablo 1979). Interest payments make up only a part of borrowing costs. Additional costs include payment for paperwork, bribes, travel costs to visit lenders, and the opportunity costs of time taken to negotiate and repay loans. For the new and small borrower, these loan-transaction costs may be several times the amount of interest paid. The reticence of many farmers to seek formal loans may reflect relatively high total borrowing costs, poor quality of financial services provided by formal lenders, and uncertainties about the permanence of the formal lender. Uncertainties about when the loan will be disbursed and inflexible terms also lessen some farmers' interest in seeking formal loans.

Low interest rates may, in fact, help explain why many farmers do not seek so-called cheap loans. Interest receipts make up a large part of most lenders' total income. As a result, low rates seriously diminish the ability and willingness of the lender to provide high quality and dependable financial services. The low rates on loans set a ceiling on the rates that can be paid for deposits and make it impossible for the lender to provide attractive savings-deposit facilities. Low rates on loans also encourage the lender to shift additional loan-transaction costs to those borrowers who are costly to serve. As Ladman points out in Chapter 9, the shifting of additional loan-transaction costs to these borrowers becomes part of the loan-rationing process used by lenders to allocate "sweet money."

Higher rates of interest might, in fact, result in *less* expensive loans for borrowers who currently incur relatively large loan-transaction costs. With higher interest rates, current large borrowers would borrow less, and lenders would be forced to seek additional business from new and small borrowers. The lender might do this by absorbing or reducing some of the loan-transaction costs imposed on individuals currently rationed by this technique. For some, the loan-transaction costs might go down more than interest charges would be increased, thus reducing total borrowing costs.

Another reason why many farmers are insensitive to changes in nominal interest rates is that interest payments make up a small part of their cash expenses. A large borrower who is highly levered may incur interest payments that consume a large part of cash flow. Borrowers of small- to medium-sized loans, however, usually are much less exposed financially, and interest payments typically make up less than 5 percent of their cash expenses. One should not expect these farmers to be highly sensitive to changes in interest rates, especially if the quality of loan services is improved and larger loans are made available.

Also, because of price and yield uncertainties, most farmers must expect substantial returns at the margin before they will make an investment. They do not borrow money at 12 percent to make investments that they expect will return 13 percent, for example. Rather, the only time they are willing to borrow money that must be repaid and that carries positive real borrowing costs is when expected rates of return are a good deal higher than the borrowing rate. Everyone will grumble about having to pay higher interest rates, but the wide margins that farmers must use in making investment decisions will result in only small adjustments in loan demand for many borrowers when rates are raised. In those cases where the real rates of interest are negative, modest increases in the rate of interest only reduce the amount of the subsidy. Many farmers will still be eager to get the loans even at higher rates of interest.

Large numbers of rural households regularly borrow from informal sources and pay interest rates substantially above those charged by formal lenders, suggesting that many borrowers will not be extremely sensitive to interest rates on formal loans. High repayment rates to informal lenders also show that borrowers protect informal credit ratings. Does this indicate that informal lenders often provide more valuable services to borrowers than do formal lenders?

Income-Transfer Mechanism

Many people believe that cheap agricultural credit is an effective way to transfer income to rural areas where poverty is concentrated; such transfers are generally consistent with social objectives. There are three ways that loans can affect income distributions: through the net returns that borrowers realize from using additional resources purchased with loans, through the income transferred via negative real rates of interest, and through loan default. The effect of all three of these processes on income is proportional to the amount of money borrowed by an individual. Small borrowers get small benefits, large borrowers get large benefits, and nonborrowers get no benefits.

Recent research has shown that most cheap agricultural credit is concentrated in relatively few loans. Chapter 10 in this volume by Gonzalez-Vega and Chapter 11 by Vogel report on some of this research. These results support the Iron Law of Interest-Rate Restrictions proposed by Gonzalez-Vega (1976). That is, the lower the real rate of interest, the more heavily concentrated will be the loans in the hands of relatively few people. This fact may be masked by formal lenders who make a number of small loans to the poor and by multiple large loans to wealthy borrowers. The modest average size of loans and the large number of loans made hide the fact that relatively few people receive most of the benefits from cheap credit. This is not due to a conspiracy. The self-interest of each lender combines with the excess demand that exists for negatively priced loans to force lenders to ration funds to their most profitable and powerful customers.

Another effect of low interest rates on loans is that they force intermediaries to pay even lower rates, usually negative in real terms, on savings deposits in rural areas. Most of the well-to-do find places to invest their surpluses in nonfinancial assets, so they are not seriously affected by the low rates paid on savings deposits. The low rates on deposits hurt poor households the most because they cannot assemble enough savings to buy lumpy, nonfinancial assets such as land and cattle. The poor are forced to accept a "tax" on their savings if they bother to open accounts or to consume their surplus. The backlash of cheap credit is that the poor take a beating on their financial savings.

Low interest rates on loans and savings have a very regressive effect on income and asset ownership in rural areas; the rich gain at the expense of the poor. Because of fungibility and the large number of participants in rural financial markets, it is impossible for governments to force financial markets to allocate significant income transfers to the poor (Von Pischke and Adams 1980).

Interest Rates and Inflation

The seventh argument for keeping interest rates low is that raising them would add to inflation. This argument is partly based on the fact that interest payments are included in price indexes used to measure inflation. Also, those who believe in cost-push inflation argue that interest payments are part of the cost of production and that raising these rates would directly fuel inflation through forcing producers to increase prices.

There are several reasons why these arguments are misleading and generally incorrect. Most importantly, they reverse the causation between inflation and interest rates. Where interest rates are not controlled, increased expectations of inflation lead to higher interest rates. It is also important to remember that an increase in interest rates has a one-time impact on a price index, whereas inflation is an ongoing process. Interest rates would have to be raised every month in order to contribute continually to this process.

The cost-push notion of inflation, when applied to the agricultural sector, is very misleading. Most segments of the agricultural sector in low-income countries include producers who have little or no control over the prices they receive for their products. They may wish that the prices of their products would increase to cover the additional costs of higher interest rates, but they have no power to exercise this wish.

There are several reasons why higher and more flexible interest rates would dampen rather than fuel inflation (Shaw 1973). Higher interest rates would allow financial markets in rural areas to mobilize via voluntary financial savings a much larger part of their loanable funds than is currently the case. This increase in self-financing would allow governments to do less deficit spending and to slow the growth in money supply. During the early 1950s the Taiwanese government used interest-rate adjustments as a major tool to control inflation (Irvine and Emery 1966). High interest rates allowed the financial system to mobilize large amounts of voluntary savings and also allowed the government to slow the creation of money in order to expand agricultural credit. Recently, at least in Brazil, rapid increases in the amount of agricultural credit have been a major factor contributing to inflation (Moura da Silva 1978). The higher interest rates would also provide more households with attractive alternatives to consumption, which would lessen the pressure on prices caused by strong consumer demand.

An equally important, yet subtle, effect of higher interest rates on inflation would be through facilitating *more* production. Higher rates would force current borrowers to economize on their use of loans. This might result in some of them producing less because the costs of borrowed liquidity would go up. These losses in production would be slight, however, because part of the borrowed liquidity would go into low-return investment and also into consumption. These losses would be more than offset by increases in output by producers who gained more access to integrated financial markets. Higher interest rates would reduce loan demand among current heavy users of credit and encourage lenders to seek new customers in order to lend the increased volume of savings mobilized by higher interest rates. This would also lead lenders to reduce loan-transaction costs that currently discourage some from borrowing.

Although it is difficult to measure or estimate the potential output that is lost by those who get too little credit, the borrowing that is discouraged by excessive transaction cost imposed on certain borrowers, and the increases in the costs of financial intermediation that are caused by excessive regulation of financial markets, they all result in large and important misallocations of resources. Many of these inefficiencies would disappear with more integrated financial markets that would result from higher-interest-rate policies. The net additional production resulting from defragmenting rural financial markets would dampen rather than fuel inflation.

The Second Best

The "second best" argument is the Goliath of the justifications for cheap agricultural credit. Many thoughtful people recognize that the agricultural sector is often penalized by policies such as overvalued exchange rates, food price controls, taxes on farm inputs, and too little public investment aimed at creating a more productive agriculture. Policymakers often feel that these "taxes" on agriculture are unavoidable because of other, more pressing considerations. They recognize that these taxes discourage production and reduce incomes in rural areas. Cheap agricultural credit is often defended as a way of offsetting the adverse production and equity effects of these taxes. Cheap credit provides the income transfer that is supposed to handle the equity problem, and it is also supposed to induce farmers to ignore the effects of the tax on the incentives to use more inputs.

There are several major weaknesses with this argument. The first is that all producers of a taxed good pay the levy, whereas only those who receive the cheap credit receive the subsidy. The tax is proportional to the amount of the good produced or sold by the farmer, but the subsidy is proportional to the size of the loan received. As pointed out earlier, because of the Iron Law of Interest-Rate Restrictions, low interest rates cause a concentration of cheap loans and result in a poor match between tax and subsidy on both equity and efficiency grounds.

The argument is further weakened when the efficiency effects are carefully evaluated. Ignoring for the moment the distributional issues already discussed, cheap credit will not overcome the inefficiencies in resource use caused by various taxes imposed on agriculture. These taxes either reduce the yields or prices of the product or increase the prices of inputs. To compensate the producer for a tax, the price of the input must be reduced enough so that the producer is induced to use the same amount of the input that would have been used without the tax. Cheap credit is supposed to substitute for these lower input prices.

Trying to use cheap credit to offset the inefficiencies in resource use caused by various taxes on agriculture, however, is like trying to sweep water up an incline. This is because of the essential property of financial instruments—their fungibility, because credit is not an input, and because most firms and households using agricultural loans have multiple sources and uses of liquidity. Loans from formal sources are only a part of this liquidity. A loan allows the borrower additional command over any real resource or service available in the market. Because of fungibility, there is no direct relationship between the cost of the loan and the willingness of the borrower to use more of an input that is taxed or to use more of the input to produce a good that is taxed. A poor investment continues to be a poor investment even though the investor has access to cheap credit!

An extreme example may help to illustrate this point. Let us assume that a government has placed a very high tax on mushrooms that are produced almost entirely for export. The tax is placed at such a high rate that mushroom growers find they are unable to make a profit producing any amount of this good. Let us also assume that all producers of mushrooms have other economic activities like growing rice, raising ducks and pigs, informal money lending, growing of marijuana, and household consumption. Let us further assume that the government has recently introduced electricity to the rural areas and has opened several color television stations. Under these conditions no additional agricultural credit, regardless of its price, would be used by any of the producers to grow mushrooms. Rather, liquidity provided by the cheap loans would be used to purchase color television sets and to purchase additional inputs for those production activities that would yield the highest net marginal returns.

Granting the cheap loans in the form of production inputs (in-kind loans) would not overcome this problem. Borrowers could always divert these inputs to other production activities or sell them in the gray market and use the cash to buy the goods or services that would give them the most satisfaction.

The "second best" argument, especially when it is applied to multiproduct and widely dispersed agricultural firms, is unsound on both equity and efficiency grounds.

Conclusions

Interest rates are critical in determining the performance of financial markets, and cheap-credit policies are a major reason for the poor performance of rural financial markets in low-income countries. They destroy the incentives for rural households to save in financial form and seriously distort the way lenders allocate loans. Arguments used to defend cheap agricultural credit are unsound, are based on value judgments, go counter to economic logic, and/or are not supported by empirical evidence. Because of the damage such arguments cause and the large amounts of money involved in agricultural credit programs, it is important that the errors be widely understood. As a minimum, policymakers who insist on continuing cheap agricultural credit policies ought to present more reliable evidence to support the assumptions on which their policies are based.

Much of the confusion about interest rates would disappear if policymakers stopped thinking of credit as an input, recognized the importance of real rates of interest, and clearly understood fungibility. Many of the problems in rural financial markets would also be eased if flexible nominal-interest-rate policies were adopted that resulted in stable and generally positive real rates of interest on both loans and deposits in rural areas. Sound policies cannot be built upon unsound assumptions and unsound arguments.

Notes

Little in this paper is totally original. I have synthesized many of the ideas of Claudio Gonzalez-Vega, Edward S. Shaw, and Robert C. Vogel. I have also drawn heavily from discussion about problems of rural finance with F.J.A. Bouman, Compton Bourne, Cristina C. David, B. M. Desai, Douglas H. Graham, Edward J. Kane, Yuzuru Kato, Jerry R. Ladman, Millard F. Long, Richard L. Meyer, J. D. Von Pischke, Edward J. Ray, and Clark M. Reynolds. I have long since forgotten which ideas are theirs and which are mine.

1. The real rate of interest is defined as the nominal rate of interest (the contractual rate) adjusted by the change in some overall price index. The real rate is equal to $[(1+i)/(1+p)]-1$, where i is the nominal rate of interest and p is the change in prices during the year.

2. Those who use this argument also ignore the burden that low-interest-rate policies place on the saver.

References

Adams, D. W, and G. I. Nehman. "Borrowing Costs and the Demand for Rural Credit." *Journal of Development Studies* 15(1979):165–176.

Datey, C. D. "The Financial Cost of Agricultural Credit: A Case Study of Indian Experience." World Bank Staff Working Paper no. 296, Washington, D.C., October 1978.

Gonzalez-Vega, Claudio. "On the Iron Law of Interest Rate Restrictions: Agricultural Credit Policies in Costa Rica and in Other Less Developed Countries." Ph.D. dissertation, Stanford University, 1976.

Harriss, Barbara. "Money and Commodities, Monopoly and Competition." In *Borrowers and Lenders: Rural Financial Markets and Institutions in Developing Countries,* edited by John Howell. London: Overseas Development Institute, 1980, pp. 107–129.

Irvine, Reed J., and Robert F. Emery. "Interest Rate As an Anti-Inflationary Inducement in Taiwan." *National Banking Review* 4(1966):29–39.

Moura da Silva, Adroaldo. "Inflacao e Mercado de Capitais." Unpublished paper, Fundacao Instituto de Pesquisas Economicas, University of São Paulo, Brazil, May 1978.

Pablo Romero, Alfredo Antonio. "Lending Activities Among Groups of Small Farmers in the Bañao Area of the Dominican Republic." Masters thesis, The Ohio State University, 1979.

Schultz, Theodore W. *Transforming Traditional Agriculture.* New Haven: Yale University Press, 1964.

Shaw, Edward S. *Financial Deepening in Economic Development.* New York: Oxford University Press, 1973.

Singh, Karam. "Structural Analysis of Interest Rates on Consumption Loans in an Indian Village." *Asian Economic Review* 10(1968):471–475.

Vogel, Robert C. "Barriers to Financial Reform." Economics and Sociology Occasional Paper no. 643, Department of Agricultural Economics and Rural Sociology, The Ohio State University, August 6, 1979.

Von Pischke, J. D., and Dale W Adams. "Fungibility and the Design and Evaluation of Agricultural Credit Projects." *American Journal of Agricultural Economics* 62(1980):719–726.

7
Credit-Rationing Behavior of Agricultural Lenders: The Iron Law of Interest-Rate Restrictions

Claudio Gonzalez-Vega

During the past three decades, formal financial institutions (FFIs) in low-income countries (LICs) have channeled large amounts of credit to agriculture. At the same time, through legal and financial controls, governments have kept at low levels the rates of interest that FFIs can charge on loans. The preferential rates charged for loans in agriculture and, in particular, those for small farmers, have been especially low. Recent financial reforms in some LICs, although increasing most rates, often have not raised the preferential rates for agriculture. As a result, interest-rate differentials between agriculture and nonagriculture have increased. These differentials have not reflected the costs and risks of FFIs lending to different borrower classes. Rather, they have reflected the political intent to favor some groups at the expense of others.

Often the preferential rates have been mandated with the best of intentions. They may have been adopted to promote socially desirable activities or to benefit marginal groups. Unfortunately, such preferential-rate policies have frequently resulted in consequences opposite of those desired and have repressed savings mobilization and formal financial intermediation in general, thus causing lower rates of economic growth. By reducing the size of domestic formal financial markets, these policies have had the effect of increasing the importance of foreign debt as a means of financing capital formation and of augmenting the dependency of LICs. By distorting the allocative functions of interest rates, these policies have prevented savings from being channeled to their most socially profitable uses.

FFIs take into account the costs and risks associated with lending to different borrower classes. If forced to charge differential interest rates, they adopt predictable rationing mechanisms that have a considerable impact on the final allocation of credit. In the discussion that follows, I explore the determinants of the behavior of borrowers and lenders under interest-rate restrictions. I examine the consequences of such controls on the final composition of loan portfolios and argue that the behavior of borrowers and lenders leads to a redistribution of loan portfolios to a relatively small number of large borrowers as well as to the exclusion from these portfolios of large numbers of small potential borrowers.

Impact of Interest-Rate Ceilings

The traditional analysis of the impact of interest-rate ceilings posits a market for credit that is characterized by an aggregate demand for loans inversely related to the loan rate of interest and an aggregate supply of deposits that is directly related to the deposit rate of interest. In this model, the imposition of a ceiling on the loan rate leads to a decline in the rate paid to depositors. As a result, fewer resources are mobilized, and the total volume of lending declines. Further, at the ceiling loan rate there is an excess demand for credit and nonprice rationing mechanisms are required to clear the market. The demands by all or some of the potential borrowers will be totally or partially frustrated.

It is increasingly recognized that these rationing processes have an unfavorable impact on small farmers, as a result of the high risks and costs associated with lending to small borrowers. The conventional analysis, however, does not explain how these rationing processes clear the market. In particular, although the conventional model shows that depositors are worse off as a consequence of the ceiling, it does not show if all borrowers (as a group) or specific borrower classes are better off. Since it does not explain how the new, smaller amounts of credit are allocated among borrower classes, this model cannot predict if the reduction in the loan rate is less or more than compensated for by a decline in the size of the loans received. Thus, the conventional analysis sheds little light on the impact of interest-rate ceilings on the allocation of resources and on the distribution of income.

The imposition of a binding ceiling on interest rates has at least three aggregate and distributive effects on the portfolios of FFIs. First, a reduction in the size of their total portfolio of assets will occur, because a drop in the rate paid on deposits reduces the ability of FFIs to attract savings. The reduction in the rate of profit caused by the ceiling also reduces their ability to attract equity capital and to borrow. Second, since ceilings on the loan rates of interest reduce the relative profitability of lending, the proportion of the total asset portfolio of the FFIs devoted to loans will decline. Third, a change in the composition of the loan portfolio of the FFIs will take place. Loan-rate ceilings alter the relative profitability of loans to different borrower classes. Depending on the rationing mechanisms adopted, the ceilings lead to changes in the relative shares of the loan portfolios going to different borrowers. These redistributions usually lead to greater portfolio concentration.

Types of Rationing

Any loan has three aspects: the size, the interest rate charged, and the noninterest terms of the loan contract. For reasons to be discussed, given the risks, transaction costs, and information costs associated with lending to different borrower classes, most FFIs try to optimize the adjustment of these three aspects of a loan to each particular borrower. When the ceilings on loan rates become binding, lenders are forced to adjust the noninterest terms of the loan contract or to reduce loan size. The result is that borrowers receive a less attractive combination of these three aspects of their loans and the profits of the FFIs decline. The welfare of both rationed borrowers and lenders could be improved by the elimination of the ceilings.

Of the three ways to clear a credit market—through interest rates, through changes in the noninterest terms of the loan contract, and through changes in loan size—the first two are examples of rationing-through-price, in contrast to rationing-through-quantities. (The non-interest terms of the loan contract may be considered as elements of the price vector of the loan, in addition to the rates charged.) The third way, however, is clearly a form of nonprice rationing. When borrowers are rationed out of the market by imposition of less attractive noninterest terms on the loans, it is the borrower who decides that the price is too high. In the event of nonprice rationing, on the other hand, the potential borrower is willing to pay the full price (all elements in the price vector of the loan), but the FFIs are not willing to grant a loan of the size demanded. In this case, an unsatisfied excess demand for credit prevails at the ruling interest rate. In practice, when ceilings on loan rates are imposed, rationing will occur through changes in both the noninterest terms of the loan contract and the loan size. Both types of rationing lead to greater loan-portfolio concentration.

Nonprice Credit Rationing

Several models of lender behavior can be used to explain rationing decisions. Portfolio theory provides insights because of uncertainty and risk; the theory of the multiproduct firm is useful because transactions costs and product heterogeneity and differentiation are important. Also, it is possible to capture uncertainty and risk within the theory of the firm by incorporating an *ex ante* premium for risk in the cost functions of the FFIs.

The application of general theories about price controls and black markets to financial markets has been useful to explain the existence of nonprice credit rationing. The analysis of the determinants of interest rates in informal credit markets of LICs and the attempts to measure transaction costs, risks of default, and monopoly profits have also helped. Theories about nonprice credit rationing, however, have been associated mostly with the controversy over the availability doctrine. Actually, the theory of nonprice credit rationing was developed to show, despite Paul Samuelson's 1952 statement to the contrary, that this type of rationing behavior is consistent with rational profit maximization, even in the absence of interest-rate restrictions. *A fortiori,* this behavior is even more likely in the presence of such restrictions.

Hodgman (1960) showed that, because of the existence of default risk, any borrower will reach a loan size beyond which he or she will not be able to obtain additional funds by promising to pay a higher interest rate. The supply of credit to an individual borrower becomes totally inelastic because each borrower's wealth and ability to repay are finite. To demonstrate the existence of nonprice rationing, however, it must be shown that an excess demand for credit persists at the rate charged in equilibrium. This requires a discussion both of supply and demand. That is, nonprice rationing occurs when the lender is unwilling to grant the loan demanded by the borrower and offers only a smaller amount. Jaffee (1971) set up a model of a lender who maximizes expected profits, taking into account possible borrower default. He formulated the lender's expected income from each loan as an explicit function of the parameters of the borrower's demand function, the probability of default, and the rate of interest charged on the loan. Within this framework, the proof of the rationality of rationing amounted to showing that the FFI can increase its expected profits by rationing some clients.

Jaffee showed that credit rationing is not profitable for a lender acting as a discriminating monopolist—one who maximizes expected profits with respect to each borrower separately and is free to charge each borrower a different interest rate. Rationing is profitable only if there are restrictions on interest-rate discrimination. That is, limited interest-rate differentiation, in the sense that FFIs have to charge identical rates to nonidentical borrowers, makes it profitable for the FFIs to supply some borrowers with less than the amount of credit they demand at the going rate. Similar behavior will occur when an inverted interest-rate structure is enforced.

Aside from usury ceilings, other legal and moral restrictions and considerations of good will make it difficult to charge widely different interest rates to different borrowers. Instead, FFIs usually justify interest-rate differentials in terms of a few objective criteria, such as industry class. A classification scheme of this type is likely to result in a tacit collusive oligopolistic agreement among FFIs. The structure of interest rates is then compressed within narrower limits and nonprice rationing occurs. Constraints on rate differentiation may also result from the information costs associated with distinguishing among different borrowers and their risk characteristics (screening costs).

Keeton (1979) showed that nonprice rationing also takes place if risk of default increases with the size of loan or if there is a moral-hazard problem. Limited liability may increase the riskiness of the project financed by the FFIs. In some cases, FFIs may find it possible to specify all relevant characteristics of the investment project as part of the loan contract and enforce such agreements by monitoring the borrower's behavior. If this cannot be done, FFIs will want to take into account the effect that the terms of the loan have on the borrower's project choice. A change in interest rates affects project choice in the same way that a change in coverage influences a policyholder's level of care in avoiding accident. This moral hazard may perform essentially the same role as interest-rate ceilings in inducing nonprice credit rationing.

Moral hazard is only one example of a broader class of imperfections that prevail in credit markets. Another type of market imperfection arises when the outcome of the investment project depends both on some state of nature to be realized at a later date and on the amount of additional resources that the borrower is willing to contribute to the project after that state is realized, but before the loan becomes due. Since the borrower receives only that part of the outcome that remains after repaying the loan, he or she will either contribute the same amount of new resources as if the entire outcome were received and repay the loan in full or will contribute no new resources and default. Since the borrower will choose the latter course whenever the amount left over after paying back the loan should be less than the opportunity cost of the new resources, an increase in the interest rate will increase the likelihood of default.

According to Fried and Howitt (1980), credit rationing exists as part of an equilibrium risk-sharing arrangement between the FFIs and the borrowers. Borrowers and lenders can benefit not only from trading loan contracts now but also from an understanding, or implicit contract, concerning the amounts they will be willing to trade, and at what prices, under various conditions in the future. This is the old "customer relationship." By means of such arrangements, borrowers and FFIs can share the risks associated with an uncertain future. By dampening the movements in interest rates, these arrangements open up the possibility of nonprice credit rationing.

Most of the imperfections and costs that explain nonprice credit rationing, even in the absence of interest-rate restrictions, exist in the rural credit markets of LICs. Uncertainty, default risks, and transactions, information, and collection costs are all particularly high in these fragmented financial markets. Moral hazard and related problems are especially acute. In these markets, FFIs find many reasons to practice one or more forms of nonprice credit rationing.

A Model of Lender Behavior

A simple model of nonprice credit rationing, further discussed in the Appendix of this chapter, is used here to illustrate the differential impact of interest-rate ceilings on access to credit by different borrower classes and on portfolio concentration. I assume that the lender is a profit-maximizing firm (this assumption is further justified in the discussion that follows) and that the lender's only source of revenue is the interest payments on loans. There are three components of the firm's lending costs: the opportunity cost of the funds, the costs of administration of the loans, and the losses due to default.

The opportunity cost of the funds is exogenously given to the lender, independently of loan size, and is identical for all borrower classes. The costs of administration, in turn, include the handling costs of the loan and the risk-reducing costs of the loan. Handling costs are incurred in recording and disbursing the loan and in receiving payments. These costs tend to be independent of the size and degree of riskiness of the loan. Thus, average handling costs decline with loan size.

Risk-reducing costs are directed at lowering the probability of default in the loan portfolio through the use of information in borrower selection and through collection efforts. These costs are not independent of loan size or of the expected losses due to default. If more resources are spent in loan evaluation and supervision, the lender can reduce losses. The lender cannot, however, completely eliminate uncertainty about repayment. Therefore, it must always include, among its *ex ante* costs, a premium for risk.

FFIs do not know, *ex ante,* if a particular borrower will repay a loan. Instead, they must estimate the probable losses due to default. This probability of default, and the corresponding premium for risk, depend on the borrower's ability and willingness to repay. This is a function of the outcome of the productive activity financed with the loan and of the value of the additional collateral offered.

In order to determine the probable losses due to default, FFIs usually distinguish among several borrower classes and estimate that a certain proportion of the borrowers in a given class will default. In addition, FFIs estimate the expected losses related to this default. It is in the interest of FFIs to distinguish among as many borrower classes as possible. However, this requires information that is costly to acquire and process, so instead FFIs set up a small number of borrower classes and estimate cost functions, including an *ex ante* premium for risk, for each class. Because of the nature of their productive activities and of the collateral offered, loans to borrowers in certain classes are riskier than loans to other borrowers. Therefore, although FFIs will charge the same premium for risk for a loan of a given size within a given borrower class, they will want to charge a different premium to borrowers in different classes.

Even though additional information reduces the required premium for risk, it also increases administration costs. In order to estimate their cost functions, FFIs must determine the optimum (least-cost) combination of information costs and the residual risk accepted. The sum of the premium for risk and the risk-reducing administration costs will be minimized when the marginal cost of additional information is equated to the marginal return of using additional information to reduce default losses.

Interest-rate restrictions and other financial regulations usually tend to restrict the use of information by FFIs. If FFIs operate with narrow margins, the evaluation of mortgageable property may be the only risk-reducing activity they can afford. As a result, the allocation of loans will be strongly influenced by the type of security offered. Under these conditions small farmers with few assets to offer will be penalized.

The costs of, and returns to, the use of information in borrower selection are a function of the degree of homogeneity among borrowers. Homogeneity makes it possible to have few borrower classes. Given the heterogeneity found among small farmers in LICs, however, FFIs ought to establish a relatively large number of classes. But interest-rate ceilings restrict the number of borrower classes that FFIs can serve. As a result of these ceilings, many small producers and new potential borrowers are thrown into the class of nonborrowers, because FFIs cannot afford the information costs involved in classifying them in one of the established classes. Since the risk premium for this residual class of potential borrowers is too high, compared to the interest-rate ceilings, these producers are excluded from the portfolios of the FFIs.

For a given borrower class, the premium for risk increases with loan size, as long as the project financed is of a fixed size; the project financed, even of variable size, shows diminishing marginal returns; the variance of marginal returns increases with loan size; or the value of the collateral offered does not increase as rapidly as loan size. Given diminishing marginal returns to the use of information, this implies that the (optimal) sum of risk-reducing costs and premium for risk increases with loan size. As a result, the marginal costs of lending are an increasing function of loan size.

As mentioned earlier, loan contracts have many dimensions. Thus, loans are viewed as nonhomogeneous products by lenders. In particular, loans to different classes of borrowers are treated as different products if the lender distinguishes among the classes and estimates different cost functions for each borrower class. It is appropriate, therefore, to use the theory of the multiproduct firm to examine lender behavior.

This is done in the model presented in the Appendix, which shows that, when the lender can behave as a perfectly discriminating monopolist, it will charge different interest rates to different borrowers, reflecting the different elasticities of demands for credit as well as the different marginal costs of lending to alternative borrower classes. If, on the other hand, loan rates are constrained, profit maximization may require nonprice credit rationing. In effect, if the constrained loan rate is higher than the marginal cost of lending for the size of loan demanded, the borrower will not be rationed, but if the constrained rate is lower than marginal cost, the lender will limit the size of the loan granted. A larger loan would simply imply an addition to costs higher than the addition to revenues and a reduction in expected profits. Depending, therefore, on the relative level of the ceilings, with respect to the various marginal cost-of-lending curves, some or all of the borrower classes may be subject to nonprice rationing, and some borrowers will receive loans smaller than those demanded.

The Iron Law of Interest-Rate Restrictions

Nonprice credit rationing is widely practiced by FFIs in LICs, and lenders employ many devices to restrict the size of the loans granted to certain borrower classes. One of the most popular mech-

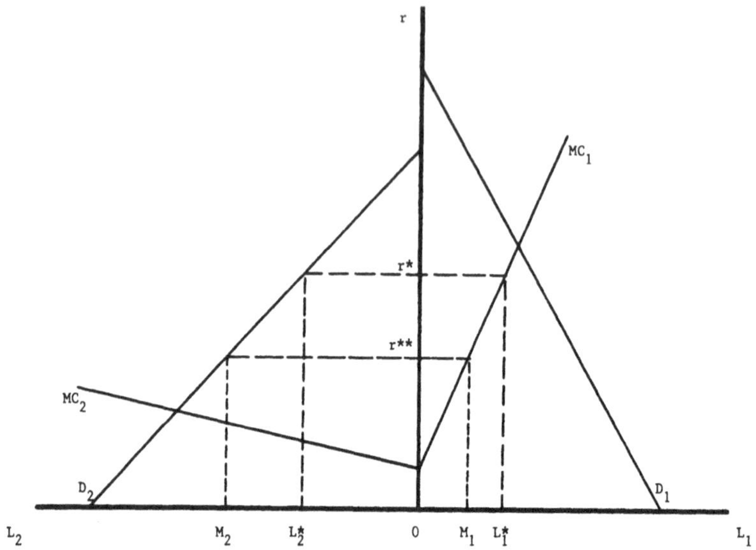

Figure 7.1 Rationed and Nonrationed Borrowers

anisms for rationing credit is to specify, for each crop, the maximum amount that can be granted per unit of land cultivated. Frequently, the proportion of total costs represented by these amounts varies significantly from crop to crop. These differences tend to reflect the perceptions of FFIs about the risks and costs associated with loans for the production of different crops. Usually the proportion financed is higher for the safer, more profitable export crops than for the small-farmer subsistence crops. The setting of these limits has also been vulnerable to pressures from growers associations, particularly in the case of public FFIs and at times when the implicit interest-rate subsidy has been substantial. Rationed borrowers are thus forced to complement the loans received from the FFIs with loans obtained in informal credit markets at higher interest rates. The extent of this additional financing reflects the extent of excess demand for credit from the FFIs.

In LICs, the loan portfolios of FFIs usually include both rationed and nonrationed classes of borrowers. When interest-rate ceilings become more restrictive, the size of the loans granted to the nonrationed borrower classes increases, while the size of the loans granted to the rationed borrower classes diminishes. This is the Iron Law of Interest Rate Restrictions.

A two-borrower case is shown in Figure 7.1. Positive loan amounts, L_1 and L_2, are measured in both directions from the origin, 0. Demand for credit curves for each borrower, D_1 and D_2, are inversely related to the real rate of interest charged, *r*. The lender's marginal cost curves, MC_1 and MC_2, increase with loan size. At a given interest-rate ceiling, r^*, the rationed borrower—represented in the right-hand quadrant—receives a loan of size L_1^*, which equates the interest rate charged with the marginal cost of lending and leaves the borrower with an unsatisfied demand for credit. The nonrationed borrower, represented in the left-hand quadrant, receives the size of loan demanded, L_2^*. As the interest-rate ceiling is lowered from r^* to r^{**}, the size of the loan granted to the nonrationed borrower increases, from L_2^* to M_2, as he or she demands a larger loan. At the same time, the size of the loan granted to the rationed borrower declines, from L_1^* to M_1 (a movement along the lender's marginal cost curve, not along the borrower's demand curve).

The changes in loan size implied by the Iron Law of Interest-Rate Restrictions cause a redistribution of the loan portfolios of the FFIs, as the nonrationed borrowers get larger shares of these portfolios and the rationed borrowers get smaller shares. Finally, when the interest-rate ceiling becomes very low, some borrower classes are excluded altogether from formal loans. A large proportion of the rural producers in LICs are in these excluded groups.

Since the nonrationed borrowers tend to be the large, wealthy, and influential producers, who are already receiving the largest loans, the behavior of the FFIs implied by the Iron Law of Interest-Rate Restrictions leads to a further concentration of the size distribution of their loans. This process of increasing concentration is accelerated by the exclusion of potential borrower classes from the credit portfolios, as the FFIs are precluded from covering their average variable costs of lending in these cases. This progressive concentration of loan portfolios and the exclusion of marginal producers from access to institutional credit significantly worsens the distribution of wealth.

High transaction costs for both lenders and borrowers limit the size of rural financial markets in LICs. When ceilings are imposed on interest rates, FFIs may be unable to cover these costs. Because of this, they will practice nonprice credit rationing and manipulate the noninterest terms of the loan contracts. The stricter terms of the contract shift some transaction costs from the FFIs to the borrowers, but this shift does not affect all classes of borrowers uniformly. Rather, it tends to restrict the access of marginal borrowers to institutional credit more than proportionately, in the fashion of the Iron Law of Interest-Rate Restrictions, and further contributes to a higher concentration of loan portfolios.

Rationing and the Lender's Objective Function

The models of lender behavior presented in this chapter are based on the assumption of profit maximization as the lender's objective. This assumption, however, is not necessary, and the results obtained *are not* dependent on it. The composition of the credit portfolios of FFIs is not a random or unconscious result; it is the consequence of lenders' attempts to optimize a given objective function within the constraints they face. That is, FFIs can be treated as rational optimizers that possess an explicitly or implicitly defined objective function and attempt to get the optimum result from their operations.

Different types of FFIs, of course, have different objective functions. Some of them are small private banks maximizing profits, whereas others are large banks attempting to maximize market shares; some of them are public-development banks attempting to maximize their political influence, and others are public or private institutions maximizing staff expenditures, managerial emoluments, or discretionary profits under different sets of constraints. Given these constraints, all of them are attempting to maximize some utility function, in terms of their managers' set of preferences, through the pursuit of either profit maximizing or nonprofit maximizing strategies or of some combination of both. Although the actual impact of interest-rate restrictions on the behavior of FFIs depends on the nature of their particular objective functions, some general considerations can be made.

For our purposes, FFIs can be grouped into two classes: those with an objective function that includes financial viability and institutional survival among the goals pursued and those with an objective function that does not include financial viability. This second group of lenders includes pilot projects not interested in a permanent presence as a lender in the rural areas. It also includes agencies set up to temporarily disburse relief loans. The first group includes all FFIs that, independently of the kinds of goals they are attempting to achieve, operate under the constraint that they must remain financially viable.

For FFIs to remain financially viable they must be able to preserve, and possibly increase, their loan portfolio in real terms. That is, they must maintain the purchasing power of their assets. To do this, their revenues must cover a significant portion, if not all, of their lending costs. To remain financially viable, therefore, FFIs must take into account revenues and costs; that is, they must have a profits strategy. As was pointed out in Chapter 3 by Bourne and Graham, if they do not, they will not survive.

In order to survive and maintain their relative importance within the financial sector, FFIs must preserve the purchasing power of the claims on resources they mobilize. Otherwise, they will be less able to serve their clients, their market shares will decline, and the political support that they need for their survival will diminish. FFIs are able to preserve the real size of their portfolios to the extent that they protect them from the eroding impact of inflation, to the extent that they collect the loans granted, and to the extent that they are able to generate sufficiently high profits.

Consider, for example, two identical FFIs, each one supplying 50 percent of the local credit market. One of them generates profits of 2 percent per year; the other generates annual profits of 12 percent. After 10 years, *ceteris paribus,* the more profitable institution will be serving 72 percent of this credit market, whereas the less profitable one will be serving only 28 percent.

Some FFIs may have continued access to the government budget, central bank rediscounting, or cheap credit from international agencies that allow them to remain temporarily viable, despite their losses. However, some measure of profitability is always included in evaluations of the performance of FFIs. International agencies and fiscal sources are usually only willing to continue with their support as long as the FFIs' losses are modest and temporary. International agencies are also judged by the success and financial strength of the FFIs they support. If FFIs' losses are high, international agencies will demand a management change or will request institutional reforms and program reorientations before they continue with their support. When the losses of FFIs are large, fiscal sources may not possess sufficient resources to continually provide the transfers needed. This is especially true of governments in LICs that are facing severe budgetary problems. Although inflationary financing from the central bank could make transfers in nominal terms possible, the ensuing inflation would erode the real value of the portfolio of the FFIs even faster.

Moreover, FFIs that receive large fiscal transfers lose their independence and are forced to accept political guidance in credit allocation. When banking and economic criteria are replaced by administrative and political decisions, the credit-rationing process becomes more vulnerable to pressures from specific borrower groups, and loan portfolios become more concentrated. Also, the reluctance of politicians to take into account creditworthiness and to enforce vigorous collection policies leads to high rates of default. These FFIs become costly and arbitrary mechanisms for political income transfers to relatively few borrowers and, unless huge fiscal transfers are forthcoming, do not long survive.

Conclusions

In most LICs, the interest rates charged by FFIs on agricultural loans have been administratively set or are constrained by regulations. As a result, these rates have been too rigid in nominal terms and too erratic and unpredictable in real terms: too low, from several perspectives; and too differentiated. FFIs have been forced to charge the lowest rates where they would have liked to charge the highest rates. This inverted structure of interest rates has accentuated the differential impact of the costs of lending on the relative profitability of loans to different borrower classes and has distorted the allocation of the loan portfolios of the FFIs among borrower classes.

The conventional model, on the basis of an aggregate demand and supply of credit, cannot explain the distributive consequences of interest-rate restrictions. This chapter has explored models of nonprice credit rationing and of rationing through the noninterest terms of the loan contracts to show how interest-rate ceilings restrict the access of small farmers to institutional credit and how this results in a high degree of concentration of the loan portfolios of the FFIs.

In particular, the chapter has shown that, according to the Iron Law of Interest-Rate Restrictions, as interest-rate ceilings become more restrictive, the size of the loans granted to nonrationed large producers increases, while the size of loans granted to rationed small producers decreases. This behavior of lenders leads to a redistribution of loan portfolios in favor of the large borrowers. Through these mechanisms, therefore, the interest-rate ceilings enforced in most of the LICs have been an important determinant of the limited access to institutional credit and the high degree of concentration of loan portfolios that characterize rural financial markets.

Appendix on Profit-Maximizing Rationing

With respect to a given borrower class, the lender's costs, as a function of loan size, have been defined as

$$C = dL + H + xL \tag{7.1}$$

where C: total cost of the loan, d: constant average opportunity cost of the funds, L: loan size, H: fixed handling costs of the loan, and

x: optimum sum of average risk-reducing costs and the premium for risk.

In turn, the lender's profit function can be defined as

$$\pi = \sum^{n} R_i - \sum^{n} C_i \tag{7.2}$$

where $R_i = r_i L_i$ and π: the lender's total profits, R_i: revenues from a loan to the ith borrower (or class), r_i: the interest rate charged to the ith borrower (or class), L_i: the size of the loan granted to the ith borrower (or class), and C_i: the total cost of the loan granted to the ith borrower (or class).

If the lender is a perfectly discriminating monopolist, it will charge different interest rates for a loan of the same size to borrowers of different classes, as well as different interest rates for loans of different sizes within a given borrower class. In this case, the first-order conditions for profit maximization are:

$$\frac{\partial \pi}{\partial L_i} = \frac{\partial R_i}{\partial L_i} - \frac{\partial C_i}{\partial L_i} = 0. \tag{7.3}$$

That is, profit maximization requires that the marginal revenue and the marginal cost of the loan be equated for the size of loan granted to each particular borrower. In these circumstances, the rates of interest charged to different borrowers will differ, reflecting both the different elasticities of the demand for credit from different borrowers and the different marginal costs of lending to them. Obviously, nonprice rationing will not occur in this case. This situation is represented for a two-borrower case in Figure 7.2.

In Figure 7.2, positive loan amounts (L_1 and L_2) are measured in both directions from the origin (0). The demand functions for each borrower (D_1 and D_2) are inversely related to the real rate of interest charged (r). Marginal revenue functions for the lender (MR_1 and MR_2) are associated with the demand functions. The lender's marginal cost functions (MC_1 and MC_2) increase with the size of loan. Profit maximization requires that marginal revenue be equated to marginal cost for each borrower. Thus, the lender must grant loans of size M_1 and M_2 and charge different interest rates, r_1 and r_2, to the two borrowers.

The simplest restriction that can be imposed on the rates of interest charged by FFIs is the requirement that they charge a uniform interest rate to all borrowers. It is assumed that FFIs are free to set this uniform rate at their most profitable level. The model can be used to show that in this case profit maximization may require nonprice credit rationing.

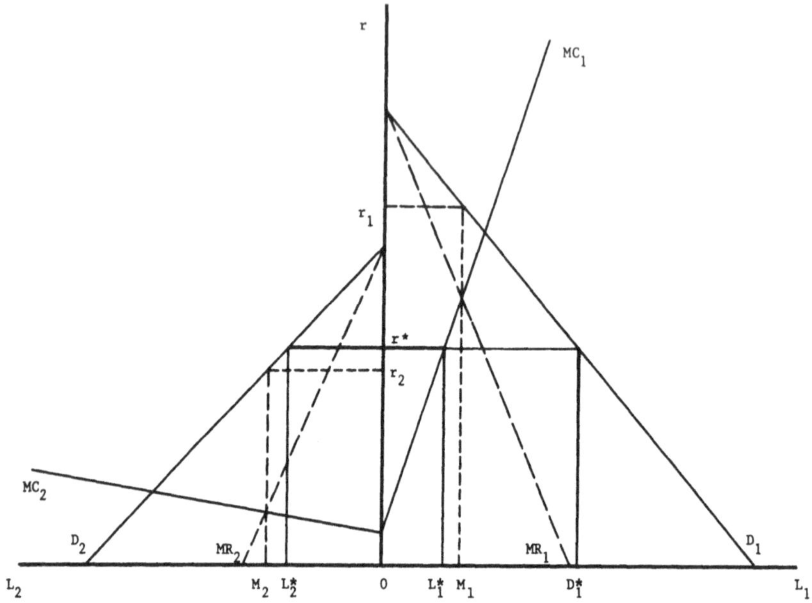

Figure 7.2 Credit Rationing with Interest-Rate Ceilings

Given the possibility of rationing—that is, the existence of individual excess demands for credit at the uniform interest rate charged by the lender—the profit-maximizing loan sizes for different borrowers can be obtained. This can be done, following Eckaus (1974), through the solution of a programming problem in which the demand functions are introduced as inequality constraints. If there is no rationing, loan size will equal the amount of credit demanded at the uniform rate charged. If there is rationing, the inequality constraint will be binding, and an excess demand for credit will exist. The programming problem consists of maximizing lender's profits, given the uniform rate charged and the size of the loans granted to different borrowers, subject to the constraints that the rate charged be the same for all borrowers and that the size of each loan be equal to or less than the amount demanded at the profit-maximizing rate.

The lender's total profits can be defined as

$$\pi = r \sum^{n} L_i - \sum^{n} C_i \tag{7.4}$$

Total profits must be maximized, subject to

$$
\begin{aligned}
&L_i - D_i \leq 0 \\
&0 \leq r \\
&0 \leq L_i
\end{aligned}
\tag{7.5}
$$

The corresponding Lagrangian function (K) is

$$K = r \sum^{n} L_i - \sum^{n} C_i - \sum^{n} \lambda_i (L_i - D_i) \tag{7.6}$$

The Kuhn-Tucker conditions for maximum profits are

$$
\begin{aligned}
&\frac{\partial K}{\partial r} = \sum^{n} L_i + \sum^{n} \lambda_i \frac{\partial D_i}{\partial r} \leq 0 \\
&\frac{\partial K}{\partial L_i} = r - \frac{\partial C_i}{\partial L_i} - \lambda_i \leq 0 \\
&r \sum^{n} [L_i + \lambda_i \frac{\partial D_i}{\partial r}] + \sum^{n} L_i [r - \frac{\partial C_i}{\partial L_i} - \lambda_i] = 0 \\
&L_i - D_i \leq 0 \\
&\lambda_i (L_i - D_i) \leq 0 \\
&\sum^{n} \lambda_i (L_i - D_i) = 0 \\
&0 \leq L_i \\
&0 \leq r \\
&\lambda_i \leq 0
\end{aligned}
\tag{7.7}
$$

These conditions imply that when credit rationing does not take place, the Lagrangian multiplier must be strictly positive. That is, if a borrower receives the size of the loan demanded, $L_i = D_i$ and $\lambda_i > 0$. On the other hand, credit rationing occurs when $L_i - D_i < 0$. In this case, the Lagrangian multiplier must be equal to zero; i.e., $\lambda_i = 0$. Therefore, when in the programming exercise one of the Lagrangian multipliers becomes equal to zero, the corresponding borrower (or class) is rationed.

The Kuhn-Tucker conditions imply that, for the Lagrangian multipliers to become equal to zero and for rationing to occur, the rate of interest charged has to become equal to the marginal cost of granting the loan. If there is no rationing, the rate of interest charged has to be higher than the corresponding marginal cost.

Therefore, when a uniform but free interest rate is enforced, if the profit-maximizing rate is less than the marginal cost of lending to a particular borrower, the lender will limit the size of the loan granted and an excess demand for credit ($D_i^* - L_i^*$) will prevail at the rate charged. If, in these circumstances, the lender granted a larger loan, as demanded, the addition to its costs would be higher than the addition to its revenues, and its expected profits would decline. The optimum uniform rate must be bounded by the rates that a discriminating monopolist would charge to the various borrowers, so that at least one class of borrowers will not be rationed.

As indicated earlier, Figure 7.2 shows a two-borrower situation where M_1 and M_2 are the profit-maximizing size of loans granted by an unconstrained discriminating monopolist, while r_1 and r_2 are the interest rates charged. The profit-maximizing interest rate set by a lender forced to charge a uniform rate to all borrowers is r^*, while L_1^* and L_2^* are the size of loans granted in this case. Given the levels of the marginal cost curves and of the uniform interest rate, one borrower is not rationed while the other one is ($L_1^* < D_1^*$).

Nonprice credit rationing will be practiced, *a fortiori,* when a binding ceiling on interest rates is enforced. Assume that a ceiling r^* is imposed on the rates of interest charged on all kinds of loans. In this case, the lender's profit function will be

$$\pi = r^* \sum^{n} L_i - \sum^{n} C_i \tag{7.8}$$

This function has to be maximized subject to

$$\begin{aligned} &L_i - D_i \leq 0 \\ &0 \leq L_i \\ &0 \leq r^* < r_i\,; \end{aligned} \tag{7.9}$$

that is, the ceiling is binding for all borrowers. The corresponding Lagrangian function is

$$K = r^* \sum^{n} L_i - \sum^{n} C_i - \sum^{n} \lambda_i\,(L_i - D_i) \tag{7.10}$$

The Kuhn-Tucker conditions for maximum profits are

$$\begin{aligned} &\frac{\partial K}{\partial L_i} = r^* - \frac{\partial C_i}{\partial L_i} - \lambda_i \leq 0 \\ &\sum^{n} (r^* - \frac{\partial C_i}{\partial L_i} - \lambda_i)\, L_i = 0 \\ &\lambda_i\,(L_i - D_i) \leq 0 \\ &L_i - D_i \leq 0 \\ &0 \leq L_i \\ &\lambda_i \leq 0 \end{aligned} \tag{7.11}$$

Again, these conditions imply that, in the absence of rationing, the Lagrangian multipliers will be strictly positive. This implies that marginal cost is lower than the given interest-rate ceiling. On the other hand, rationing implies that $\lambda_i = 0$. Thus, when rationing is taking place, the marginal cost of the loan is being equated to the ceiling interest rate. Depending on the relative level of the ceiling, with respect to the marginal cost curves of lending, some or all of the borrowers may be subjected to nonprice credit rationing.

Notes

Among the many friends who have influenced my ideas on rural finance, I want to especially acknowledge Dale W Adams, Ronald I. McKinnon, Edward S. Shaw, and Robert C. Vogel.

References

Baltensperger, Ernst. "Credit Rationing: Issues and Questions." *Journal of Money, Credit, and Banking* 10(1978):170–183.

Eckaus, Richard. "Monopoly Power, Credit Rationing, and the Variegation of Financial Structure." *3d Annual Meeting, Capital Markets Development Program.* Washington, D.C.: Organization of American States, 1974.

Fried, Joel, and Howitt, Peter. "Credit Rationing and Implicit Contract Theory." *Journal of Money, Credit, and Banking* 13(1980):471–487.

Gonzalez-Vega, Claudio. "Interest Rate Policies and Small Farmer Credit Programs in LDCs." In *AID Spring Review of Small Farmer Credit,* vol. 19, edited and published by the Agency for International Development. Washington, D.C.: June 1973.

———. "On the Iron Law of Interest Rate Restrictions: Agricultural Credit Policies in Costa Rica and in Other Less Developed Countries." Ph.D. dissertation, Stanford University, 1976.

———. "Interest Rate Restrictions and Income Distribution." *American Journal of Agricultural Economics* 59(1977):973–976.

Hodgman, Donald R. "Credit Risk and Credit Rationing." *Quarterly Journal of Economics* 74(1960):258–278.

Jaffee, Dwight M. *Credit Rationing and the Commercial Loan Market.* New York: John Wiley, 1971.

Kane, Edward J. "Good Intentions and Unintended Evil: The Case Against Selective Credit Allocation." *Journal of Money, Credit, and Banking* 9(1977):55–69.

Keeton, William. *Equilibrium Credit Rationing.* New York: Garland Publishing, 1979.

Shull, Bernard. "Commercial Banks as Multiproduce Price Discriminating Firms." In *Banking and Monetary Studies,* edited by Deane Carson. Homewood, Ill.: Richard D. Irwin, 1963.

8
Agricultural Lending Costs in Honduras

Carlos E. Cuevas
Douglas H. Graham

Even though large amounts of funds have been channeled through credit institutions by governments and donor agencies, relatively little attention has been given to the costs of financial intermediation in low-income countries. It has been assumed that these costs were negligible and that they had little effect on the behavior of financial market participants. Recent research in Bolivia on borrowers' loan-transaction costs, reported in Chapter 9, and work in India and Jamaica appear to challenge this assumption (Saito and Villanueva 1981; Nyanin 1982). Our research reinforces these recent findings and also shows that loan-targeting and loan-reporting requirements imposed on lenders by governments and donor agencies significantly increase costs of financial intermediation.

It is useful to recognize four sets of costs in financial intermediation: (1) the expenses incurred by the depositor in searching out and making deposits; (2) the resources used by the lender in servicing deposits and other funds collected; (3) the intermediary's costs of transacting loans; and (4) those costs incurred by the borrower in negotiating, obtaining, and repaying a loan. In the discussion that follows we concentrate on the lenders' loan-transaction costs. We report on an analysis of agricultural lending costs in a private commercial bank (PCB) and a government-owned agricultural development bank (ADB) in Honduras. We also describe how use of donor-agency funds affected lending costs in the private bank.

Background

The Honduran financial system has been increasingly controlled by the government over the past 10 years, as rates of inflation have increased (Graham and others 1981). The controls have included interest-rate ceilings, manipulation of reserve requirements, and setting of lending targets. Because of the agrarian nature of Honduras, formal agricultural lenders have been the focus of much of this concern. There are 16 commercial banks and several government-owned development banks in the country. The 2 banks selected for our lending-cost analysis accounted for over one-quarter of the value of all new loans made by Honduran banks in 1981, the year of the study. These 2 banks also granted nearly half of the value of new formal loans made in Honduras for agricultural purposes in that year. Agricultural loans accounted for almost three-quarters of the ADB's loan portfolio and for about one-seventh of the PCB's loans. The total value of agricultural loans made by the ADB was approximately three times that of the PCB.

We focused on the nonfinancial (administrative) costs of both banks. Provisions for bad debt were excluded from the analysis because of the different accounting criteria used in the two institutions. A large representative sample of branches for both banks was selected. The ADB branches surveyed accounted for 55 percent of the ADB's loan portfolio and for 49 percent of its total nonfinancial costs. These percentages were 86 percent and 88 percent, respectively, for the PCB branches selected.

Branch income statements were the basis for our cost estimates. Identification of the direct credit-operations expenses and their functional breakdown were drawn from branch-level surveys in both institutions. These surveys consisted of questionnaires administered by us in interviews with branch managers, credit analysts, accounting personnel, and clerical employees.

Administrative Costs of Banks

As shown in Table 8.1, the average lending cost per loan made by the PCB was almost 7 times that of the ADB. However, the average size of loan made by the PCB was about 22 times that of the ADB. In part, this helps explain the sharp difference in average costs per unit of money lent by the two banks. Ignoring loan defaults, the PCB had loan-transaction costs of only 2.5 percent of the value of its loans, compared to ADB costs of 8.4 percent (line 2).[1] Although difficult to document, part of the dissimilarity in costs was also related to differences in the sources of funds for lending. In 1981 three-fifths of the money lent by the ADB came from rediscount lines with the Central Bank or from external aid donors, whereas only 7 percent of the PCB's liabilities were from these sources. Deposits

Table 8.1 Lending and Deposit Mobilization Costs in a Commercial Bank and a Development Bank in Honduras

	Costs	Commercial Bank	Development Bank
1.	Average lending cost per loan	Lps. 1,748 1/	Lps. 260 1/
		%	
2.	Average lending cost per lempira lent	2.5	8.4
3.	Lending costs/overall costs	33	77
4.	Costs of deposit mobilization and other services/overall costs	67	23
5.	Branch level costs/total lending costs	77	43
6.	Personnel costs/total lending costs	41	27
7.	Loan evaluation costs/total lending costs	45	16
8.	Loan monitoring costs/total lending costs	4	7
9.	Loan recovery costs/total lending costs	14	6

Source: Bank income and expenditure statements and branch-level surveys.

1/ 1 U.S. dollar = 2 lempiras

were 91 percent of all the PCB's loanable funds, but only 40 percent for the ADB. Accordingly, lending costs made up a much larger proportion of overall costs in the ADB than in the PCB, 77 percent versus 33 percent (line 3 in Table 8.1). These differences in the sources of funds between the two banks caused dissimilarities in the makeup of their costs, as will be discussed later.

It can also be noted from the data in Table 8.1 (line 5) that more than three-quarters of the PCB's lending costs were incurred at the branch level, whereas only 43 percent of the ADB's lending costs occurred in its branches. The ADB's operations were much more centralized than the PCB's. The large incidence of special lines of credit and externally funded projects in the ADB forced this centralization. The central office spent a good deal of time preparing reports to justify these external funds, an activity that could not be handled by branches.

Another major difference between the two banks is shown in the proportion of total administrative costs involved in salaries and other personnel costs (line 6). Because the ADB made much smaller loans and was required to be more concerned with development objectives, one would expect the personnel costs would have been relatively higher in the ADB than in the commercial bank. We were surprised to find the opposite. Personnel costs made up over 40 percent of the PCB's total administrative costs, but only a bit more than a quarter of the ADB's costs. The main explanation for this is that the commercial bank paid much higher salaries to its employees than did the development bank (it also expected higher levels of employee productivity). The information in Table 8.1 (lines 7–9) also shows that the PCB spent much more on loan evaluation, less on loan monitoring, and much more on loan recovery than did the ADB. These figures provide very strong insights into why the ADB has much more serious loan-recovery problems than the PCB: The ADB spends less time and effort extending and recovering loans than does the private bank! In doing so it also rewards its employees less than does the PCB.

Donor and Government Funds

Because the ADB received a large part of its funds from the government or donor agencies through the Central Bank, only a small part (23 percent) of its total administrative costs resulted from nonlending efforts (Table 8.1, line 4). The opposite was true for the private bank. About two-thirds of its total administrative costs resulted from nonlending activities, mainly deposit mobilization. Even though the rediscounted funds from the Central Bank were usually extended to the ADB on concessionary terms, these funds were not cheap. In most cases these rediscount lines carried targeting, documenting, and reporting requirements that imposed a good deal of extra effort and cost on the ADB.

To shed more light on the effect these external funds have on the loan-transaction costs of the two banks, we documented the branch-level costs for a subsample of PCB branches that handled relatively large amounts of funds provided by an international donor. We were able to document and separate the lending costs incurred in managing the bank's own funds as well as targeted funds provided by the donor through rediscount facilities in the Central Bank. This was done by two loan-size categories: less than 125,000 lempiras and 125,000 lempiras or more. The donor funds were all targeted to agricultural loans of under 125,000 lempiras. The information we collected (Table 8.2) shows the costs incurred per loan and per lempira lent by the

Table 8.2 Private Commercial Bank Branch Lending Costs by Source of Funds, End Use of Loans, and Loan Size

Source of Funds and End Use of Loans	Loan Size: Less than L. 125,000			Loan Size: L. 125,000 or more		
	Average Cost per Loan (Lps.)	Average Loan Size (Lps.)	Cost Per Lempira Lent (%)	Average Cost Per Loan (Lps.)	Average Loan Size (Lps.)	Cost per Lempira Lent (%)
Bank's Own Funds						
Agriculture	995	31,777	3.1	1,319	471,571	0.3
Industry	642	48,542	1.3	850	364,173	0.2
Housing	774	10,699	7.2	1,026	250,000	0.4
Commerce	642	39,672	1.6	850	250,200	0.3
Consumption	642	11,381	5.6	-	-	-
Other	642	39,090	1.6	850	257,440	0.3
Donor's Funds						
Agriculture	5,450	69,664	7.8	-	-	-

Source: Surveys of selected bank branches.

bank in handling the specified loan applications. (For the subsample of branches studied, central-office costs added 0.6 percent as an overhead cost to the branch-level costs reported here.)

As can be noted from the information in Table 8.2, there were large differences in administrative costs by loan-size groups. As expected, the large loans were less expensive to administer per unit of money lent than were the smaller loans. However, we found surprisingly large differences in the lending costs by end use of funds. Even though the costs per loan did not show important variations across different end uses, average loan sizes by end use varied considerably, particularly in the loan category of less than 125,000 lempiras. This implies important differences in the costs per lempira lent. Although PCB loans of under 125,000 lempiras for industrial purposes only involved administrative costs of 1.3 percent, loans for housing and real estate had costs of 7.2 percent. Loans made for agricultural purposes in the smaller loan-size category had midrange administrative costs of 3.1 percent.

The most interesting figure in the table is the administrative cost per unit of money lent for the agricultural loans made from donor funds. These loans involved an average cost per loan operation five times as large as the costs of extending agricultural loans from the bank's own funds. Yet the average size of donor-funded agricultural loans was more than twice the size of agricultural loans financed with the bank's own resources. As a result, branch costs of agricultural loans made from donor funds amounted to 7.8 percent of the value of the loans made, more than twice the cost of agricultural loans extended from other funds managed by the PCB. Adding central-office overhead costs to branch expenses pushed the total administrative costs on these agricultural loans to 8.4 percent. It is clear that the higher cost per unit of money lent in the case of the donor's funds did not result from a portfolio of small-sized loans. Instead, it was a result of a far more complicated and costly set of procedures associated with the administration of the donor's funds, as compared to the use of the bank's own funds.

Again, ignoring default risks, the administrative costs on donor funds far exceeded the 3–4 percent spread allowed on these loans for administrative costs. Because of other larger profitable activities, the PCB could tolerate these administrative losses. Unless margins are increased, or administrative costs reduced, it is unlikely that the PCB will be enthused, however, about becoming heavily involved in underwriting the relatively large administrative costs of handling donor funds. Being a government bank, the ADB does not have the luxury of avoiding the punishment involved in handling large amounts of targeted money.

Conclusions

This study has emphasized the contrasts in the structure of lending costs and overall organization between a public-sector and a private-sector bank serving agriculture in a less developed country. It is clear that the source of funds to these institutions strongly influences the composition of their loan portfolios and their lending costs. The private bank, relying more on local deposits, is more cautious and efficient in evaluating and screening loans at the branch level and, in general, delegates more decision making to branches. The public-sector bank is far more centralized, with a heavy overlay of administrative costs associated with the loan-targeting criteria of external sources of finance. External donor agencies probably impose higher lending costs on the on-lending institutions than they realize. Unrealistically low administrative margins contribute to the financial unviability of their client institutions. Concessionary-priced credit programs are not cheap to the institutions required to on-lend these funds. This may compromise their future as viable financial institutions. International donors and local governments should either reconsider their administrative cost margin policy or alter the costly features of the loan-targeting policies. Otherwise they must accept the negative consequences of subsidizing permanently the financial institutions receiving their funds.

Notes

We wish to express our gratitude to the Bureau of Science and Technology, Office of Multisectoral Development, AID/Washington, and to the Agricultural Development Office of the U.S. AID Mission in Tegucigalpa, Honduras, for their generous support of the research behind this work. Also, we wish to thank officials of the National Agricultural Development Bank (BANADESA) and a private commercial bank (to remain anonymous) for their cooperation in allowing us to undertake this study in their institutions. The usual disclaimers apply.

1. In 1981, delinquency rates (loans overdue/total portfolio) were approximately 5 percent in the PCB and 50 percent in the ADB.

References

Bhatt, V. V. "Development Banks in the Financial System." Seminar Paper no. 15. Washington, D.C.: Economic Development Institute, International Bank for Reconstruction and Development, 1979.

Cuevas, Carlos E. "Intermediation Costs and Scale Economies of Banking Under Financial Regulation in Honduras." Ph.D. dissertation, The Ohio State University, 1984.

Graham, Douglas H., and others. "An Assessment of Rural Financial Markets in Honduras," 2 vols. Report prepared for the Agency for International Development in Honduras by the Department of Agricultural Economics and Rural Sociology, The Ohio State University, December 1981.

Nyanin, Ohene O. "Costs of Agricultural Lending, Institutional Viability, and Lender Behavior in Jamaica." Ph.D. dissertation, The Ohio State University, 1982.

Saito, Katrine A., and Delano P. Villanueva. "Transaction Costs of Credit to the Small-Scale Sector in the Philippines." *Economic Development and Cultural Change* 29(1981):631–640.

World Bank. *Agricultural Credit Sector Policy Paper.* Washington, D.C.: World Bank, May 1975.

9
Loan-Transactions Costs, Credit Rationing, and Market Structure: The Case of Bolivia

Jerry R. Ladman

Many less developed countries have small-farmer credit programs, often financed by foreign aid, that are designed to promote development and rescue farmers from reliance on informal market credits. Almost all feature concessionary interest rates. Often these programs have not reached the large number of small farmers envisioned by governments and aid donors. Most rural poor continue to do without loans or to use informal lenders.

Recently, convincing agruments have been made by Adams (1971), Gonzalez-Vega (1977), Ladman and Tinnermeier (1981), and others that concessionary interest rates are the major factor contributing to this lack of success. Cheap credit leads to credit diversion, low-lender revenues, and political intrusions into credit allocation. These results are exacerbated by inflation. The recommended policy is to raise the real interest rate—an approach that highlights the role of interest rates in rationing credit.

Several authors have explored the role of loan-transactions costs in credit rationing. These costs include the noninterest expenses incurred by both lenders and borrowers in making (obtaining), servicing (implementing), and collecting (repaying) loans. Donald (1976, pp. 120–136) discussed problems with credit-delivery systems of agricultural banks. In Chapter 7 Gonzalez-Vega shows the role of lender transaction costs in the profitability (or loss) of a lending institution. Assuming that loan procedures and paperwork do not vary with loan size, a lender can reduce costs per unit of money lent by making large loans. Gonzales-Vega also reasons that such action will be most often employed where concessionary interest rates and an excess demand for credit prevail.

Adams and Nehman (1979) examined how borrowing behavior is affected by total borrowing costs, including transactions costs and interest payments. They presented evidence from several countries showing how borrower transactions costs lead to high borrowing costs from many formal lenders. They concluded that relatively large transactions costs discourage the rural poor from borrowing from these sources.

This chapter further probes the role of transactions costs, especially for the borrower, as a credit-rationing mechanism and demonstrates how these costs play an important role in the structure of financial markets in rural areas. The discussion is largely based on information from Bolivia, a country that has many small farmers and has received considerable foreign aid for credit programs.

Transactions Costs

Credit conditions and the set of procedures that are followed by a lender in making, servicing, and collecting loans are here termed a credit delivery system (CDS). To obtain a loan, a farmer not only must assume the agreed-upon conditions of the loan but also must go through the procedures that are required by the lender's CDS. The costs associated with the steps the farmer undertakes to complete these requirements result in borrower transactions costs. In general, these costs are the out-of-pocket outlays required to obtain documents, pay commissions and bribes, and travel to and from the lender's office, as well as the opportunity costs of time involved to complete all required procedures. If there are delays in loan approval or disbursements, the farmer may incur additional transactions costs associated with obtaining a temporary loan from another lender.

It should be noted that the steps followed by the borrower are not mirror images of those of the lender. For example, a borrower may present documents that require considerable time and money to acquire; the lender, on the other hand, only requires a short time to examine and file them.

Reasons for Transactions Costs

Many lender procedures are aimed at gathering information about a prospective borrower. This is done mainly to protect the lender's funds by determining the prospective borrower's creditworthiness and to provide internal control on funds lent. Lenders also incur transactions costs when they have employees supervise credit. In the cases of government development banks, patronage and bureaucracy might also cause some procedures to be incorporated into the CDS simply to make work for bank employees on the public payroll.

CDSs will vary considerably among different lenders. There are differences in the terms and conditions of the loans as well as in lender and borrower transactions costs. Within any country a continuum of lenders could be established, ranked in terms of complexity of CDSs. An intercountry comparison would likely show similarity of rankings among different lenders. At the end of the scale denoting the least complex CDS (but the one with the most flexible and highest interest rates) would be the informal lenders. These lenders generally operate within a small geographic area and are able to accumulate reliable information on creditworthiness of their clientele. Based on this knowledge, they extend credit without resorting to paper work or documents to provide additional information. Morover, since they are independent businesspeople, they do not need to maintain elaborate records to justify their actions. As a result, their CDSs are simple and result in low lender, as well as low borrower, transaction costs.

At the other extreme would be an agricultural development bank with a complex CDS that might include a lot of loan supervision and rigid interest rates. Because it is a public institution, detailed paper work and documents to back up all actions for purposes of internal control and financial responsibility are important. Operating in many sites, the bank uses standardized procedures at all locations. This type of operation leads to intrinsically high lender and borrower transactions costs.

Between these two extremes are other institutions such as credit unions and commercial banks. Their CDSs and associated transactions costs will vary depending upon the strength of their reasons for collecting information, their means of collecting it, and their services.

Lender Behavior

Lender transactions costs are assumed to be more or less constant, irrespective of loan size. As Gonzalez-Vega (1977) has demonstrated, a lender—such as a development bank—that has high transactions costs is motivated to lower those costs per unit of money lent. This can be accomplished in several ways. The most direct is to simplify the CDS. For example, supervised credit functions and costs can be cut by eliminating these services or by transferring them to the agricultural extension service. Another means is to reduce procedures and documentation. However, in this regard, the lender may be constrained by banking codes.

In practice these constraints may not be important because lenders have learned that transactions costs are an effective means to ration credit, especially when they must charge concessionary interest rates and hence face excess demand for loans. Because of this they have little incentive to change the CDS, but rather are motivated to use the high borrower transactions costs associated with the CDS to help ration credit by raising borrowing costs to nonpreferred clients while simultaneously lowering lender costs. This can be accomplished in several ways. First, some of the lender's costs can be transferred to the borrower. One example is the practice of making the farmer spend time and money to visit the lender rather than vice versa. Another example is the making of group loans, where many of the costs of obtaining information and loan repayment are shifted to the group.

A second way to lower costs is to focus on repeat borrowers about whom the lender has already accumulated considerable information, rather than on new borrowers about whom relatively little information is on hand. Third, the average loan size can be increased by lending to large farmers and for high-cost enterprises. This may imply making longer-term loans, which the lender would be willing to do if the expectations are that the future rate of inflation will be low and/or that there will be no increase in the interest rate. To shift the portfolio in these directions it may be necessary to impose complementary nonprice rationing mechanisms such as collateral and credit sanctions for selected enterprises (Ladman 1974).

Borrower Behavior

Assume that a farmer has a set of farm enterprises and associated technologies that can be used to produce a combination of farm products. Further, assume that the farmer must rely upon credit to undertake any of these investments and that the demand for credit will be derived from the expected productivity of the resources employed as a result of using a loan (Ladman 1970). The demand schedule (*DD*) in Figure 9.1 consists of the locus of present values of the marginal value products (MVP) resulting from the resources employed using successive loan units. The demand for credit is net of risk associated with the enterprise selected and credit use. AR and ABC in Figure 9.1 represent average revenue and average borrowing costs incurred by the borrower.

Assume the farmer is working with a single lender. The farmer who uses credit must incur borrowing costs (BC) that are imposed by the lender's CDS. These consist of interest costs (IC) and constant

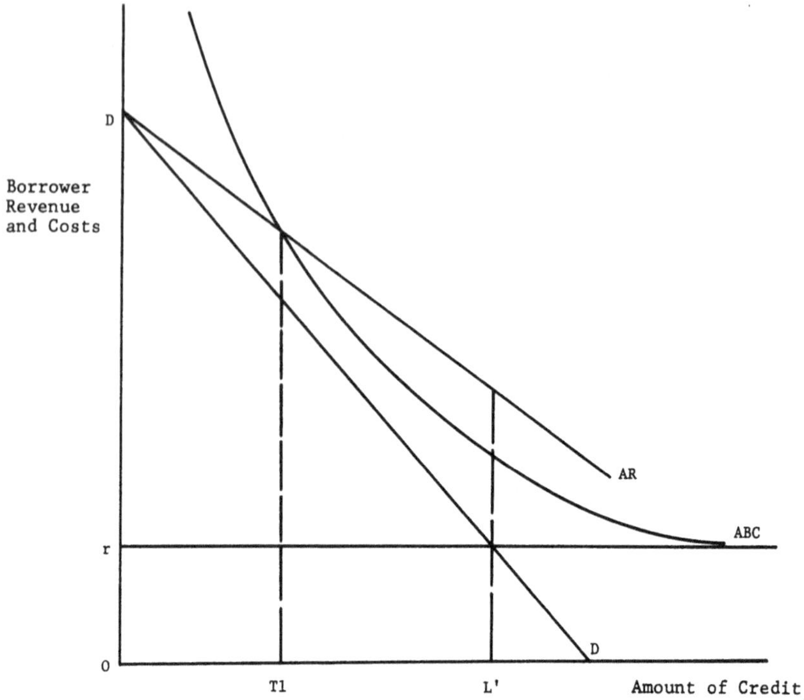

Figure 9.1 Borrowing Costs and Revenues: One Lender

borrower transactions costs (BTC). The former are equivalent to the product of a constant nominal interest rate (r) and the loan size (L). The latter arise from out-of-pocket costs and opportunity costs of the borrower's time spent in carrying out loan procedures. They are assumed not to vary with loan size. Revenue (R) resulting from borrowing is net of costs of the resources purchased with borrowed funds, but is not net of borrowing costs.

Assume that there are no delays in credit delivery that cause the farmer to lose revenue or to temporarily resort to other lenders. (It should be noted, however, that such delays often occur, especially when farmers are dealing with lenders that have complex and time-consuming CDSs that require multiple reviews of loan applications.)

Assume the borrower is a profit (π) maximizer and thus would seek a loan only if he or she expected $\pi > 0$, i.e., R > (IC + BTC). Furthermore, the borrower would maximize π by borrowing up to the point where r = MVP, i.e., where the marginal cost of borrowing, the additional interest payment, is equal to the marginal value product from additional resources purchased with borrowed funds.

The profit statement can be expressed in terms of average revenue (AR) and average borrowing cost (ABC) by dividing all terms by the size of loan, *L*. ABTC is defined as the average borrower transaction cost and r is average interest cost. In this form

$$I = \frac{L(\pi)}{L} = L\left[\frac{R}{L} - \left(\frac{IC}{L} + \frac{BTC}{L}\right)\right] = \tag{9.1}$$

$$L[AR - (r + ABTC)] = L[AR - ABC]$$

Figure 9.1 shows the profit-maximizing condition. With *DD* the demand schedule, the farmer would want to borrow *L′*, where *r* = MVP and π would be *L′*(AR−ABC).

The borrower transaction costs have at least three impacts on profitability. First, *ceteris paribus*, larger BTC means less profits for borrowers. Second, there is a minimum loan size below which the borrower would not be willing to borrow from a lender. This level (T1) is the borrowing threshold and is the level where ABC = AR and BC = R. Clearly, for any given *r*, the larger the borrower transactions costs, the higher the borrowing threshold. Third, the out-of-pocket cost threshold (T2) is part of T1 and represents the amount of outlay the farmer must make in applying for a loan. Examples are payments for documents and travel expenses. A farmer who does not have the funds to exceed this threshold will not be able to obtain credit.

Even a farmer who did have the T2 funds might not want to attempt to borrow because of facing some probability that the loan application would be rejected and the accompanying risk of losing the threshold money. If this were the case, then the borrower would implicitly weight these costs by a risk factor and would not apply for the loan if the probable loss exceeded an acceptable level. Such a situation would be very important for first-time borrowers who do not know what to expect from a lender. Experienced borrowers who know the probability of loan rejection is high also would not apply.

In summary, the farmer would be willing to borrow *L* from the lender if $T1 < L \leq L'$, if he or she had funds available in the loan application phase that were at least equivalent to T2, and if he or she was willing to risk those funds. A farmer who did not have T2 or was not willing to risk the funds would not be able to borrow from the lender. It is important to note that first-time borrowers may have larger borrower transaction costs and borrowing and out-of-pocket thresholds than repeat borrowers because they must present information and documents that need not be furnished again by repeat borrowers. Compared to repeat borrowers, first-time borrowers would have smaller profits and a greater possibility of not exceeding the two thresholds.

Choice of Lender

Now assume there are two lenders, I and II, in the market (subscripts I and II are used to denote variables related to each lender). Further, assume that the farmer will choose the lender that offers the largest expected profit (π) given interest rates r_I and r_{II}, transaction costs BTC_I and BTC_{II}, and demand for credit *DD*, subject to the constraints and associated risks of the out-of-pocket expenses $T2_I$ and $T2_{II}$. Thus for any loan size *L*, the farmer would choose lender I, be indifferent between I and II, or choose II depending upon relative expected profits $\pi_I \gtreqless \pi_{II}$ subject to covering and risking the out-of-pocket loan access costs T2 for the preferred lender. A farmer unable to cover T2 for that lender would be forced to a second-best (less preferable) situation of borrowing from the other lender if he or she could cover T2 for that lender. A borrower who could not cover T2 or was not willing to risk funds in applying for credit from that lender would be forced to go without credit.

For any loan size, *L*, the preference for borrowing from one of the two lenders can be rewritten as a function of average borrowing costs, i.e., $(r_I + ABTC_I) \gtreqless (r_{II} + ABTC_{II})$.[1] The level of *L* where the farmer would prefer to use one lender or the other should *L* rise or fall is the point of indifference.

It is quite possible that the shape of *DD* would be such that a farmer would not choose to work with a lender because the borrowing threshold exceeds the optimum loan size, in which case the particular lender is not within the farmer's feasible set of lenders. In this situation the farmer would still likely want to work with a lender that had a CDS embodying a low out-of-pocket threshold, even though it might mean paying a high interest rate (Ladman 1971).

To illustrate how transactions costs influence the borrower's choice of lender, assume I and II are a moneylender and an agricultural bank, respectively. Further, assume that the moneylender's interest rate r_I greatly exceeds the bank's rate r_{II}, while the transaction costs of borrowing from the moneylender (BTC_I) are very small compared to those of borrowing from the bank (BTC_{II}). As a consequence $T1_I < T1_{II}$ and $T2_I < T2_{II}$.

As shown in Figure 9.2, the farmer would be indifferent between the two lenders at L'', where $\pi_I = \pi_{II}$; would prefer the bank at loan sizes greater than L'', where $\pi_I < \pi_{II}$, if he or she has funds that can be risked to cover $T2_{II}$; and would prefer to work with the moneylender at loan sizes less than L'', where $\pi_I > \pi_{II}$, if he or she is willing to risk funds to cover $T2_I$. Farmers preferring the bank would want to borrow L_{II} because at that level of credit they would

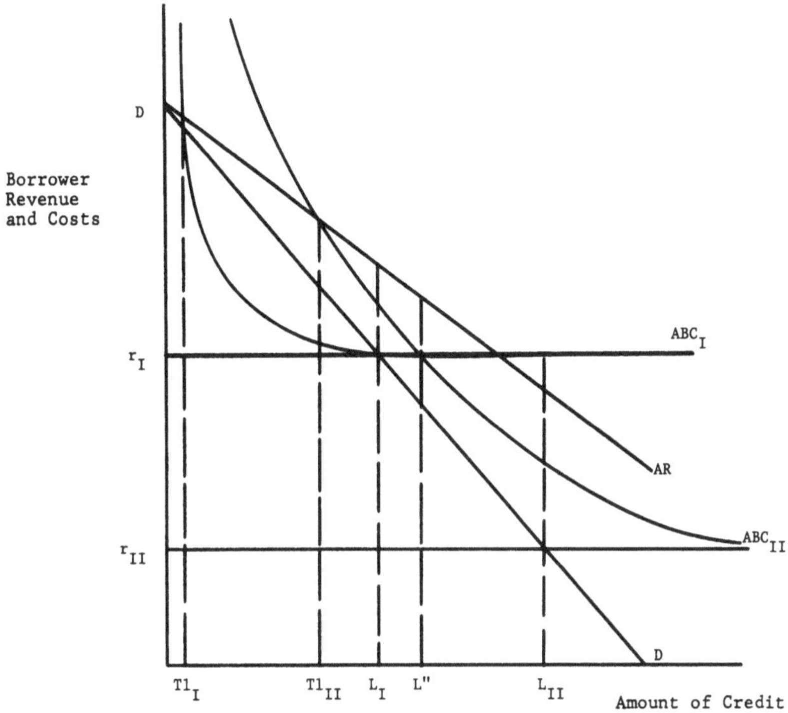

Figure 9.2 Borrowing Costs and Revenues: Two Lenders

maximize their profits. Likewise, those preferring the moneylender would want to borrow L_I.

The farmer who prefers the bank but cannot cover—or is not willing to risk—$T2_{II}$ would be forced to borrow from the moneylender, but would not use more than L_I credit. If a farmer prefers the moneylender but cannot cover—or is not willing to risk—$T2_I$, he or she would be forced to go without credit.

It is possible that due to the shape of *DD* the farmer would be excluded from operating with the bank because $T2_I > L_{II}$. In other words, the high transaction costs associated with a bank loan exclude the farmer from including the bank within the feasible set of lenders.

Market Structure

The previous sections show how transactions cost influence lender and borrower behavior. It should be clear that transactions costs have an important impact on the structure of financial markets in rural areas. Indeed, they provide an explanation of why several credit institutions can operate side by side even though they charge considerably different rates of interest. Lenders with CDSs that embody high lender transactions costs will gravitate toward larger loans, whereas those with low costs will be content to make smaller loans. Likewise borrowers seeking small loans will often prefer to work with lenders who charge high interest rates but who impose low transactions costs upon borrowers. When seeking larger loans, borrowers may prefer to work with lenders who impose larger transactions costs but charge a lower interest rate.

As a result of this convergent behavior the aggregate demand for credit in these markets is segmented. In the case of two lenders, the segment associated with higher rates of interest, lower borrower transactions costs, and smaller loans corresponds to the moneylenders' portion of the market. The second segment—associated with lower rates of interest, higher borrower transactions costs, and larger loans—corresponds to the agricultural banks' portion of the market.

Partitioning of the aggregate demand will tend to occur at an aggregate loan volume where across all farmers the average costs of borrowing from both lenders are equal; that is, where, in the aggregate, farmers are indifferent between the two lenders. This condition will be determined by the CDS of each lender. Mandates, rules, and operating procedures governing the lenders' CDSs will determine BTC_I, BTC_{II}, and r_{II}. Conditions of competition will determine r_I. If there is perfect competition among moneylenders, r_I will be kept at a level that is commensurate with the opportunity costs of lending for nonagricultural purposes and/or other investment opportunities. If conditions of nonperfect competition prevail, r_I will be kept at some level at which a portion of the moneylender's return on investment consists of monopoly profits.

Changes in borrower transactions costs or in interest rates associated with either lender will change the partitioning of the market. If either the interest rate or borrower transactions costs rise for a lender, more borrowers will prefer to seek their credit from other lenders and thus shift the partition accordingly, *ceteris paribus*.

Concessionary interest rates play an important role in structuring financial markets. Assume an agricultural bank charges concessionary rates and faces an excess demand for credit. The bank would need mechanisms to ration credit among its potential clients. If borrower transactions costs were raised as a result of the bank's action, some potential borrowers would go to other lenders or go without credit. Because more farmers would now prefer to borrow from moneylenders, there would be a corresponding shift in moneylenders' share of the overall market.

The Bolivian Case

In 1975 the Bolivian Agricultural Bank (BAB) initiated a small-farmer credit program with financing from the U.S. Agency for International Development (AID), and the remainder of this chapter deals with activities under this program in the Upper Valley of Cochabamba, an area densely populated by land-reform beneficiaries. These activities illustrate the importance of transaction costs in credit rationing.

AID and BAB jointly established the conditions of the short- and medium-term small-farmer loans. First, for the then conventional reasons, a concessionary interest rate was adopted, and this assured an excess demand for credit. Second, in an effort to ration credit toward target farmers and enterprises, borrower-eligibility and loan-purpose criteria were established. Third, because of legal requirements, previous BAB operating procedures, and the conventional wisdom surrounding small-farmer credit, a complex CDS was adopted that caused large transactions costs for both lenders and borrowers. This CDS required several meetings of the bank agent and the farmer, considerable paperwork, and the presentation of several documents.

At the ouset, BAB wanted to disburse funds rapidly to demonstrate farmer demand, justify the program, and possibly to obtain a second loan from AID. In order not to exclude large numbers of small farmers, several important nonprice rationing features were eliminated. Collateral requirements were reduced to those of the expected harvest, for crop loans, and the items purchased with livestock and equipment loans. Many farmers did not have an authentic title to their land, so substitute documentation was arranged. An important effect of these actions was to increase the excess demand for cheap loans.

Because of the high lender transactions costs embodied in the CDS, BAB established procedures that would ease the pressure on itself and place more responsibility for obtaining information on the borrower. The farmer had to obtain all of the required documents and provide them to the bank and was expected to carry out all transactions at the bank office rather than at the farm site, excepting one on-site visit by the BAB agent. Furthermore, BAB decided to make most loans to groups of farmers.

In another move to lower lender transactions costs and rapidly disburse funds, BAB opted to put most of its portfolio in larger and medium-term loans rather than short-term production loans.[2] In response to farmer demand, the typical loan was to finance one year of crop production and the acquisition of oxen or dairy cows. The loan was to be repaid in installments over a three- or four-year period.

The effects of the CDS chosen by BAB are clear. Their measures, designed to lower their costs and rapidly disburse funds, rationed credit away from small farmers who wanted smaller and short-term loans and placed loans in the hands of those wanting larger and medium-term loans. Simultaneously, on the side of borrower transactions costs, farmers who could not surpass the out-of-pocket or borrowing thresholds were excluded from borrowing. Some farmers who could meet these thresholds found it more profitable to borrow from other lenders.[3] The result was that farmers who sought smaller loans did not go to BAB, whereas those seeking the larger loans were more than willing to incur the heavy transactions costs associated with borrowing because it was the most profitable alternative among their sources of credit. Thus, in the presence of an excess demand for credit, it was both BAB's actions and the effect of those actions on borrowers that served to ration the credit among farmers.

The effect of the credit-rationing features of BAB's small-farmer credit program is clearer if one understands the structure of rural financial markets in the Upper Valley. In 1979 there were three types of lenders in the area making most of the loans: moneylenders, BAB, and a multipurpose cooperative (Ladman and Torrico 1981). In this chapter we report on the first two. Data on average loan terms and transactions costs in 1979 are presented in Table 9.1.

BAB loans had a mean size of $3,695 (all figures are in U.S. dollars) and a term of 60 months and carried interest rates of 13 percent. In sharp contrast, moneylender loans had a mean size of $480, a term of 3 months, and an interest rate of 48 percent. Given these interest rates, lender and borrower transactions costs explain how the market is partitioned among lenders.

BAB borrowers incurred an average of $135.95 in total transactions costs; of this $94.75 were out-of-pocket costs and $41.20 were time costs (the equivalent of 16.5 days). Of the total, $69.66 was incurred in the application phase. Thus the prospective borrower from BAB had to project profits, above interest charges, in excess of $135.95 (the borrowing threshold) and have on hand $50.28 for out-of-pocket costs (out-of-pocket threshold). Moreover, the borrower had to be willing to risk $69.66 of out-of-pocket and time costs before knowing whether or not the loan would be accepted. In practice, however, a borrower was usually informed of the probable decision at an early stage of the negotiation, based on the eligibility criteria, so the risk cost was not as high as it would appear. Clearly, the magnitude of these figures served to ration many small farmers out of working with BAB. Moreover, the fact that the farmer had to go through the full loan application procedures, after being told by the bank agent

Table 9.1

AVERAGE TERMS OF LOANS AND COSTS FOR MONEYLENDERS AND THE BOLIVIAN AGRICULTURAL BANK IN THE UPPER VALLEY, COCHABAMBA, 1979 (U.S. Dollars)[a]

	Moneylender	Bolivian Agricultural Bank[c]
Length of Loan	3 mos.	60 mos.
Loan Size	$480	$3,695
Annual Interest Rate	48%	13%
Lender Transactions Costs per Loan	Very Low	Very High
Total Borrower Transactions Costs	$4.35	$135.95
Total Out-of-Pocket Costs	$3.80	$ 94.75
Application Phase Out-of-Pocket Costs	$3.50	$ 50.28
Total Time Costs[b]	$ .55	$ 41.20
Application Phase Time Costs[b]	$ .45	$ 19.38
Total Borrower Transactions Costs in Application Phase	$3.95	$ 69.66

a/ Rate of exchange: 20 Bolivian pesos = 1 U.S. Dollar.

b/ Time valued at $2.50 per 8-hour day.

c/ Figures for the Bolivian Agricultural Bank are for borrowers who were members, but not leaders, of groups formed to receive loans. Leaders transactions costs were higher due to the additional tasks they undertook on behalf of the group.

Sources: Ladman and Torrico, Kvaran, and lender and borrower surveys carried out in 1979.

that it was very likely a loan would be granted, strongly suggests that the information and documents collected by BAB were not critical to the loan decision. Rather, they were procedures that the bank used to satisfy internal and legal requirements and also to ration credit among farmers.

In sharp contrast, borrowers from moneylenders incurred an average of only $4.35 in total transactions costs; $3.80 were out-of-pocket costs and $.55 time costs. Most of these costs, $3.95, were incurred in the application phase. Our survey of moneylenders and their clients in 1980 showed the reasons for low transactions costs. A farmer usually lived near the moneylender and needed to make only one or two short trips to inquire about and obtain the loan. The moneylender, knowing clients well, did not require collateral or need to collect much additional information and could make a decision on the spot. Most of the borrower's expense was in registering the loan with the local small-claims judge. Clearly, these small borrower transactions costs had little effect on credit rationing by moneylenders; the interest rate they charged was far more important.

Given a credit demand schedule, the interest rates, and borrower transactions costs associated with both lenders, the borrower's point of indifference between the two lenders in terms of loan size would be $376. At this point the average total borrowing costs (interest and transactions costs) would be 49.2 percent of the loan. The credit demand schedules may be summed across all farmers. The aggregate demand for credit would be partitioned at a loan volume corresponding to the sums people want to borrow from moneylenders, the remainder being desired from BAB.

The partitioning of the market between BAB and moneylenders shows the two lenders are providing different services. The moneylender provides credit quickly, on a short-term basis, and in relatively small amounts. In contrast BAB provides credit for longer-term investments and in much larger amounts. Moreover, BAB credit is not quickly obtained—the complex CDS procedures require weeks or sometimes months to complete.

It is doubtful that the small-farmer credit program in the Upper Valley has had much effect on the moneylenders' market, because BAB is lending for purposes that do not directly compete with those of moneylenders. Indeed, a 1980 survey of moneylenders showed they saw no decline in their business after BAB began its program.

Conclusions

The chapter stresses the important role of lender and borrower transactions costs as rationing mechanisms and how these costs affect credit allocation as well as the structure and performance of rural financial markets. For any lender the larger the size of transactions costs, assuming a fixed interest rate, the greater will be the rationing power of transaction costs. As demonstrated by the Bolivian case, when concessionary interest rates are present, lenders will rely heavily on transactions costs to ration credit.

Small-farmer credit programs are often criticized for not reaching large numbers of farmers. For example, in the Upper Valley of Bolivia about 1.2 percent are reached by BAB (Ladman and Torrico 1981, p. 87). Transactions costs are important in forcing this outcome. Large

BAB borrower transactions costs cause many potential borrowers to seek loans from moneylenders. Similar phenomena would be expected in rural financial markets in most low-income countries, especially when concessionary interest rates are used.

A lender will attract more clients when borrower transactions costs for loans are lowered. Agricultural banks that want to reach more farmers must lower these costs, but there are sound and rational reasons why banks are unable or unwilling to do so. First, some of these costs are necessary to collect information vital to extending good loans. The costly procedures and documents employed often are based on a banking code that a bank cannot alter. Second, for those procedures that are determined internally by the banks, there may be a reluctance to simplify them. This may seem paradoxical given that the concessionary interest rate generates low bank revenues and that the banks therefore would appear to have an incentive to lower costs. However, there is no paradox, because the banks can use borrower transactions costs as a credit-rationing mechanism. Thus, as the Bolivian experience shows, the incentive is not to change the CDS but rather to shift transactions costs to the borrower with the double consequence of rationing credit and lowering bank operating costs.

Strong arguments have been made to eliminate concessionary interest rates. If this were to occur, and if borrower transactions costs were not lowered accordingly, more farmers would be excluded from borrowing from the banks and forced to seek other lenders, resulting in a new partitioning of the market. This is not likely to occur, however, because banks no longer would face an excess demand for credit and would seek more efficient credit delivery systems that would lower borrower transactions costs. It is highly likely that the elimination of concessionary interest rates is the key to lowering transactions costs and allowing agricultural banks to serve a larger number of small farmers. Unless this is done the incentives to reduce these costs will be absent and many small farmers will continue to rely on moneylenders and other sources of credit.

Notes

The research for this paper was funded by the U.S. Agency for International Development. The author alone is responsible for its content. Appreciation is expressed to Dale W Adams, Peter Kilby, and Hannes Kvaran for comments that helped clarify some of the concepts presented.

1. The work is shown as follows:

1. $\pi_I \gtreqless \pi_{II}$
2. $(R - BC_I) \gtreqless (R - BC_{II})$ by substitution
3. $BC_I \gtreqless BC_{II}$ by subtraction of R and multiplication by -1
4. $(IC_I + BTC_I) \gtreqless (IC_{II} + BTC_{II})$ by substitution
5. $[(IC_I + BTC_I)/L] \gtreqless [(IC_{II} + BTC_{II})/L]$ dividing by L to obtain
6. $(r_I + ABTC_I) \gtreqless (r_{II} + ABTC_{II})$.

2. It was rational for BAB to make medium-term loans. At that time the rate of inflation was considerably less than the concessionary rate, and BAB's expectations were that the interest-rate level and structure would remain the same. There had been little change in inflation in the previous 10 years. As a result it was to their advantage to lend for several years rather than to make short-term loans, recycling their funds. The transactions costs of relending would be considerably higher than those of administering outstanding loans.

3. The study by Miller and Ladman (1981) supports this point. High transactions cost were shown to be important factors in impeding small farmers in southern Bolivia from using BAB loans.

References

Adams, Dale W. "Agricultural Credit in Latin America: A Critical Review of External Funding Policy." *American Journal of Agricultural Economics* 53(1971):163–172.

Adams, D. W, and G. I. Nehman. "Borrowing Costs and the Demand for Rural Credit." *Journal of Development Studies* 15(1979):165–176.

Donald, Gordon. *Credit for Small Farmers in Developing Countries.* Boulder, Colo.: Westview Press, 1976.

Gonzalez-Vega, Claudio. "Interest Rate Restrictions and Income Distributions." *American Journal of Agricultural Economics* 59(1977):973–976.

Kvaran, Hannes. "An Analysis of the Bolivian Agricultural Bank's Group Loans for Small Farmers." Ph.D. dissertation, Department of Economics, Arizona State University, forthcoming.

Ladman, Jerry R. "An Expanded View of the Demand for Short-Term Capital." *Canadian Journal of Agricultural Economics* 18(1970):172–174.

______. "Some Empirical Evidence in Unorganized Rural Credit Markets." *Canadian Journal of Agricultural Economics* 19(1971):61–66.

______. "A Model of Credit Applied to the Allocation of Resources in a Case Study of a Sample of Mexican Farms." *Economic Development and Cultural Change* 22(1974):279–301.

Ladman, Jerry R., and Ronald L. Tinnermeier. "The Political Economy of Agricultural Credit: The Case of Bolivia." *American Journal of Agricultural Economics* 63(1981):66–72.

Ladman, Jerry R., and Jose Isaac Torrico. "Informal Credit Markets in the Valle Alto of Cochabamba, Bolivia." In *1981 Proceedings of the Rocky Mountain Council on Latin American Studies Conference,* edited by John

J. Brasch and Susan R. Rouch. Lincoln: Office of International Programs, College of Business Administration, University of Nebraska, 1981, pp. 83–89.

Miller, Calvin, and Jerry R. Ladman. "Factors Impeding Credit Use in Small-Farm Households in Bolivia." Unpublished paper, Department of Economics, Arizona State University, 1981.

10
Cheap Agricultural Credit: Redistribution in Reverse

Claudio Gonzalez-Vega

Two of the main characteristics of rural financial markets in low-income countries (LICs) are limited access to institutional credit and a high degree of concentration of the loan portfolios of formal financial institutions (FFIs). That is, only a small proportion of the total number of rural producers receive loans from FFIs and, among those with access to institutional loans, a very small group captures a very large share of the total amount of credit disbursed. It has been estimated that on the average only about 15 percent of the farmers in Asia and in Latin America, and no more than 5 percent of the farmers in Africa, have had access to institutional credit. In addition, usually fewer than 20 percent of the total borrowers of the FFIs have received 80 percent of the total amounts of agricultural credit disbursed. This means that in LICs 3 percent of the total number of agricultural producers have been the beneficiaries of at least 80 percent of the credit disbursed by FFIs.

As a result of their participation in the formal rural financial markets, these few privileged borrowers have increased their incomes in more than one of the following ways: through the profits received as a consequence of the increased command over resources permitted by the loans, through the free transfer of income implicit in underpriced credit, and through the resource transfer implicit in partial or total default. Since not all rural producers have enjoyed these "benefits" and not all borrowers have received them to the same degree, this differential access to cheap credit has impacted income distribution significantly. This chapter explores some of the reasons why this impact has been substantial and undesirable.

Credit Access

Limited access and a high concentration of the loan portfolios of FFIs characterize the evolution of all institutional credit markets in LICs. These problems are particularly acute in the case of rural financial markets. Since the majority of the population in LICs lives and works in rural areas, the income-distribution implications of these features are particularly important.

Factors associated with both the demand and supply of credit explain limited access and the high degree of concentration of loan portfolios. Low average returns and high risks associated with many agricultural activities limit the demand for agricultural credit. High transactions costs, for both borrowers and lenders, further reduce the size of these markets and restrict loan access for many rural producers.

The high degree of concentration in loan portfolios of FFIs is frequently explained by the underlying concentration of wealth and political power. If there are a few wealthy producers who own a significant share of the total assets of the community, it is not surprising that they also receive a significant portion of the credit. There is increasing evidence, however, that the distribution by size of loans of the credit portfolios of the FFIs is more concentrated than the distribution of income, the distribution of the value of the agricultural output, or the distribution of land. Credit concentration, therefore, requires an additional explanation.

Initial wealth is an important determinant of differential access to loans. In fragmented capital markets, on the other hand, limited access to credit explains a substantial part of the different rates of growth of wealth through time. That is, differential access to credit is not only a consequence but also a cause of differences in wealth. Policymakers concerned with income inequalities have emphasized redistribution of land as a solution to these concentration problems. Financial reform has been much less popular, however, although access to credit is as crucial as access to land for an adequate command over resources. In many cases financial policies, particularly the imposition of interest-rate ceilings, have further restricted access to credit and have aggravated the problem of unequal wealth distributions.

Through several types of controls most LICs have kept nominal interest rates fixed during long periods. In real terms these rates have often been negative, erratic, and unpredictable. In addition, preferential rates have been established to favor agriculture and other priority sectors. I argue in this chapter that these interest-rate policies have significantly contributed to the concentration of the loan portfolios of FFIs and have accentuated restrictions on access to institutional credit. The modification of these policies is a necessary, although not a sufficient, condition for greater equity in the rural areas.

Interest rates influence income distribution in several ways. As the relative price of the present in terms of the future, they influence savings and investment flows and therefore affect the intertemporal distribution of income between present and future generations. As the price of financial assets, interest rates affect the composition of wealth portfolios and the distribution of income among asset holders. As a component of the costs of borrowing, interest rates also affect the distribution of income between lenders and borrowers and between those with access and those without access to credit. Interest rates also affect the functional distribution of income.

This chapter focuses on the impact that the loan rates of interest charged by the FFIs have on the distribution of income among borrower and nonborrower classes. For these purposes, rural producers may be classified into groups according to their size (large-small), their wealth (rich-poor), the length of their banking relationship (new client–old client), or the uncertainty associated with their productive activities (safe-risky). Any of these classifications is relevant for the analysis as long as it is related to the credit-rationing behavior of FFIs or as long as it is closely correlated to such classifications.

Credit and Income

The income of any producer is determined by productive opportunities and by command over resources that permit taking advantage of these opportunities. Command over the required inputs depends on the producer's own initial endowment, which is a result of previous savings efforts and of access to resources external to the producer's enterprise through credit.

In fragmented capital markets, potentially productive opportunities are poorly correlated with command over resources. Given the heterogeneity of farmers, varied investment opportunities arise from the unique individual circumstances of each producer. Given investment indivisibilities and low levels of income, past savings are frequently insufficient to take advantage of such opportunities. Therefore, many producers with attractive investment options cannot finance them. Access to credit becomes a crucial precondition for these producers to take advantage of new investment opportunities. Fragmentation implies, in turn, that other producers with abundant resources are

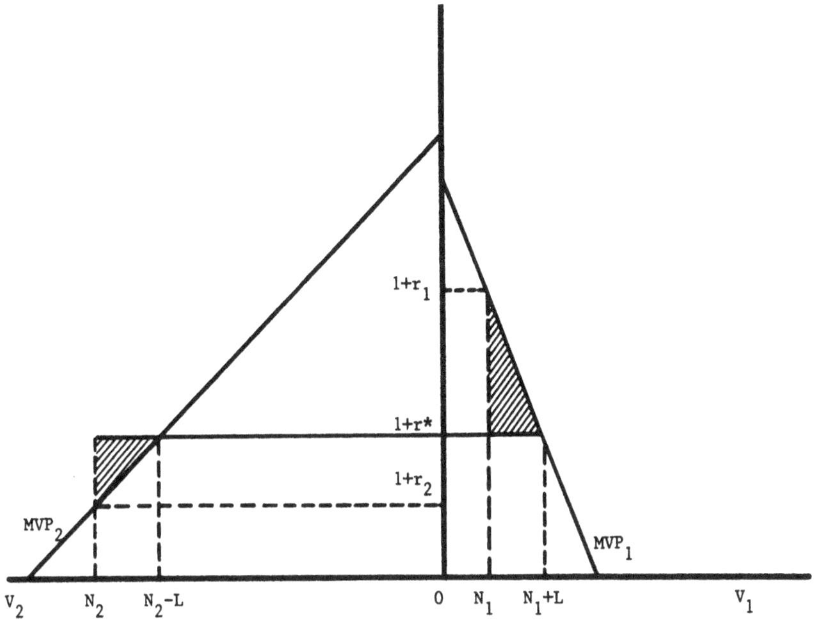

Figure 10.1 Self-financing and Impact of a Loan.

forced to invest them in low-return activities, sometimes even at negative real rates of return.

When producers lack access to credit markets they are forced to self-financing. This, in turn, leads to a wide dispersion in rates of return and to gross social inefficiencies. Such a situation is represented in Figure 10.1 for a two-producer case. In this figure, positive amounts of variable inputs (V_1 and V_2) are measured in both directions from the origin (0). The productive opportunity of each producer is represented by the corresponding curve of the marginal value of the product of the variable inputs employed (MVP_1 and MVP_2). Diminishing marginal returns are assumed throughout.

Given their initial endowments of variable inputs (N_1 and N_2), the gross income of each producer is represented by the area under the curve. Income differences are explained in terms of the different productive opportunities and of the different initial endowments ($N_2 > N_1$). For the same amount of variable inputs, the marginal rate of return is higher for the large producer than for the small one. The superiority of the large producer, however, is assumed to be relatively greater in terms of initial endowments than in terms of productive opportunities. Thus, under conditions of self-financing, the marginal rate of return of the large producer will be lower than the marginal rate of return of the small producer (that is, in equilibrium, $r_2 < r_1$). This is a situation frequently encountered in the rural areas of LICs.

Given these differences in marginal rates of return both producers can increase their incomes through a direct loan, of size *L*, from the large producer to the small one, at the rate of interest r^*. After repaying the principal plus the interest on the loan $(1 + r^*) L$, the small producer has increased income by the equivalent of the shaded area in the right-hand quadrant of Figure 10.1. At the same time, the large producer obtains an increase in income, over that previously earned from his or her own productive activity, equivalent to the shaded area in the left-hand quadrant of Figure 10.1.

Although the incomes of both producers increase, as a result of a better allocation of resources, the income of the small producer increases more, if the marginal returns to the variable inputs employed by this producer decline more rapidly than the marginal returns to the variable inputs used by the large producer. The assumption that diminishing marginal returns are more pronounced for small than for large producers is a reasonable one, in view of the smaller stock of fixed inputs and possibly less favorable access to technologies of the former. If this is the case, credit not only improves the allocation of resources but also improves income distribution. That is, the net gain of the small producer will be larger than the net gain of the large one, as represented by the shaded areas in Figure 10.1.

In summary, income differences among producers are due to differences in productive opportunities and in initial endowments. Access to credit for the acquisition of variable inputs reduces differences that are due to diverse initial endowments. Access to credit for investment in physical or human capital, in turn, may also tend to eliminate income differences due to differences in productive opportunities. In this static context, therefore, access to credit is crucial for the generation of higher incomes.

Credit and Growth

In a dynamic context, access to credit increases the rate of growth through time of the producer's initial endowment (the producer's wealth). In any period, the producer's net income (Y) is given by

$$Y = a\,(N + L) - iL, \tag{10.1}$$

where a: average rate of return of the variable inputs employed, N:

producer's initial endowment (wealth), L: size of the loan received, and i: rate of interest paid on the loan.

Under the assumption that all of the producer's net income is added to wealth each period, the rate of growth (g) through time of the producer's initial endowment is given by

$$g = \frac{Y}{N} = \frac{a\,(N + L) - iL}{N} = a + R\,(a - i) \qquad (10.2)$$

where $R = L/N$ is the leverage ratio.

That is, the rate of growth of the producer's wealth is directly associated with the average and marginal rate of return on the variable inputs used by the producer as well as with the leverage ratio, whereas it is inversely related to the rate of interest paid on the loan. These three variables, however, are not independent. Even if the rate of interest paid is given, the average rate of return will be inversely related to the leverage ratio, if decreasing marginal returns are present. As long as the marginal rate of return on the variable inputs employed is higher than the rate of interest paid, the rate of growth of the producer's wealth will increase as access to credit increases (the size of loan L increases).[1]

The impact of differential access to credit on the rates of growth of wealth can lead to dramatic differences in future endowments and therefore in the level of incomes through time of different producers. Assume that, initially, two producers X and Z possess identical productive opportunities and identical initial endowments. That is, $a_x = a_z = a(V)$, for any given level of variable inputs used, and $N_x = N_z = N_0$, in the initial period 0.

Assume that in each period both producers add to their initial endowments all of their net income. Assume that, while producer Z has access to credit, producer X does not. The rates of growth of their initial endowments will be

$$\begin{aligned} g_x &= a_x \\ g_z &= a_z + R\,(a_z - i) \end{aligned} \qquad (10.3)$$

After n periods of time, the wealth of these producers will be

$$\begin{aligned} N_n^x &= (1 + g_x)^n\, N_0 = (1 + a_x)^n\, N_0 \\ N_n^z &= (1 + g_z)^n\, N_0 = [1 + a_z + R\,(a_z - i)]^n\, N_0 \end{aligned} \qquad (10.4)$$

Therefore, after n periods of time the relative size (W) of their endowments will be

Table 10.1 Hypothetical Increases Through Time of a Firm's Relative Wealth Under Various Assumptions of the Real Rate of Return, Interest Rates, and Leverage Ratios

a	r	R	W n=5	W n=10	W n=20
.25	.20	1	1.2	1.5	2.2
.25	.05	1	2.1	4.4	19.5
.25	.05	3	7.1	50.4	2,542.3
.25	-.10	3	21.1	444.8	197,859.3
.10	-.30	4	89.1	7,938.0	63,011,755.0

a: Average rate of return, in real terms

r: Interest rate, in real terms

R: Leverage ratio

W: Relative wealth (ratio of borrower's wealth with respect to nonborrower's wealth)

n: Number of periods

$$W = \frac{[1 + a_z + R\,(a_z - i)]^n}{(1 + a_x)^n} \tag{10.5}$$

That is, W indicates how many times the wealth of the producer with access to credit is larger than the wealth of the producer without access to credit. If in the initial period both producers have the same wealth, $W = 1$, the differences that will exist after some time will be directly related to the number of periods that have passed (n), the difference between the average rates of return, a_x and a_z, the leverage ratio (R), and the rate of interest paid (i). Table 10.1 illustrates the impact on W of these variables, under the assumption that the average rate of return is constant.

For example, given a constant real average rate of return (a) of 25 percent, if each year one of these two producers receives a loan equal to 3 times his or her initial endowment, at a real rate of interest of minus 10 percent (r), and the other producer does not receive any loans, after 5 years (n=5) the wealth of the former will be more than 21 times larger than the wealth of the latter. After 20 years, the wealth of the borrower will be almost 200,000 times larger than the wealth of the nonborrower!

This simulation illustrates the magnitude of the impact of differential access to credit on rates of growth of wealth and on income distribution. Differences in the rate of growth of wealth among producers depend on differences in average rates of return earned and rates of interest paid. The most dramatic differences, however, are directly related to the leverage ratio (R). That is, access to credit, in comparison to the producer's initial endowment, is the most important determinant of the relative level of the producer's wealth in the future. Therefore, access to credit is a key mechanism for influencing the distribution of wealth through time.

Nature of Interest-Rate Policies

In most LICs the interest rates charged by FFIs have been administratively set or constrained by usury ceilings. These rates have been kept at low nominal levels in the presence of high rates of inflation. As a result, in real terms many of these rates have been negative. Also, they have not reflected the opportunity costs of the claims on resources transferred by FFIs to their borrowers, they have not equated the supply and demand for institutional loans, and they have not covered the costs and risks associated with lending to some borrower classes. Most importantly, these low interest rates have implied the transfer of a substantial subsidy to the relatively few, not so poor, beneficiaries of FFIs loans.

Interest rates not only have been kept low, but differentiated and inverted rate structures have often been enforced. That is, interest-rate differentials have not reflected the costs and risks associated with lending to different borrower classes. Rather, they have resulted from policymakers trying to favor some sectors and activities at the expense of others. Typically, the borrower classes favored with preferential rates, like small farmers, are associated with the highest costs and risks for the FFIs. Thus, FFIs have been forced to charge the lowest rates on loans to those borrower classes to which they would want to charge the highest interest rates. As a result of these discrepancies, the borrower classes that the authorities intended to favor have been harmed.

Recent interest-rate reforms, that in some countries increased all but the preferential rates, have significantly widened the differentials within the inverted interest-rate structure and have thus accentuated credit rationing and the concentration of the loan portfolios. For example, in the mid-1970s, while the commercial interest rates and government bond rates reached 50 percent per annum and more in Brazil, the interest rates charged on agricultural loans were kept at 15 and 17 percent per annum. Substantial inefficiencies in credit allocation and inequities in income distribution resulted.

Nature of the Interest-Rate Subsidy

When loan interest rates do not reflect the social opportunity cost of the claims on resources transferred, plus the social cost of disbursing them, a subsidy is implicit in the credit transaction. Income distribution is affected in two ways: directly, because of the implicit subsidy, and indirectly, because of the differential influence of the restrictions on access to credit.

Suppose, very conservatively, that the social costs of the loan are, in real terms, 10 percent per annum. If the nominal rate of interest charged is 15 percent per annum, but the rate of inflation is 65 percent per annum, then the real rate of interest charged is minus 30 percent per annum.[2] If a positive rate of 10 percent should have been charged, while a negative rate of minus 30 percent was actually charged, there is a rate of subsidy of 40 percent implicit in this credit transaction. That is, 40 cents out of every dollar lent represents an outright, free transfer of resources, a gift.

The magnitude of this subsidy can be substantial. Suppose that the total volume of agricultural credit disbursed by the FFIs represents 60 percent of the gross value of the domestic agricultural output. In this case, the total amount of the subsidy, the grant transferred, will be equivalent to 24 percent of the value of this output. This is a very sizable transfer of resources, and its impact on income distribution is very significant. Because the subsidy implicit in underpriced credit can be so substantial, it is not surprising that policymakers value it as a powerful instrument for income redistribution. Unfortunately, the subsidy seldom reaches the poor. Rather, the vested interests of the groups that eventually capture the subsidy create serious political obstacles for interest-rate reform in agricultural credit programs.

The main claim of this chapter is that credit, in general, and interest-rate subsidies, in particular, are an impotent tool for income redistribution. The mechanism is inefficient, because the same redistributive objectives could be achieved at much lower social costs by other means. Even as a second-best solution, the subsidy is not justified, because it is ineffective; that is, it is intrinsically incapable of achieving the desired redistributive goals. Further, under most circumstances, it is perverse. It leads to a redistribution "in reverse," actually accentuating the concentration of wealth instead of alleviating it. This is the case because the direct impact of the subsidy is regressive and its indirect impact further restricts access to institutional credit and further concentrates the loan portfolios of FFIs in the hands of a few large borrowers.

Direct Impact of the Subsidy

To become a beneficiary of the interest-rate subsidy, a producer must first become an institutional borrower. Access to cheap credit, however, is very restricted. As a consequence, a large portion of the total number of producers is excluded from this subsidy. Moreover, the amount of the free grant is directly proportional to the size of the loan received. That is

$$G = [r^* - r]\ L(W) \tag{10.6}$$

where G: the amount of the grant, L: size of the loan, W: the borrower's wealth, r^*: the social opportunity cost of the claims on resources lent, and r: the rate of interest charged on the loan.

The larger the loan, the larger the grant. In addition, since there is a high correlation between previous wealth and the size of the loan received, the wealthier the borrower, the larger the grant. As a result, large producers have access to large loans and to the accompanying large grants. Medium-size producers have access to small loans and to the associated small grants. Small producers get few or no loans and thus few or no grants. A similar result is obtained with respect to the income transfer implicit in default. A large borrower who does not repay the loan receives a larger implicit grant than a small delinquent borrower. Usually large borrowers represent a small proportion of the number of defaulters but a very high proportion of the unpaid portfolio.

Moreover, as indicated in Chapter 7, when the rate of subsidy $(r^* - r)$ increases, large nonrationed borrowers[3] get access to larger loans than before and the magnitude of their grants increases. The size of loans to rationed borrowers, on the other hand, declines, and the magnitude of their grants could increase or decline depending on the relative position of the intermediaries' marginal cost curve of lending to them.

There is one more way in which underpriced credit has a direct unfavorable impact on impact distribution. The resources freely transferred to the privileged borrowers are collected by the FFIs through the exploitation of savers and of holders of financial assets, by means of the inflation tax, which reduces the purchasing power of their assets. In most LICs, the size distribution of the borrowers of FFIs is much more concentrated than the distribution of holders of claims of the financial system. As a consequence, the majority of the population pays a substantial tax that is used to finance a subsidy enjoyed by a few privileged borrowers.

Indirect Impact of the Subsidy

Interest-rate restrictions also influence income distribution through their differential impact on access to credit. The nature of this impact depends on the rationing behavior adopted by FFIs when the ceilings are imposed. Most of the likely mechanisms for rationing adopted by the FFIs tend to redistribute loan portfolios in favor of some borrower classes (e.g., large, safe, well-known borrowers).

For these purposes, producers can be classified into three groups, according to the nature of their access to institutional credit: (1) nonrationed borrowers; that is, producers who receive all the credit that they demand at the rate of interest charged by FFIs; (2) rationed borrowers; that is, producers granted FFIs loans smaller than the size they demand at the going rate of interest, so that they are left with an unsatisfied excess demand for institutional credit; and (3) excluded borrowers; that is, potential or previous borrowers whom FFIs are not willing to serve at the constrained interest rates.

In general, for FFIs with a profits strategy, if the maximum rate of interest that can be charged covers the marginal costs of lending to a particular borrower, that borrower's demand will be satisfied. If, on the other hand, this maximum rate of interest does not cover the marginal costs of lending, the FFIs will reduce the size of the loan granted below the size of the loan demanded, until the rate of interest and marginal costs are equated. Finally, when the maximum rate of interest does not cover the average variable cost of granting the loan, FFIs will exclude the borrower from their portfolios.

Lending costs tend to be particularly high in rural financial markets. There is a great diversity among rural producers, and the information required for borrower selection—concerning entrepreneurial ability, productive opportunities, and access to resources—is expensive to collect. Risks are also particularly high, as a result of the importance of exogenous factors in determining the outcome of investment efforts, and creditworthiness is difficult to ascertain. Even if, *ex post,* small producers tend to be less delinquent than some of the larger producers, it is difficult for lenders to choose from the heterogeneous mass of farmers.

One of the consequences of these high costs and risks of lending is that rural producers in general, and small farmers, in particular, are among the rationed classes of borrowers. When ceilings on interest rates are imposed or lowered, the amounts of credit demanded by all classes of borrowers increase. However, according to the Iron Law of Interest-Rate Restrictions (discussed in Chapter 7), only the size of the loans granted to nonrationed borrowers increases. In the case of the rationed borrowers, the size of loan granted declines, and in certain circumstances these borrowers are excluded from the loan portfolios altogether.

Conclusions

The most important conclusion of this chapter is that interest-rate ceilings redistribute the loan portfolios of FFIs in favor of nonrationed borrowers and modify the access to credit by different producer classes. Since access to credit is a crucial determinant of differences in the growth of wealth through time, these changes in loan size significantly influence income distribution. Nonrationed borrowers tend to be the largest and most influential producers, and interest-rate restrictions lead to the concentration of credit portfolios in their favor.

The most crucial aspect of financial markets, for rural producers, is their degree of access to credit. Ironically, the policies that have attempted to keep the price of credit artificially low have, at the same time, modified access in unwanted ways: The access of the large and influential producers to the loan portfolios of the FFIs has been improved, while at the same time the access of the small producers has been limited or even eliminated. Interest-rate restrictions have also penalized numerous small savers who have received low returns on their financial assets. Therefore, policies of interest-rate restrictions not only have reduced efficiency in the allocation of the economy's resources but also have reduced the financial viability of the FFIs and have contributed to more concentrated distributions of wealth and of income in the rural areas of the LICs—the reverse of what most policymakers say they want to do.

Notes

Among the many friends who have influenced my ideas on rural finance, I want to especially acknowledge Dale W Adams, Ronald I. McKinnon, Edward S. Shaw, and Robert C. Vogel.

1. This can be shown by taking the total differential of Equation 10.2 to demonstrate that the impact on the growth rate of wealth of a larger loan is

$$\frac{dg}{dL} = \frac{\partial a}{\partial L} + R\frac{\partial a}{\partial L} + \frac{R}{N}(a - i) = \frac{N + L}{N}\frac{\partial a}{\partial L} + \frac{a - i}{N}. \quad (10.7)$$

However, the marginal rate of return, *r*, is equal to

$$r = (N + L)\frac{\partial a}{\partial L} + a. \tag{10.8}$$

Therefore

$$\frac{dg}{dL} = \frac{r - i}{N} \tag{10.9}$$

2. $r = (i - p)/(1 + p)$, where r: real rate of interest, i: nominal rate of interest, and p: rate of inflation.

3. These are borrowers who receive loans of the size they demand. Rationed borrowers, on the other hand, receive loans smaller than those demanded.

References

Adams, Dale W, Harlan Davis, and Lee Bettis. "Is Inexpensive Credit a Bargain for Small Farmers? The Recent Brazilian Experience." *Inter-American Economic Affairs* 26(1972):47–58.

Araujo, Paulo F. Cidade de, and Richard L. Meyer. "Politica de Credito Agricola no Brasil: Objectivos e Resultados." In *Ensaios Sobre Politica Agricola Brasileira,* edited by Alberto Veiga. São Paulo: Secretaria da Agricultura, 1979.

Gonzalez-Vega, Claudio. "Small Farmer Credit in Cost Rica: The Juntas Rurales." In *AID Spring Review of Small Farmer Credit,* vol. 2, edited and published by the Agency for International Development. Washington, D.C., 1973.

———. "On the Iron Law of Interest Rate Restrictions: Agricultural Credit Policies in Costa Rica and in Other Less Developed Countries." Ph.D. dissertation, Stanford University, 1976.

———. "Interest Rate Restrictions and Income Distribution." *American Journal of Agricultural Economics* 59(1977):973–976.

———. "Interest Rate Restrictions and the Socially Optimum Allocation of Credit." *Savings and Development* 4(1980):5–28.

Ladman, Jerry R., and Ronald L. Tinnermeier. "A Model of the Political Economy of Agricultural Credit: The Case of Bolivia." *American Journal of Agricultural Economics* 63(1981):66–72.

McKinnon, Ronald I. *Money and Capital in Economic Development.* Washington, D.C.: Brookings Institution, 1973.

Shaw, Edward S. *Financial Deepening in Economic Development.* New York: Oxford University Press, 1973.

11
The Effect of Subsidized Agricultural Credit on Income Distribution in Costa Rica

Robert C. Vogel

Subsidized agricultural credit has been very popular in low-income countries, on the usual assumption that such policies improve the welfare of small farmers. It is argued that small farmers will be unable to borrow or will be able to borrow only small amounts at high rates of interest unless they are aided by low-interest loans. It is my conclusion, however, that subsidized credit policies in Costa Rica have, in fact, made income distributions more unequal. The lion's share of the credit subsidy, which turns out to be very substantial, has been captured by large farmers, whereas the access of small farmers to credit may even have been reduced.

This Chapter focuses on Costa Rica because it presents a particularly favorable case for subsidized agricultural credit to make the distribution of income more nearly equal. In Costa Rica subsidized agricultural credit is allocated by four commercial banks, all of which are owned by the government. Thus, it cannot be argued that the allocation of credit is the result of profit-maximizing behavior by private commercial banks or that the credit subsidy could be allocated to make the distribution of income more nearly equal if those commercial banks were in the hands of the government. The period for this analysis is the mid-1970s because it coincides with a detailed study of income distribution and the most recent agricultural census in Costa Rica. Moreover, two features of the Costa Rican economy that are important for the following analysis have largely persisted: the structure of interest rates and the upsurge of inflation that began in the mid-1970s.

The largest bank (Banco Nacional de Costa Rica) has been a government bank since it was founded in 1914, and the other three commercial banks were nationalized in 1948, so that all of them have had many years to adjust to carrying out government credit policies. Moreover, by the mid-1970s the three smaller banks had more than 30 regional offices, and the Banco Nacional had more than 100, 60 of which were rural credit offices (Juntas Rurales de Credito Agricola) specializing in credit for small farmers.[1] It would be difficult to imagine a banking system better designed and more oriented toward carrying out policies of subsidized agricultural credit to benefit small farmers.

The subsidy in agricultural credit in Costa Rica and other low-income countries does not take the form of explicit payments to the recipients of credit. Rather, the subsidy is implicit, as the interest rates charged to credit recipients are below the interest rates that would be charged in competitive markets. The first section of this chapter is concerned with estimating the total amount of the interest-rate subsidy to recipients of agricultural credit in Costa Rica. In the second section the allocation of this credit subsidy among different classes of borrowers is examined, and in the last section implications for the distribution of income are discussed. In addition, I suggest some reasons for the highly unequal distribution of agricultural credit and draw some conclusions for agricultural credit policies.

The Amount of the Credit Subsidy

In Costa Rica, as in many other low-income countries, interest rates on bank agricultural loans are set far below the interest rates that would be determined in competitive markets for agricultural credit. As of the mid-1970s, Costa Rican banks were charging interest rates of 8 or 9 percent on agricultural loans (with an additional 2 percent or less for commissions and other charges on some of these loans). Small farmers have consistently been given preferential treatment with interest rates of 8 percent and no commissions or other charges, while interest rates, commissions, and charges for larger farmers vary slightly depending on the product financed. Agriculture tends to be favored relative to other sectors, as interest rates on bank loans for nonagricultural activities in the mid-1970s ranged as high as 13 percent (plus commissions and other charges of 2 percent).[2]

To estimate the amount of the interest-rate subsidy on bank agricultural loans, it is necessary to have some idea of how high interest rates would be under competitive conditions. First, the impact of inflation on interest rates must be taken into account, and a distinction between nominal and real rates of interest must be made. During the 1950s and 1960s Costa Rica experienced rates of inflation averaging only about 2 percent per year as measured by the consumer price index. However, the rate of inflation increased slightly during the late 1960s and early 1970s and accelerated sharply in 1973. In 1974 the Costa Rican consumer price index increased by 30 percent, and the rate of inflation as measured by the wholesale price index was 40 percent. Even using the conservative 30 percent figure as the relevant indicator of the rate of inflation, Costa Rican lenders in 1974 would have had to charge 30 percent interest just to avoid reducing their real wealth by making loans.[3]

What real rate of interest would equate the supply and demand for credit in Costa Rica? It would certainly not be a negative real rate of interest, as long as potential lenders had any productive outlets for their funds and as long as potential borrowers had any productive investment opportunities. Moreover, competitive credit markets would not determine a single equilibrium real rate of interest, but rather a range of interest rates depending on risks and administrative costs. In fact, it would be surprising if under competitive conditions loans for agriculture in general and small farmers in particular did not carry interest rates above average because of the greater risks and administrative costs.

A conservative estimate of the real rate of interest that would be determined in competitive markets for agricultural credit in Costa Rica would be at least 10 percent. A survey of agricultural credit in Costa Rica in 1969 (before the arrival of high rates of inflation) indicated that informal lenders typically charged interest rates of 18 or 24 percent on loans to farmers (Vogel and Gonzalez-Vega 1969). Studies of agricultural credit in other low-income countries suggest that such interest rates can be largely attributed to risks and administrative costs and not to monopoly power (Bottomley 1975; Long 1968).

With a negative real rate of interest of 20 percent on bank agricultural loans and a conservative estimate of an equilibrium real rate of interest of 10 percent for agricultural lending under competitive conditions, the total amount of the subsidy going to the recipients of Costa Rican agricultural credit during 1974 can readily be computed. During 1974 the average amount of agricultural credit outstanding from the four commercial banks was slightly over 1.6 billion colones (US$187 million).[4] The interest-rate subsidy of 30 percent, together with the average amount of credit outstanding, implies a total subsidy of about 480 million colones (US$56 million). To put this subsidy in perspective, it should be noted that Costa Rican gross domestic product (GDP) for 1974 was approximately 13 billion colones (US$1.5 billion), so that the subsidy amounted to almost 4 percent of GDP. Moreover, the agricultural sector accounted for about 20 percent of Costa Rican GDP, so that the subsidy to the recipients of bank agricultural loans was equivalent to almost 20 percent of value added in Costa Rican agriculture.

Most of the subsidy to recipients of bank agricultural loans was paid by holders of bank deposits. They received a negative real return for making funds available to the banking system for lending; that is, they had to pay an inflation tax of 20 to 30 percent depending on the type of deposit held. Unfortunately, no data are available to identify precisely who these individuals were. However, it is likely that individuals with low incomes held a higher percentage of their wealth in the form of currency and deposits (because of their requirements for transactions balances and precautionary reserves) than did individuals with high incomes who had a wider range of opportunities to hedge against inflation. An indication of the better alternatives available for the wealthy is given by the behavior of the amount of banking-system bonds outstanding. In the late 1960s these bonds accounted for almost 10 percent of the banking system's resources. However, they had dwindled to less than 2 percent by 1974, as a result of the impact of inflation and the low nominal rates of interest paid on these bonds. The former holders of these bonds, largely the wealthy, were able to find more attractive alternatives when an inflation tax of more than 20 percent was imposed. Such behavior also illustrates that high rates of inflation, uncompensated by high rates of interest, substantially reduce the resources available to the banking system for lending.

The Distribution of the Credit Subsidy

A picture of the main beneficiaries of subsidized bank agricultural credit can be obtained from the size distribution of agricultural loans disbursed during 1974 by the Commercial Department and the Rural Credit Department of the Banco Nacional. The data from the Banco Nacional are particularly useful for two reasons: (1) the Banco Nacional accounted for about 60 percent of the total amount of agricultural credit disbursed by the banking system during 1974; and (2) as mentioned earlier, the Banco Nacional through its Rural Credit Department is supposed to be particularly dedicated to making credit available to small farmers. The data from the Banco Nacional are presented in Table 11.1, and the pattern is striking. Loans of more than 500,000 colones (US$58,343) accounted for more than 55 percent

Table 11.1 Banco Nacional, Commercial and Rural Credit Departments Size Distribution of Agricultural Loans Disbursed During 1974

Size of Loan (Colones)	Percent of Total Number of Loans	Percent of Total Amount of Credit	Cumulative Percentages: Number of Loans	Cumulative Percentages: Amount of Credit
1-5,000	52.4	3.3	52.4	3.3
5,001-10,000	17.7	3.5	70.1	6.8
10,001-20,000	13.2	5.2	83.3	12.0
20,001-40,000	6.2	4.6	89.5	16.6
40,001-100,000	6.0	9.9	95.5	26.5
100,001-500,000	3.3	17.9	98.8	44.4
Over 500,000	1.2	55.6	100.0	100.0

Source: Banco Nacional.

of the agricultural credit disbursed by the Banco Nacional, but for only 1.2 percent of the total number of agricultural loans made by the bank. The largest 10 percent of the agricultural loans accounted for more than 80 percent of the agricultural credit disbursed by the bank, but on the other hand the smallest 50 percent (loans under 5,000 colones, i.e., under US$583) accounted for less than 5 percent of the agricultural credit disbursed by the bank.

These findings for the Banco Nacional are largely confirmed by data from a second commercial bank, the Banco Anglo Costarricense.[5] Table 11.2 presents the size distribution of agricultural loans disbursed during 1974 by the Commercial Department of the Banco Anglo. Loans of more than 100,000 colones (US$11,670) accounted for more than 40 percent of the agricultural credit disbursed by the Banco Anglo, but for less than 5 percent of the total number of agricultural loans made by that bank. On the other hand, loans under 10,000 colones (US$1,167) accounted for more than 50 percent of the agricultural loans made but less than 10 percent of the agricultural credit disbursed by the Banco Anglo.

The recipients of the large agricultural loans from the Costa Rican banking system are the principal beneficiaries of the credit subsidy. Who are they? Unfortunately, no data are available on the incomes, land holdings, or other forms of wealth of the recipients of bank agricultural loans. However, enough evidence is available to reach a

Table 11.2 Banco Anglo Costarricense, Commercial Department Size Distribution of Agricultural Loans Disbursed During 1974

Size of Loan (Colones)	Percent of Total Number of Loans	Percent of Total Amount of Credit	Cumulative Percentages Number of Loans	Cumulative Percentages Amount of Credit
1-5,000	33.8	3.6	33.8	3.6
5,001-10,000	20.7	5.8	54.5	9.4
10,001-20,000	17.3	9.5	71.8	18.9
20,001-40,000	14.2	15.1	86.0	34.0
40,001-100,000	10.4	24.1	96.4	58.1
100,001-500,000	3.2	22.0	99.6	80.1
Over 500,000	.4	19.9	100.0	100.0

Source: Banco Anglo Costarricense, unpublished records.

definite (and obvious) conclusion: Large agricultural loans are received by large farmers, that is, wealthy farmers with high incomes. Three pieces of evidence are sufficient to reach this conclusion. First, 75 percent of the number of agricultural loans disbursed by the banking system during 1973 went to small farmers.[6] This is consistent with the conclusion that the largest 10 percent of bank agricultural loans, accounting for 80 percent of bank agricultural credit disbursed during 1974, went to large farmers. Second, one would not expect banks to make large loans to small farmers because of the high risks involved. This is confirmed by a survey of agricultural credit in Costa Rica carried out in 1969, which found that bank officials responsible for making agricultural loans placed heavy emphasis on the prior economic success of their clients and on the ability to provide good guarantees (Vogel and Gonzalez-Vega 1969). Finally, this same survey found a high positive correlation between the size of bank loans and the size of farmers as measured by the area of the farm, the area cultivated, and the number of workers employed.

The amount of the credit subsidy going to the large farmers who received the largest 10 percent of bank agricultural loans in 1974 can readily be calculated. As indicated above, a conservative estimate of the total amount of the agricultural credit subsidy for 1974 is 480 million colones (US$56 million).[7] Approximately 80 percent of bank agricultural credit and hence about 80 percent of the subsidy went

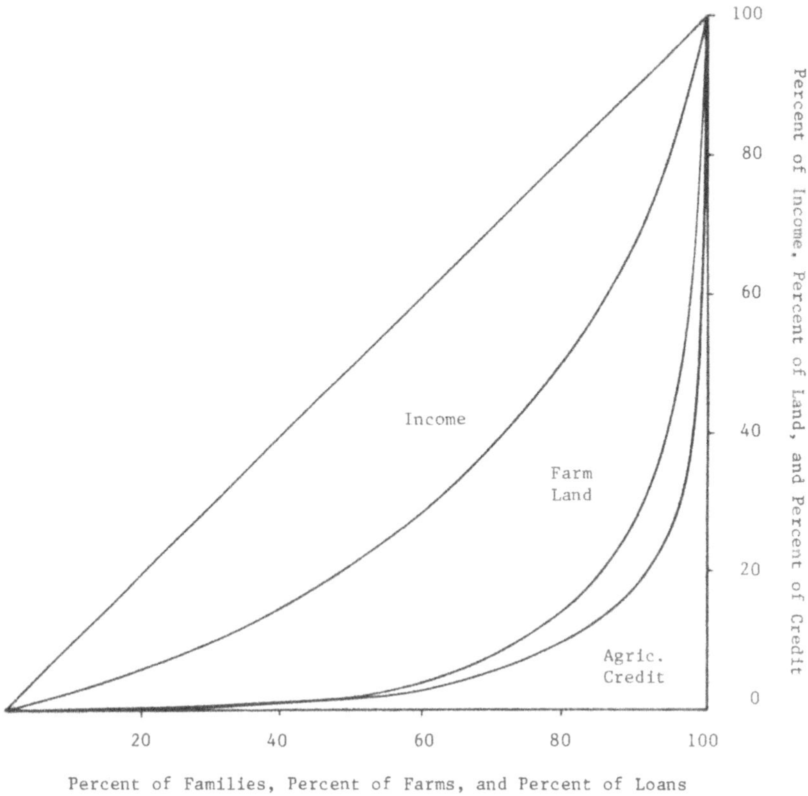

Figure 11.1 Lorenz Curves for Income, Farmland, and Agricultural Credit Distribution in Costa Rica

to the large farmers who received the largest 10 percent of the loans. In short, these farmers received a credit subsidy of approximately 385 million colones (US$45 million) during 1974 from the Costa Rican banking system.

The Impact of the Credit Subsidy on Income Distribution

To assess the effects of this distribution of bank agricultural credit on the distribution of income, it is useful to begin by comparing the distributions of income, land, and agricultural credit in Costa Rica. Figure 11.1 plots three Lorenz curves: one for agricultural loans disbursed by the Banco Nacional during 1974, a second for the distribution of land holdings by size of farm (given in the 1973 *Censo Agropecuario*), and a third for the distribution of income in Costa

Rica in 1971.[8] The curves clearly show that the distribution of land is much more unequal than the distribution of income and that the distribution of credit is still more unequal. Moreover, the concentration of land and credit is understated for two reasons: (1) many individuals own more than one farm and receive more than one agricultural loan from the banking system; and (2) there are many rural Costa Ricans whose main occupation is agriculture who own no land and receive no bank agricultural loans.

According to the 1973 census, there are approximately 200,000 rural families in Costa Rica, but there are only 81,562 farms (only 62,585 with more than 1 hectare), and only 44,019 agricultural loans were disbursed by the banking system in 1974. Not all rural Costa Ricans are engaged in agriculture, but on the other hand some farms (especially large farms) are owned by urban Costa Ricans who also receive agricultural loans (often the largest loans). Of the 5,646 farms in Costa Rica containing more than 100 hectares, one-third are run by a manager, with the owners presumably absent. In addition, the 1969 survey of Costa Rican agricultural credit revealed numerous instances of farmers receiving more than one bank agricultural loan, particularly in cases involving large loans or large farms (Vogel and Gonzalez-Vega 1969).

Figure 11.1 and the forgoing discussion provide a picture of the extent of inequality in the distribution of bank agricultural credit, but some additional assumptions are necessary in order to evaluate the impact of the credit subsidy on the distribution of income. First, it seems reasonable to assume that the subsidy accompanying the 80 percent of bank agricultural credit that is contained in the largest 10 percent of the loans goes primarily, if not entirely, to individuals in the top 10 percent of the income distribution. There are approximately 35,000 Costa Rican families in the top 10 percent of the income distribution who, under these assumptions, would be receiving the 4,400 largest bank agricultural loans disbursed during 1974. Thus, even for this group, only about 1 family in 8 would be receiving a large agricultural loan from the banking system, even if it is assumed that there is no more than 1 such loan per family. In addition, 4,400 large bank loans would not reach all 5,646 farms of more than 100 hectares in Costa Rica, even if it is assumed that there is no more than 1 such loan per large farm. These figures, together with the evidence discussed at the end of the second section, suggest that it is not unreasonable to assume that large agricultural loans go to those in the top 10 percent of the income distribution. If anything, this may underestimate the concentration of bank agricultural credit.

Removing the credit subsidy of 385 million colones (US$45 million) from the top 10 percent of the income distribution would reduce the share of these families in total income from 34.4 percent to approximately 30 percent. In 1974 the average income of a family in the top 10 percent of the income distribution was about 90,000 colones (US$10,500), and averaging the 385-million-colones subsidy among the 4,400 large agricultural bank loans yields an average credit subsidy of 87,500 colones (US$10,210) per loan. These figures suggest that the impact of the credit subsidy on the incomes of those families receiving the subsidy is likely to be quite substantial and that at the same time the credit subsidy is likely to be concentrated among the highest-income families within the top 10 percent of the income distribution.[9] Distributing the 385 million colones evenly among the remaining 90 percent of Costa Rican families would raise the share of those families in the bottom half of the income distribution from 20.9 percent to over 23 percent and the share of those families in the bottom 10 percent from 2.1 percent to over 2.5 percent.

Besides the direct effects of subsidized agricultural credit on the distribution of income, there are two indirect effects of subsidized interest rates that may be equally important. The first is that low interest rates may encourage the substitution of capital for labor by those farmers who are the recipients of bank loans. This effect can be seen in Costa Rica, for example, in the expansion of the labor-saving beef-cattle industry and in the replacement of labor by electric milking machines in the dairy-cattle industry. This reduction in the demand for labor by farmers who receive low-interest-rate bank loans will tend to reduce agricultural wages and agricultural employment. Moreover, farmers who do not receive bank credit (but who might have received credit if interest rates were not controlled at low levels) may also be forced to reduce their demand for agricultural labor because of the lack of complementary inputs.

The second indirect effect concerns the farmers who might have received bank credit if interest rates were not controlled at low levels. To this point it has been assumed that the allocation of credit is not affected by charging subsidized interest rates. However, there is evidence that large farmers not only receive most of the credit subsidy but also receive a larger share of agricultural credit than they would if interest rates were not controlled at low levels (Gonzalez-Vega 1977). Access to credit allows individuals to earn higher incomes; otherwise, in the long run loans would not be repaid, and individuals would no longer be able to borrow. Consequently, the redistribution of agricultural credit away from small farmers results in a further worsening of the distribution of income.

What is the evidence that large farmers increase their share of agricultural credit at the expense of small farmers in the presence of subsidized rates of interest? As indicated in the first section, the equilibrium interest rates that would equate the supply and demand for agricultural credit are far above the interest rates being charged by the banking system on agricultural loans. At these low interest rates the demand for agricultural credit greatly exceeds the supply, and some form of rationing must occur. Even neglecting the role of political influence and family connections in the allocation of subsidized bank agricultural credit, there are good reasons for the Costa Rican banks to allocate the lion's share of subsidized agricultural credit to large farmers (Vogel 1979). Risks will be lower on the average on loans to large farmers because they have more assets and higher incomes, which make repayment more secure than in the case of small farmers. Administrative costs per dollar lent will also tend to be lower on large loans to large farmers because of the fixed costs of lending and because the more favorable risk situation of large farmers implies lower costs for credit investigations. Moreover, in Costa Rica interest rates are set lower on loans to small farmers than on loans to large farmers. Thus the returns from lending to small farmers are lower while the costs are higher.

Conclusions

A study of loan delinquency in Costa Rica has shown that delinquency rates are low for agriculture in general and for small farmers in particular (Vogel 1981). This evidence has often been used to conclude that Costa Rican agriculture is highly productive and that small farmers are particularly good risks. However, because of the substantial subsidy that accompanies bank credit, the repayment of loans gives no indication that agricultural undertakings are profitable in Costa Rica. Moreover, the particularly low delinquency rates for small farmers reflect the ability of Costa Rican bank officials to select farmers with the best repayment potential. The fact that small farmers have lower delinquency rates than large farmers thus indicates that loans to small farmers are rationed more severely than loans to large farmers because of the lower returns and higher costs of lending to small farmers.

Removal of the interest-rate subsidy on bank agricultural credit would have several effects that would tend to make the distribution of income more nearly equal in Costa Rica. First, a surprisingly large proportion of the subsidy goes to large farmers in the form of large loans. Second, the demands for, and hence the incomes of, agricultural laborers tend to be reduced, and agricultural laborers are undoubtedly in the lower deciles of the income distribution. Third, small farmers, who would have access to bank credit in the absence of low subsidized interest rates, find their income is reduced because credit is rationed more severely to them than to other groups.

Only the first effect has been quantified, and it alone implies that the distribution of income could be made significantly less unequal by allowing interest rates to rise to their equilibrium level. Although the other two effects have not been quantified here, each may be very important in making the distribution of income in Costa Rica as unequal as it is. Moreover, raising interest rates to their equilibrium level can simultaneously remove the direct subsidy effect and deal with the indirect effects of the reduced demand for agricultural labor and the more stringent rationing of bank credit to small farmers. Thus, credit subsidies, which have often been attacked for their perverse effects on economic efficiency, can also be attacked for making the distribution of income more unequal.

Notes

An earlier version of this paper was presented at the April 1977 meeting of the Rocky Mountain Council for Latin American Studies in Tucson, Arizona. The author wishes to thank Dale W Adams, Jerry Ladman, and Claudio Gonzalez-Vega for helpful comments.

1. Rural credit offices were initially established in 1914 as part of the Banco Internacional de Costa Rica, and by October 1915 there were 27 such offices. The most significant feature of the rural credit offices is their relatively high degree of decentralization and the important role of local residents in making credit decisions (Gonzalez-Vega 1973).

2. By the late 1970s, but before the financial reform in late 1978, a slightly higher structure of interest rates was in effect: 8 to 11 percent on agricultural loans and as high as 18 percent on certain nonagricultural loans (commissions and other charges continued to range from 0 to 2 percent).

3. Even if expectations do not adjust immediately to higher realized rates of inflation (and adjustment should be rapid under such circumstances as the high rates of inflation experienced in Costa Rica in 1973 and 1974), continuing inflation in Costa Rica should bring eventual adjustment. Inflation in Costa Rica was just under 10 percent per year for 1976–1978 but rose again to 20 percent per year at the end of the decade.

4. Agricultural credit includes loans for crops and livestock. The average for 1974 is based on month-end figures for December 1973 and for each month of 1974, as reported by the Banco Central de Costa Rica in *Credito y Cuentas Monetarias.* The amount of new bank agricultural loans disbursed during 1974 was almost as great, more than 1,400 million colones. For

conversion of colones to dollars, the official exchange rate of 8.57 that prevailed at the time is used.

5. The Banco Anglo accounts for almost 15 percent of agricultural credit from the banking system. The Banco de Costa Rica accounts for almost 25 percent of agricultural credit, and the Banco Credito Agricola de Cartago accounts for less than 5 percent. However, no data on the size distribution of agricultural loans were available from these other two banks.

6. As of the mid-1970s small farmers were defined as having net incomes of less than 25,000 colones (US$2,920) and total bank loans of less than 100,000 colones (US$11,670).

7. The estimate of 480 million colones is based on the average amount of bank agricultural credit outstanding during 1974, whereas the figures for the size distribution of bank loans are based on the amount of agricultural credit disbursed during 1974. If there is a significant correlation between the size of the loan disbursed and the length of time for which the loan is granted, then the size distribution of loans disbursed will not give an accurate picture of the size distribution of loans outstanding. However, the data available on the maturities of Costa Rican agricultural loans suggest that the size distribution for loans disbursed is an accurate representation of the size distribution for credit outstanding.

8. See Cespedes (1973) for the figures on Costa Rican income distribution. This study is based on a survey of approximately 3,000 families, divided among rural areas (about 60 percent), the metropolitan area of San José (about 25 percent), and other urban areas (about 15 percent). The income-distribution figures plotted in Figure 11.1 are for all Costa Rica because, as indicated in the text, it is likely that a significant number of farm owners and recipients of agricultural credit live in urban areas. Average income in the metropolitan area is more than 50 percent above the national average and somewhat more concentrated (Gini coefficient = .44) than in rural areas (Gini coefficient = .37), where average income is about two-thirds of the national average. Other urban areas have an average income about 25 percent above the national average and are intermediate in concentration (Gini coefficient = .39). See Jain (1975) for a summary of recent surveys of income distribution in Costa Rica, including the survey by Cespedes. This summary indicated that the Cespedes survey was representative, as well as being the most recent survey, and that the distribution of income in Costa Rica tended to be less equal than in other Latin American countries. Figures on income distribution are also available from the Costa Rican censuses, but these figures include only labor income.

9. In considering the impact of subsidized credit in general on the distribution of income, it should be remembered that agricultural credit represents slightly less than half of total credit outstanding from the banking system.

References

Bottomley, Anthony. "Interest Rate Determination in Underdeveloped Rural Areas." *American Journal of Agricultural Economics* 57(1975):279–291.

Cespedes, Victor Hugo S. *Costa Rica: La Distribucion del Ingreso y el Consumo de Algunos Alimentos.* San Jose, Costa Rica: University of Costa Rica, 1973.

Gonzalez-Vega, Claudio. "Small Farmer Credit in Costa Rica: The Juntas Rurales." In *AID Spring Review of Small Farmer Credit,* vol. 2, edited and published by Agency for International Development. Washington, D.C.; 1973.

______. "Interest Rate Restrictions and Income Distribution." *American Journal of Agricultural Economics* 59(1977):973–976.

Jain, Shail. *Size Distribution of Income: A Compilation of Data.* Washington, D.C.: World Bank, 1975.

Long, Millard F. "Interest Rates and the Structure of Agricultural Credit Markets." *Oxford Economic Papers* 20(1968):275–288.

Vogel, Robert C. "Subsidized Interest Rates and the Rationing of Agricultural Credit in Developing Countries." In *Problems and Issues of Agricultural Credit and Rural Finance,* edited and published by the Bangladesh Bank. Dacca, 1979.

______. "Rural Financial Market Performance: Implications of Low Delinquency Rates." *American Journal of Agricultural Economics* 63(1981):58–65.

Vogel, Robert C., and Claudio Gonzalez-Vega. *Agricultural Credit in Costa Rica.* San Jose, Costa Rica: Agency for International Development, July 1969.

12
Rural Credit and Positive Real Rates of Interest: Brazil's Experience with Rapid Inflation

João Sayad

Negative real rates of interest have been blamed for such aspects of the unsatisfactory performance of rural financial markets in many low-income countries as the concentration of loans among wealthy farmers, the small share of self-financing in the farming sector, the shortage of medium- and long-term loans, and the weak formal financial institutions in rural areas. The low degree of financial intermediation, market segmentation, and limited savings also have been blamed on these negative rates. Low real rates of interest are singled out as the most important features of financial repression.

In this chapter I analyze the conceptual and operational difficulties of defining and charging positive real rates of interest where very rapid inflation exists. My discussion is based on recent events in Brazil. Brazil's experience may be helpful in determining appropriate interest-rate policies in other countries that suffer from high rates of inflation.[1]

Agricultural Credit in Brazil

Agricultural policy in Brazil has emphasized heavily subsidized credit provided by a government bank, the Banco do Brasil, and by private commercial banks that are required to lend not less than 20 percent of their demand deposits to the rural sector. During the 1960s nominal rates of interest on rural credit ranged from 0 to 15 percent a year with rates of inflation of 30 to 40 percent a year. Since 1971 nominal rates have been gradually increased as inflation accelerated;

in 1981, nominal interest rates on agricultural loans varied between 45 percent and 70 percent a year with inflation averaging near 100 percent a year. High nominal interest rates are part of a general economic policy aimed at curtailing interest-rate subsidies. Since rural credit and low interest rates have been the most important elements of Brazilian agricultural policy, the recent increase in nominal interest rates represents an important change in strategy. It appears that policymakers are moving toward the goal of providing agricultural loans at positive real rates of interest, the topic discussed in this chapter.

Table 12.1 shows the amount of rural credit supplied by the Banco do Brasil and other commercial banks from 1970 to 1980. As can be noted, there was a very large increase in the nominal amount of formal rural loans made in the country over this 11-year period. There was also a very large increase in the purchasing power of the rural loan portfolio; the value of the rural portfolio increased more than three times in real terms. Column 3 in Table 12.1 shows the ratio of agricultural loans to gross agricultural domestic product. Compared to other low-income—as well as high-income—countries, Brazil's ratio is very large. In the mid-1970s the volume of formal agricultural loans in Brazil substantially exceeded the value of agricultural output. The amount of credit subsidy associated with the high negative real rates of interest for this sector represented almost 30 percent of the value of agricultural product in 1979 (column 8). This subsidy came to approximately US$3 billion in 1980.

Rural credit subsidies have been distributed as unequally as the rural credit itself. Table 12.2 shows the distribution of rural credit across different farm-size groups. As can be noted, the large farm-size groups received very large amounts of loans in comparison with the total value of their agricultural output (column 6). In 1975 those in the largest farm-size group (more than 10,000 hectares) received loans equal to three-quarters of the total value of their output, whereas those in the smallest farm-size group (less than 10 hectares) received only 6 percent of the value of their output in loans.

Real Rates of Interest

A widely used definition of the real rate of interest considers the mean rate of inflation as a nonrandom variable, which is defined as

$$r = \frac{1 + i}{1 + p} - 1 \tag{12.1}$$

where *r* is the real rate of interest, *i* the nominal rate, and *p* the

Table 12.1 Selected Data on Agricultural Loans, Inflation, Interest Rates, Subsidies, and Gross Agricultural Product in Brazil, 1970–1980

	Value of Agricultural		Ratio	Average Rate of		Median Rate of		Ag. Credit Interest-Rate Subsidies as Percent of Ag. GDP	
	(1)	(2)	(3)	(4)	(5)	(6)	(7)	(8)	(9)
Year	Loans Out-Standing*	Gross Domestic Product	1/2	Infla-tion****	Real Ag. Interest Rates	Inflation	Real Ag. Interest Rates	Average Inflation (5)x(3)	Median Inflation (7)x(3)
	Billion Current Cruzeiros			%	%	%	%	%	%
1970	12	17	.71	19	- 3	15	-.3	2	2
1971	18	24	.75	19	- 3	15	-.3	2	2
1972	24	31	.77	19	- 3	15	-.3	2	2
1973	37	44	.84	19	- 3	15	-.3	4	2
1974	63	66	.95	28	- 4	20	- 4	10	4
1975	105	88	1.19	27	-11	24	- 8	13	10
1976	159	138	1.15	38	-20	30	-13	23	16
1977	227	237	.96	41	-23	37	-19	22	18
1978	298	321	.93	41	-17	37	-13	16	12
1979	494	521	.95	74	-31	60	-20	29	19
1980**	813	1,293***	.63	74	-31	60	-20	20	13

Sources: Unpublished reports prepared by the Comissao de Financiamento da Producao (CFP) and the Secretaria de Planejamento (SEPLAN)

* Year end outstanding balances. In 1980 one U.S. dollar exchanged for 84 cruzeiros, while in 1970 the exchange rate was about 5.

** Preliminary data reported in the Gazeta Mercantil, January 23, 1981.

*** Estimated by the author.

**** Average rates of inflation for the subperiods defined in Table 12.4.

Table 12.2 Distribution of Rural Loans in Brazil According to Farm Size, 1970-1975 (in 1978 Cruzeiros)

Farm Size Class in Hectares	Total Value of New Rural Loans (000,000)		Average Value of New Loans per Farm		Ratio of Loans to Gross Product Value	
	1970	1975	1970	1975	1970	1975
	(1)	(2)	(3)	(4)	(5)	(6)
Less than 10	1,697	3,263	673	1,254	.05	.06
From 10 to 100	10,212	28,982	5,279	15,262	.14	.19
From 100 to 1,000	12,895	45,095	31,091	101,072	.24	.35
From 1,000 to 10,000	4,820	19,915	136,058	502,290	.24	.42
10,000 and more	1,230	3,827	849,287	2,102,458	.36	.75
Total	30,854	101,081	6,266	20,244	.17	.26

Source: Paulo Fernando Cidade de Araujo, *Analise da Politica de Credito a Agricultura Brasileira*, unpublished doctoral thesis, Escola Superior de Agricultura "Luiz de Queiros," University of São Paulo, Piracicabo, São Paulo, Brazil, 1980, p. 109. Original data was drawn from the 1970 and 1975 *Census of Agriculture*.

mean rate of inflation. I will argue that inflation should be viewed as a random variable because it has an unknown value, different values for each time period considered (even when the annual average is well known), and different rates of price increase by sectors and products and should be considered a random variable defined over time and over different sectors. In the following discussion I assume that borrowers and lenders can correctly forecast only the expected average rate of inflation for the entire economy. The analysis focuses on the *ex post* values that inflation might have across sectors and products.

When the rate of inflation is low, relative to the real rate of return on investments, the assumption of nonrandomness for the rate of inflation is harmless. If, for example, the average rate of inflation is 5 percent a year, and the nominal rate of interest 8 percent a year, the *ex ante* real rate of interest is 2.9 percent. If inflation is, in fact, a random variable that can assume values between 3.5 percent and 6.5 percent, the *ex post* real rate of interest will assume values between 1.4 and 4.4 percent. In this case, assuming that the real rate of return on investments is 10 percent a year, the difference between minimum and maximum values for the *ex post* real rate of interest is not very important and may be ignored by borrowers.

If inflation moves to higher levels, the variance in the real rate of interest may become a more serious problem, however. Assume an economy that experiences an average inflation rate of 50 percent per year, where investment has a real rate of return of 10 percent. In this case an average *ex post* real rate of interest of 3 percent a year implies a nominal rate of interest of 54.5 percent. If inflation rates can assume values across sectors and products of between 35 and 65 percent a year, the *ex post* real rates of interest will lie between 14.4 and minus 6.4 percent. The distribution of actual inflation rates around its mean value will make a substantial difference for borrowers, depending on what happens to the prices of their products. If the rate of increase in the price of a borrower's products happens to lie closer to the lower interval of the range of inflation rates, highly leveraged borrowers may lose not only their profits from the new investment but also some assets and wealth. Thus, when inflation rates assume high values relative to the real rate of return on investment, the definition of real rates of interest must consider the variability of sector- and product-specific price changes around the average value of inflation.[2]

This chapter analyzes the definition of real interest rates and the difficulties of charging positive real rates. I do this by looking at the distribution of inflation rates and considering real rates of interest

Table 12.3 Summary Characteristics of the Variability of Wholesale Price Indexes Across 50 Different Product Groups in Brazil 1971-1980

Year	Annual Rate of Change %	Standard Deviation %	Skewness %
1971	19	11	1.9
1972	19	14	1.5
1973	18	11	0.3
1974	34	24	1.9
1975	27	16	1.3
1976	47	29	3.4
1977	38	15	0.6
1978	41	18	0.6
1979	72	26	1.0
1980	110	48	2.1

Source: Conjuntra Economica, and Indices Economicos, Suplemento Especial - vol. 33, no. 11, 1980

as random variables across different sectors and through time periods. The next section presents the statistical evidence on the distribution of inflation rates in Brazil from 1970 to 1980. Then I analyze the consequences of these distributions on financial contracts with positive real rates of interest.

Recent Inflation in Brazil

Over the years Brazil has had substantial inflation. As a result, there is a large number of measures of price change available in the country. The analysis that follows is based on 50 wholesale price indexes for agriculture and industry calculated monthly by the Getulio Vargas Foundation from January 1970 to December 1980. The most important characteristics of these indexes can be seen from the data in Table 12.3, which shows the mean rate of inflation for each year of the period, the standard deviation (calculated as the squared difference between each product group's rate of price increase and the average), and the skewness.[3]

Analysis of these 50 price indexes showed the following: (1) the standard deviation of the rate of inflation was positively associated with the mean, (2) the coefficient of variation was positively correlated with the mean inflation rate, and (3) the skewness was positive.[4] This was also true of the distribution of inflation rates across different product groups; it was asymmetrically skewed to the right during most of the period. In other words, more than 50 percent of the sectors included in the sample had a rate of inflation below the mean. A fourth characteristic was that the degree of asymmetry was positively correlated with the coefficient of variation. Thus, when inflation accelerated and the range of possible rates of inflation increased, the number of sectors that lagged behind the mean inflation rate increased.

Table 12.4 presents the characteristics of the variability of the rates of price increase for the agricultural and industrial sectors separately. For this analysis the data were grouped into six subperiods during which the rate of inflation had consistent behavior (constant, steadily increasing, or steadily decreasing). The table indicates the following additional characteristics of the variability of inflation rates: (1) the standard deviation of price changes for products within the agricultural sector was larger than that for the product groups within the industrial sector in all the subperiods; (2) both distributions were skewed to the right for most periods, and the median for the industrial and the agricultural sector was lower than the mean (with the exception of periods 2 and 3 for the agricultural sector); and (3) the rates of agricultural price increase not only had a larger standard deviation but also had a higher degree of asymmetry, particularly in periods 5 and 6.

It is instructive to analyze the variability of the average rate of inflation over time for both sectors. Table 12.5, which presents the mean, the standard deviation, and the coefficient of variation of the average agricultural and industrial prices over the same subperiods considered before, permits an analysis of the behavior of the average rate of price increase for both sectors when the rate of inflation is changing. Data in the table indicate the following additional characteristics of the variability of rates of price increase: (1) the mean rate of inflation was higher for the agricultural sector than for the industrial sector when inflation was increasing, and the reverse was true when inflation eased; (2) the standard deviation and the coefficient of variation for the mean agricultural and industrial rates of price increase were positively correlated with the mean inflation rate; and (3) the mean rate of price increase for the agricultural sector had a larger standard deviation than that for the industrial sector, indicating

Table 12.4 Characteristics of the Distribution of Rates of Price Increase in Brazil for Agriculture and Industry, 1970-1980

Period (Month/Year)	Mean	Standard Deviation	Median	Skewness
	%	%	%	%
Period 1 (01/70 - 10/73)				
Agriculture	26	19	23	27
Industry	17	11	15	18
Average	19	13	15	20
Period 2 (11/73 - 10/74)				
Agriculture	24	23	28	24
Industry	28	21	20	30
Average	28	21	20	29
Period 3 (11/74 - 09/75)				
Agriculture	22	25	17	23
Industry	28	19	26	28
Average	27	20	24	28
Period 4 (10/75 - 12/76)				
Agriculture	61	55	38	67
Industry	33	18	30	34
Average	38	29	31	41
Period 5 (01/77 - 12/78				
Agriculture	54	35	47	55
Industry	39	14	36	39
Average	41	19	37	42
Period 6 (01/79 - 12/80)				
Agriculture	88	58	67	93
Industry	72	35	59	74
Average	74	40	60	77
All Periods				
Agriculture	48	46	38	50
Industry	37	28	30	38
Average	38	32	31	40

Source: Conjuntura Economica, various issues

Note: This table is based on 100 price indexes for the agricultural sector and on 40 price indexes for the manufacturing sector published by the Getulio Vargas Foundation.

Table 12.5 Characteristics of the Distribution of the Average Agricultural and Industrial Price Indices Over Time in Brazil, 1970-1980

	Periods (Month/Year)					
Price Index	01/70- 10/73	11/73- 10/74	11/74- 09/75	10/75- 12/76	01/77- 12/78	01/79- 12/80
Agricultural						
Mean	23	27	23	53	50	71
Standard Deviation	3	8	9	15	17	32
Coeff. of Variation	15	31	39	29	35	46
Industrial						
Mean	16	27	29	35	39	66
Standard Deviation	2	7	4	5	3	31
Coeff. of Variation	9	25	14	15	81	47

Source: Conjuntura Economica, Various issues and Indices Economicos, Retrospecto na Nova Base, Suplemento Especial, vol. 33, no. 11.

that over time agricultural prices changed more and presented a larger range of possible values in each month than industrial prices.

Problems in Setting Real Interest Rates

The variability in the intra- and intersectoral rates of price increase makes it difficult to define the real rate of interest for specific sectors and enterprises in Brazil. Because the rates of price increase vary substantially across sectors and enterprises through time, the use of an average, economy-wide inflation index to set nominal interest rates will result in some borrowers paying much higher real rates of interest than others. Furthermore, for some of these borrowers, nominal interest rates equal to the average rate of inflation may represent negative leverage if the inflation rate is high.The effects of large standard deviations and coefficients of variation are analyzed in Table 12.6. The table presents the possible *ex post* real rates of interest that result when inflation is associated with a constant standard deviation of inflation rates, a constant coefficient of variation, and an increasing coefficient of variation. The probable values of inflation rates are calculated by adding and subtracting an amount equal to twice the standard deviation.

The last column of Table 12.6 shows that the range of possible values of *ex post* real rates of interest increases when the standard deviation increases with inflation. Since standard deviation and the coefficient of variation are positively associated with the average inflation rate, the problem is aggravated, and one may conclude that higher inflation rates and higher real rates of interest will increase financial risks of investment. Comparison of the results for a 20 percent inflation rate and a 100 percent inflation rate shows that, even with an increasing coefficient of variation (and a higher standard deviation), the range of possible values of the *ex post* rate of interest increases when inflation increases. Thus inflation increases the risk of default for even a zero real rate of interest on loans for two reasons: It increases the standard deviation, and it increases the coefficient of variation.

The asymmetry of the distribution of rates of price increase causes obvious difficulties for setting interest rates; in Brazil more than half of the product groups experienced product price increases of less than the average rate of inflation. If this pattern of price increases continues, positive real rates of interest on loans will cause negative leverage for the majority of the sectors considered. If the degree of asymmetry increases when inflation rates increase, paying positive real rates of interest becomes more risky for borrowers because inflation

Table 12.6 Ex-Post Real Rates of Interest for Different Rates of Inflation and Different Standard Deviations

Average Rate of Inflation	Assumptions	Standard Deviation	Minimum Value of Inflation	Maximum Value of Inflation	Range in Real Rates
20%	constant standard deviation	.01	18	22	-2 ____ +2
	increasing standard deviation	.02	16	24	-4 ____ +4
	const. coeff. of variation	.03	14	26	-6 ____ +6
	increasing coeff. of variation	.04	12	28	-8 ____ +8
40%	constant standard deviation	.01	38	42	-2 ____ +2
	increasing standard deviation	.04	32	48	-8 ____ +8
	const. coeff. of variation	.06	28	52	-12 ____ +12
	increasing coeff. of variation	.10	20	60	-20 ____ +20
100%	constant standard deviation	.01	98	102	-2 ____ +2
	increasing standard deviation	.06	88	112	-12 ____ +12
	const. coeff. of variation	.15	70	130	-30 ____ +30
	increasing coeff. of variation	.25	50	150	-50 ____ +50

increases the range of possible *ex post* real rates of interest and because an even larger number of product groups and borrowers will be paying higher real rates of interest.

The differences between agricultural and industrial rates of inflation pose some additional difficulties. As pointed out earlier, the dispersion in rates of inflation in Brazil, as measured by the standard deviation, is larger in the agricultural sector than in the industrial sector. This implies that an equal real rate of interest for both sectors will increase financial risks for the agricultural sector more than for the industrial sector. If inflation is accelerating, a nominal rate of interest equal to the inflation rate and common to both sectors represents, on average, a higher real rate of interest for the industrial sector than for the agricultural sector.

The problems in charging real rates of interest are more severe during periods of changing rates of inflation. When inflation is going up, the average rate of inflation (as well as the standard deviation) for the agricultural sector is larger than the average rate of inflation for the industrial sector. When inflation declines, the average rate of inflation for agriculture becomes smaller than the average for the industrial sector, although the same characteristics of the standard deviation remain. Thus, during periods of changing monetary policy it is very difficult to forecast the trend of rural and industrial prices and therefore the feasible nominal rates of interest for both sectors. The setting of real rates of interest on the basis of past rates of inflation might not be feasible for the agricultural sector if inflation is expected to decline.

Finally, these results change the estimated subsidies implicit in rural credit programs in which the rate of inflation is used to calculate the real rate of interest. The data in Table 12.1 illustrate how subsidies are estimated by the difference between inflation rates and interest rates multiplied by outstanding rural loans (columns 8 and 9). They represent a larger proportion of agricultural domestic product when the average rate is used (column 8), but become smaller when the median is used (column 9), particularly in more recent years, when inflation rates have increased.

Conclusions

The conventional definition of real rates of interest is based upon the average rate of inflation within an economy and assumes that inflation has no significant effect on relative prices. Under these assumptions financial assets and liabilities can be protected against inflation by rates of interest above the average rate of inflation.

Empirical evidence from a highly inflationary setting in Brazil does not support these assumptions. Inflation has been associated with changes in relative prices.

In terms of the possibilities for reforming rural credit policies, these findings suggest the following guidelines. First, increases in nominal interest rates for rural loans should not be implemented together with changes in general monetary policy, since under these circumstances the variance of sector- and product-specific inflation rates is even higher. Second, the results suggest that rural credit as well as other financial contracts might be subject to growing default risks during periods of high inflation. It is also important to emphasize that pricing policies and other market distortions worsen the domestic terms of trade for many agricultural products. This contributes to a wide dispersion of agricultural prices that makes many farm enterprises vulnerable to abrupt interest-rate readjustments. In this context, price adjustments and price-support programs stand out as important alternative policy instruments that might decrease the variance of nominal prices and, at the same time, represent an effective incentive for agricultural production.[5] Finally, the findings of this chapter suggest that proposals for changing the real rates of interest on agricultural loans have to define how these rates are calculated, and care must be taken to consider the feasibility of such changes for the finances of borrowers.

It is useful to analyze some alternative measures for protecting financial assets against inflation and decreasing the undesirable effects of inflation on financial savings. One consideration is the identification of the best price index to measure inflation and real rates of interest. The mean rate of inflation is an overestimate of the product price changes that most sectors and borrowers experience. Some borrowers may not be able to pay an interest rate equal to the mean inflation rate; inflation is an average of a basket of goods, and products like oil, transportation, and imported raw materials have had prices growing faster than others. Some borrowers may not be able to pay that average inflation rate unless they invest a large proportion of their money in exactly those products whose prices are growing faster than the average.

Thus, the first conclusion is that one has to consider different price indexes or alternatively calculate the real rate of interest with a discount. The Brazilian experience clearly illustrates this point; monetary correction after 1974 has been subject to different types of "discounts" that subtract explicitly the effect of oil prices or bad harvests on price indexes.[6]

The problem is not completely solved by charging a lower rate of interest. The previous discussion has shown that high inflation rates increase the risks of default, especially in the agricultural sector, which has flexible prices. One could imagine that if interest rates in the agricultural sector were linked to the price of the products that are being financed, the borrower would not face increased risk. The borrower would have a liability linked to the price of the product to be sold in the future. Loans for rice would earn an interest rate equal to the change in the nominal prices of rice plus a real rate of interest. Loans for sugar production would earn an interest rate equal to the changes of sugar prices plus an agreed real rate of interest. The rural loan would be expressed in the same unit of account as the farmer's assets, and inflation would not increase the risk of default. This policy would transfer most of the risks of inflation and changes in agricultural prices to the lender.

It is difficult to find a simple solution for correcting the risks that inflation represents for financial assets and liabilities. Higher nominal rates of interest and some types of indexing represent an incentive for lenders during periods of high rates of inflation, but there is no way of decreasing the risks that high rates of inflation create for many financial contracts. If current inflation is a net result of changing relative prices and is persistently high and variable, there is no convenient way that lenders and real financial savings can be satisfactorily protected, on the one hand, and all borrowers protected, on the other.

Notes

I have discussed many aspects of this paper with Decio Kadota and Adroaldo Moura da Silva. Arne Disch also gave me editorial suggestions.

1. See Baer and Beckerman (1980) and Beckerman (1978) for background on this issue.

2. The definition of the real rate of return on investment also becomes complex if inflation is a random variable. In the text I ignore this issue and assume that 10 percent is the average real rate of return.

3. The results in Table 12.3 are based on monthly data. However, for convenience only yearly data are presented in this table.

4. These characteristics have also been observed in the U.S. economy (Vining and Elwertowski 1976).

5. This conclusion concerning price-support programs is also presented in Sayad (1983) based on different considerations.

6. See Baer and Beckerman (1980) and Beckerman (1978) on this point.

References

Baer, Werner, and Paul Beckerman. "The Trouble with Index Linking: Reflection on the Recent Brazilian Experience." *World Development* 8(1980):677–703.

Beckerman, Paul. "Index Linked Brazilian 'Inflation Feedback' Mechanism." Faculty Working Paper no. 517, University of Illinois at Urbana-Champaign, 1978.

Kadota, Decio, and Adroaldo Moura da Silva. "Inflacão e Preços Relativos: O Caso Brasileiro 1970–1980." *Encontro da Anpec.* Unpublished conference proceedings. Nova Friburgo, 1980.

McKinnon, Ronald L. *Money and Capital in Economic Development.* Washington, D.C.: Brookings Institution, 1973.

Sayad, João. "Inflacão e Agricultura." *Pesquisa e Planejamento Economico* 9(1977):1–32.

______. "The Impact of Rural Credit on Production and Income Distribution in Brazil." In *Rural Financial Markets in Developing Countries: Their Use and Abuse,* edited by J. D. Von Pischke, Dale W Adams, and Gordon Donald. Baltimore: Johns Hopkins University Press, 1983.

Vining, Daniel, Jr., and Thomas C. Elwertowski. "The Relationship Between Relative Prices and the General Price Level." *American Economic Review* 66(1976):699–708.

Part 3

Politics and Finance

13 Overview of Relationships Between Politics and Finance

Dale W Adams
Douglas H. Graham
J. D. Von Pischke

In most countries political considerations play a large role in financial markets, especially those in rural areas. That these markets have always been a prominent exercise area for politicians stems partly from government need to regulate money supplies. Manipulation of financial markets, however, typically goes well beyond the bounds of simply supervising the creation of money. In many countries, financial markets are more thoroughly regulated than other markets. The controls include interest-rate regulation almost everywhere, restrictions on the range of services that lenders can provide, geographic limitations on intermediaries, and attempts to force lenders to allocate certain portions of their loan portfolios to specific people or activities.

Politicians are generally confident of their ability to control financial markets. New lines of credit for various development activities are prominent policy tools in most low-income countries. It is becoming increasingly clear, nevertheless, that the control politicians have over financial systems is more shadow than reality. By nature, financial intermediaries are innovative. They are able to mine loopholes that exist in virtually every regulation. The net result of this mining is that the original intent of the policymaker is often evaded by the intermediary, and the social costs of financial intermediation are increased through evasion. Because of the diffused nature of financial intermediation, it is difficult for anyone, especially the harried policymaker, to know exactly what intermediaries are doing. It is easier for policymakers to assume that financial mandates are largely followed.

Even in those cases where the economic results of cheap-credit programs fall short of expectations, policymakers are generally tenacious in continuing to push these programs. In a few cases researchers have documented that cheap credit is concentrated in the hands of relatively few people, that it results in inefficient allocation of resources, and that it may seriously undermine the financial integrity of the intermediary. Even with that information in hand, policymakers insist on going ahead with credit policies and programs that are very similar to those that have failed in the past. It is increasingly apparent that one must delve into the political economy of financial markets to understand why these policies persist.

The four chapters presented in Part 3 outline some of the most important aspects of the political economy of rural financial markets. Kane's chapter focuses on the reaction of financial intermediaries to regulations affecting their economic well-being. He points out that intermediaries often evade the intent of regulation through various innovations. This, in turn, causes governments to impose further regulations in attempts to reduce evasion, and this forces intermediaries to devise ways to evade the intent of new regulations. The net result of these cycles of regulation and evasion is to increase the costs of financial intermediation. These additional costs would be eliminated if market forces played a more prominent role in rural financial markets.

Blair points out in his chapter that judging the performance of financial markets only on the basis of economic criteria of efficiency and equity may not expose the reasons for the persistence of damaging policies. He argues that one ought to look at cheap credit as political patronage; that the political system may be using cheap credit as a way of rewarding those in the society who help to sustain governments. Cheap credit is a desirable tool for rewarding the friends of the regime. It is very easy to initiate or expand cheap-credit programs.

In addition to direct interventions in financial markets, politics can also have major impacts on these markets through general economic policies. In his chapter, Ray discusses the problems that overall economic policies may create for financial markets. By nature, financial markets are a service sector to productive activities. If various government policies cause yields and/or prices of agricultural products to be low, and also elevate input prices, it will be difficult to make large numbers of good loans to farmers. Strong loans are best made to firms that enjoy profits. Suppressed agricultural incomes also limit the amount of money that people have to deposit in financial markets. Vigorous agriculture leads to healthy financial intermediaries, whereas a sick agriculture causes sick lenders.

David expands on this theme in her chapter by pointing out how various policies dampened agricultural incentives in the Philippines and affected rural financial markets. She stresses that cheap credit does not make an unprofitable enterprise profitable. If given access to cheap credit, individuals will direct the use of additional funds provided by loans to those activities that give the borrower the most profit or satisfaction. Thus, cheap credit does not eliminate the inefficiencies in resource allocation caused by price and yield distortions.

All of the authors in this part stress the importance of politics on the performance of rural financial markets. It is increasingly obvious that critical policy changes in rural finance will not be made until some of these political considerations have been addressed.

14 Political Economy of Subsidizing Agricultural Credit in Developing Countries

Edward J. Kane

Development plans in many countries include regulatory schemes for controlling the volume, terms, and distribution of agricultural finance. The professed strategy is to make agricultural credit cheap enough to encourage farmers to adopt modern methods of production and thereby to increase agricultural output for the nation as a whole. As pointed out by several other authors in this volume, such policies are sometimes also justified as offsets for distorted exchange rates and product-price discrimination that favor importers and urban consumers over agricultural producers. Typically, banking institutions set up to specialize in agricultural development loans (generically termed "agricultural development banks" throughout my discussion) are mandated to make credit for small farmers and remote agricultural regions particularly abundant and especially cheap.

Although adherents maintain that agricultural development banks and other credit-allocation strategies to promote economic development are theoretically sound, practical results have been very disappointing in country after country. The long-run consequences of development-promoting credit-allocation policies invariably run counter to their ostensible goals. The analytical framework set forth in this chapter explains how the predictable response of economic forces to financial-market regulation makes it impossible to keep credit-allocation policies on target over long periods of time.[1]

Agricultural Development Banks and the Problem of Finance

For government planners in a developing nation, the problem of finance centers on how to acquire sufficient funds to support the various programs targeted in development plans. Funds raised from foreign sources are called external finance; funds raised from domestic sources are called internal finance. A parallel distinction between internal and external finance relates to sources of funds used to pay for expenditures in excess of income by individual spending units within a country (i.e., by firms, households, and government agencies).

These distinctions treat finance as a matter of delivering funds to would-be deficit spenders. But funds delivery is merely one side of the finance coin; funds generation is the second side. To deliver funds to deficit spenders, development planners and financial-services firms must first gather loanable funds. Apart from running down previous accumulations of wealth and making use of foreign borrowing or government tax receipts, this involves tapping into funds accumulated by spending units that voluntarily or involuntarily run an expenditure surplus.

Inasmuch as an agricultural development bank can draw funds from international donors and the local government, it seldom competes simultaneously for domestic deposits. But ignoring private funding leaves a financially incomplete institution that cannot survive without continuing subsidies. Most agricultural development banks function like philanthropic institutions. They do not truly "finance" their own operations by borrowing loanable funds for their own account at market interest rates and seeking energetically at least a break-even rate of repayment. They are organized to receive funds from domestic or foreign donors and to lend them out on subsidized terms to designated beneficiaries (Von Pischke 1980).

In principle, an agricultural development bank acts as a retail distributor for the domestic government or international donor that supplies it with loanable funds. Although the funding source tends in the short run to assess the quality of an agricultural bank's performance strictly by bureaucratic criteria, in the long run it wants the institution to realize a surplus. These conflicts in performance criteria put agricultural banks and their employees through a repeating two-stage life cycle.

Initially, the institution and its employees are judged not by the institution's bottom line, but by how quickly they can lend out the funds the sponsor delivers to the bank and by how well they appear to exclude applicants other than intended beneficiaries from receiving loans. Compared to a profit-oriented institution, too little emphasis is placed on project evaluation, credit-screening procedures, and contractual safeguards (such as collateral) that affect the probability that loan funds are actually paid back on schedule. Emphasizing borrowers' repayment capacity would impact immediately and unfavorably on the institution's initial goals, whereas improvement in payback experience would not be visible to the sponsoring agency or government until a much later date.

After several years, the economic costs of these bureaucratically "successful" lending priorities come to outweigh their ongoing political benefits. As repayment problems mount, the institution comes under fire, and its original managers either jump ship or are pushed overboard. In this stage, strengthening the institution's balance sheet becomes the dominant objective. Operating costs are cut and lending officers concentrate on borrower repayment capacity. But this emphasis on the financial viability of the bank's loan portfolio tends increasingly to exclude from access to program funds the beneficiaries originally targeted by the funding source. Eventually, bureaucratic pressures to serve this group renew the cycle.

In establishing guidelines to be followed by loan officers at agricultural development banks, assessment of borrowers' repayment capacity is only one of several problems facing bank sponsors. Their most fundamental difficulties flow from the fungibility of credit. A fungible good is one that can freely replace—or be replaced by—other goods of a similar nature or kind. Fungibility refers to the ease with which perfectly equivalent substitute arrangements can be established and is an essential property of loan funds that resists erasure by program restrictions and government regulations (Von Pischke and Adams 1980). It is nearly impossible without full borrower cooperation to ascertain—either before or after the fact—the true use of a loan. Just because loans are made to persons who are farm owners or farm operators or because loans are secured by agricultural land, equipment, or crops does not prevent the proceeds from being expended in unauthorized pursuits. Even making loans payable in kind or in special currencies that are redeemable only for agricultural inputs cannot guarantee that the purchase of the designated products was the marginal expenditure ultimately financed by the additional liquidity provided by the loan. The ostensible restriction can be neutralized as long as the goods can find their way through intermediate trades in gray or black markets into the hands of others.

Government and Financial Markets

Financial markets may be defined as the set of institutional arrangements by which a nation's citizens exchange current funds or commitments against future funds or commitments. When they are allowed to operate without government subsidies, financial-service firms are arbitrageurs by nature: They borrow funds to lend them out again at a profit. Precise institutional arrangements differ in form from nation to nation, but in almost every society self-regenerating financial intermediaries offer a similar set of economic benefits to those who supply funds to them: fiduciary pooling of individual accumulations of wealth, formal schemes for sharing risk, individualized payment and safekeeping services, and detailed record-keeping.[2] The universality of this pattern suggests that in financial intermediation economies of scope may be more important than economies of scale. It appears cheaper to produce intermediation services in combination at multifunction firms than to produce them separately in a series of specialized single-function intermediaries.

In every country and in every era, governing authorities almost always impose restrictions on financial-services firms. Politicians calculate a policy's effects predominantly in the short run and in terms of its impact on the chances of staying in office (Downs 1957). They are attracted to economic policies in which short-run balance of costs and benefits is favorable, especially policies in which long-run costs are disguised and widely spread across the population. Government interference in the workings of financial markets looms as a quick and administratively convenient way for politicians either to penalize or to reward specific segments of the population. The explicit marginal costs of such interference are extremely low in the short run. These costs are low because, whether or not a particular government interferes with credit-allocation decisions, it is already active in establishing the credibility of private financial contracts.

Financial markets can be no better than the quality of the contracts they feature. Participants depend on a system of legal sanctions to make financial contracts enforceable. The trick in any contract is to establish a set of incentives that make it highly likely that both sides will perform. Whether a commitment is unconditional or contingent on stipulations designated in the contract, the market value of the associated instrument depends in essential ways on the particular system of laws that governs its enforceability. Since final performance typically turns out to be more painful *ex post* for one side of the contract than the other, the penalties that may be imposed on a defaulting party closely affect the probability of contract compliance. For example, the most important difference between finance-company and loan-sharking operations is the extent to which extralegal penalties for default, such as violence to persons and property, may be threatened and exacted.

Even in the freest society the government must inevitably serve as referee in civil disputes. Costs incurred in serving this function make the government a contingent partner in collecting damages suffered by either side of any unfulfilled financial contract. As a partner, it is natural for the government to look for ways to safeguard its interests. Precisely because transactions in financial markets require governmental rulemaking and careful documentation, governments must always monitor these markets. It is natural for lawyers (though less natural for economists) to suppose that a government—merely by stepping up the degree of monitoring—can readily mandate who receives credit and on what terms. To the legal mind, interference in financial markets looks like an easy opportunity to redistribute benefits from financial intermediation in politically advantageous ways.

Although a country's financial markets and institutions are shaped importantly by its inherited legal system and cultural traditions, contemporary changes in arrangements for delivering financial services express the interplay of recognizable political and economic forces. This chapter uses a conceptual framework developed in Kane (1977 and 1981) to interpret the interaction of political and economic elements in the evolution of programs for subsidizing credit for agricultural development. Although the presentation focuses on contemporary problems of channeling credit to agriculture in developing countries, the scheme is potentially useful in explaining financial change in any country and in any era.

Political Economy of the Regulatory Dialectic

Political economy is the name by which the study of economics was known before twentieth-century academic specialization led economists and political scientists to adopt a less holistic vision of economic and political processes. Taking an old-fashioned perspective, this chapter maintains that the dynamic interaction of these processes is the driving force in institutional change.

The paramount explanatory concept is the "regulatory dialectic." This philosophical word *dialectic* represents a careful way to characterize the dynamic workings of a process that operates more or less like a playground seesaw. A dialectical process is one whose outcomes are governed over time by two opposing forces. As the respective forces gain and lose momentum, they push outcomes first one way and then the other. However, because the gains in momentum of both sides are inherently self-canceling, neither side can ever permanently dictate the result.

In the regulatory dialectic, the opposing forces differ in the manner in which power is amassed and in the precise real-world arenas where they are expressed. On the political side, power is accumulated by coalition building and is expressed in legislative activity or government decrees. On the economic side, power is gained by accumulating wealth and is exercised by purchasing or borrowing financial and productive resources and employing them efficiently.

In regulated markets, economic and political forces offer a lagged response to every action taken by the other side. The sequence of mutual action and reaction may be likened to the progression of alternating moves in a chess game or to the unfolding of successive tennis shots in a sustained volley. At each step along the way, opposing players develop advantages for their side intended to meet and overcome disadvantages previously imposed on them by their opponents.

My analysis depicts the flow of events in a regulated market as a three-stage process, driven by alternating acts of political and economic arbitrage. The individual stages—which deliberately parallel Hegel's famous triad of thesis, antithesis, and synthesis—are conceived as acts of regulation, avoidance, and re-regulation. Although Hegelian processes are essentially seamless, in analyzing the role of subsidized credit in strategies for national development it is convenient to start each sequence with an exogenous political effort to intervene in a particular set of markets.

Although lags are visible both between the regulation stage and the avoidance stage and between avoidance and re-regulation, in most countries the re-regulation lag tends to be considerably longer than the avoidance lag. I attribute this to differences in the structure of incentives for timely action facing managers of regulatory agencies. In particular, traditions of bureaucratic procrastination and of gradually phasing in the impact of important changes in operative regulations simultaneously reduce the risk of avoidance activity to regulatees and retard the pace of regulatory realignment.

From the point of view of a regulatee, regulation may be characterized either as a taxlike forcible taking of potential income (Posner 1971) or as a type of "negative innovation" that destroys selected economic opportunities. Holding other things equal, regulation increases the cost of doing business. Just as waves of positive innovations account in Schumpeterian theory for growth and fluctuations in economic activity, so the regulatory dialectic can explain the nesting of long, intermediate, and short cycles in specific regulated industries.

In any society, self-interest leads individuals to strive to accumulate both economic wealth and political clout. Once accumulated, individuals will express their economic and political power advantageously and will respond to others' efforts to exercise power against them. In modern mixed economies, political power and economic power collide almost perpetually in a dual process of arbitrage. Powerful political coalitions press for changes in taxes and regulations intended to alter in their favor market determinations of how income and wealth are to be distributed. Similarly, economically powerful persons seek to avoid the tax and regulatory burdens that political efforts to redistribute wealth propose to lay on them. The conflict may be described as the rule of legal force versus the "law of one price," defined later in this chapter.

Why Regulate?

Political power resides in being able to mobilize what may be called an "effective political majority" to place legal restraints on persons or firms with whom one deals. What matters is controlling a majority of votes in the forum where a crucial policy decision is actually made. Such a forum need not be an open one. In the United States, the relevant forum for legislative decisions sometimes reduces to a 10-person House-Senate Conference Committee that, in reconciling differences in legislation previously passed by the two houses, can fix the final form of a new law. In regulatory matters, the relevant forum may reduce to the governing board of a particular agency, to their top staff advisers, or to a pivotal group of military officers. Particularly in the self-appointed oligarchies that dot the landscape of the developing world, the crucial forum may not even by a governmental institution.

Even in a democratic society, an effective majority seldom needs to command a numerical majority of the voting population. When the government actively interferes in the marketplace, the numerical majority invariably becomes an exploited political minority. Unlike parties whose interest in government regulatory action is direct and immediate (e.g., providers of regulated goods and services and employees of regulatory agencies), the average citizen has a small stake in the typical regulatory action. The net benefits an individual has at stake in a proposed regulatory change closely condition his or her willingness to study the pros and cons of an issue and to spend his or her own resources to support lobbying efforts seeking to influence the outcome.

In contemporary democracies, the ostensible purpose of a given regulation is seldom the purpose that actuates the coalition that pushed it into law. The true purpose of real-world systems of economic regulation is seldom to promote greater economic efficiency in the long run. Lobbying activity seeks primarily to employ government power to redistribute current income and wealth from politically weak to politically powerful sectors. Coalitions form to persuade elected politicians to set up and to oversee for their benefit detailed systems of economic regulation (Stigler 1971). Legislative processes help politicians to disguise and to legitimize beggar-my-neighbor political activity by special interests. If coalition members were to throw their weight around openly, they would alert the numerical majority of the need to protect themselves from the coalition. By delegating the detailed operations of regulatory schemes to a semi-autonomous financial agency, elected officials erect still another layer of cosmetic shielding. Regulatory bureaus insulate sponsoring coalitions and their agent politician from being blamed for the unpopular long-run consequences of specific regulatory decisions.

As political institutions, agricultural development banks are unusual in that the wealth being allocated—and sometimes even the ostensible purposes of the allocation system—may come in significant part from outside the nation. International development assistance agencies may disrupt the workings of the domestic regulatory dialectic by making external funds available to finance specific sectors (e.g., small farmers) that are perceived as being neglected by indigenous institutions. Negotiations over the shape of the credit-allocation program between domestic politicians and international donors add another dimension of political activity.

Whatever ostensible purposes the domestic sponsors of an externally funded agricultural development bank may profess, an additional intention is to serve politically powerful domestic groups. Unlike regulations that have been demanded by an effective domestic majority, regulations adopted to please an external donor may well be deliberately sabotaged both in the design and execution stages by domestic politicians. In response to the funding opportunity, the effective domestic majority develops to shape a system of regulations that, appearances aside, is meant to frustrate some or all of the goals of the external donor. The problem is to accomplish this subtly, without alienating officials of the donor agency enough to cause them to reduce greatly their planned contribution of foreign exchange.

Subterfuge in political purpose tends also to promote subterfuge and corruption in bank operations. No matter how many formal bureaucratic safeguards are established to earmark funds for agricultural purposes or for small farmers in particular, career incentives within the bank and opportunities for personal enrichment invariably predispose loan officers toward allowing funds to flow to uses that are only apparently agricultural and to wealthy persons whose connections with farm operations may be tenuous.

Processes of Economic Circumvention

Establishing a preferential borrowing rate for specific classes of agricultural borrowers represents a political attempt to violate the tendency toward price equalization that economists call the "law of one price." Unlike governmental laws that depend on a system of external policing and penalties for enforcement, the law of one price derives its force from individuals' pursuit or their own self-interest.

Borrowing at a below-market interest rate enriches the borrower by an incremental "wedge" equal to the product of the interest-rate differential and the amount borrowed. The more one actually borrows, the greater is the wealth transfer that takes place. Hence, even eligible borrowers want to obtain program funds for unauthorized uses. Additional demands for funds come from lenders and ineligible borrowers and arise from arbitrage profits that they can earn once they find ways to circumvent the credit-allocation program.

Ineligible borrowers recognize that they can gain wealth either by misrepresenting or transforming the status of their loan request. Ineligible borrowers are willing to incur substantial amounts of implicit interest, either to achieve eligibility or to persuade loan institutions (perhaps by bribing loan officers) to overlook their ineligibility. Similarly, lending institutions can improve their balance sheets by relabeling or recollateralizing what would otherwise be ineligible contracts to divert program funds to unintended uses. These reactions illustrate the so-called balloon principle, which describes how an attempt to squeeze one side of a balloon (or credit market) creates excess pressure that is displaced into the unregulated part.

Credit-allocation programs try to force lenders to act against their economic interests. Rather than put funds to the most profitable use, institutions are supposed to lend funds to targeted beneficiaries. But the more profits a lender forgoes, the greater the economic pressure it feels to allocate current funds flows away from the targeted population.

Arbitrage pressures summarized in the law of one price explain why preferential loan schemes require continual and close bureaucratic supervision of lending-institution screening procedures. As long as a wedge of excess value can be found in program loans, a fringe of unsatisfied borrowers exists. The harder the unsatisfied borrowers compete for program funds, the more the intended loan subsidy tends to be converted into elements of implicit interest.

This is because the eagerness of unsatisfied borrowers allows lenders to extract additional value in the form either of bribes to loan officers (which lead to unlawful *evasions* of program provisions) or of lawful nonpecuniary compensation to the institution. Nonpecuniary compensation is collected by tightening unregulated features of the loan contract, such as the degree of credit risk or promises of profitable ancillary business. Either form of compensation may be usefully conceived as implicit interest paid by the borrower, the imposition of which tends to squeeze marginal borrowers out of the loan market.

Given enough time, competitive financial markets inevitably transform preferential loan rates into a system in which market clearing occurs primarily through variations in implicit interest. In the long run, competition among borrowers and lenders requires that the sum of explicit and implicit interest a borrower pays for program funds should rise to the market rate of interest. However, implicit interest often diverts economic resources from their best use. The degree of waste embodied in a particular market-clearing interest combination varies principally with the amount of political energy channeled into the program. Potential ways of conveying implicit interest are so diverse that further governmental restrictions can stop them only by compromising increasingly higher forms of economic and personal freedoms.

In some agricultural credit programs, circumvention becomes a cooperative game played by lenders and borrowers at the expense of the external sponsors and the intended beneficiaries of the program. Every technique for lender avoidance has a counterpart technique in the sphere of borrower avoidance.

Even without lender connivance, borrowers find it easy to misrepresent both the purpose of their loan requests *ex ante* and the effect that loan accommodation has *ex post* on their economic activities. Taking account of all relevant costs, every borrower wants to raise funds as cheaply as possible. But costs of repackaging the documentation supporting a loan request to conform to the requirements of a credit-allocation program are typically a minor element in funds costs. Because loan funds are fungible, the purposes for which a borrower can *demonstrate* a need for funds include any expenditures he or she plans to make during the time interval covered by the loan. Merely by relabeling various features of a proposed loan contract, a borrower can substitute cheap program loans for market sources of finance, with little or no effect on the allocation of his or her resources to agricultural pursuits. Von Pischke (1980) describes several such creative devices for borrower avoidance.

It is hard for borrowers skilled or lucky enough to obtain program funds to refrain from using them to arbitrage financial and nonagricultural investment opportunities. No matter how cheaply funds have been borrowed, an optimizing borrower must put them to the most advantageous use he or she has available. In this way, loans made for agricultural purposes may end up supporting consumption or real estate purchases.

Finally, we must recognize that borrowers should be willing to offer favors and kickbacks to program personnel in exchange for access to subsidized funds. Patterns of corruption in government subsidy programs are considered extensively by Sanchez and Waters (1974).

Over time, the wedge between market rates of interest and the explicit loan rate mandated in a program of subsidized agricultural credit tends to be filled by methods of extracting implicit interest. However, the forms that implicit interest takes and its distribution between program personnel and their employers differ importantly from one institution to another. Unsatisfied borrowers will learn to bid in the currencies that elicit the delivery of loan funds. When career incentives constrain loan officers to promote the development bank's economic welfare, they will look to borrowers with good collateral, strong balance sheets, and solid business prospects. However, loan officers who can safely enrich themselves through loan administration must be expected to do so. Hence, the better an agricultural development bank's systems of incentive payment and information auditing and the more severe the penalties that a given society imposes on corrupt behavior, the more likely it is that corrupt allocational criteria will give way to lawful forms of implicit interest.

Although subsidized loan programs may achieve a good portion of their intended distribution effects in the short run, they impose unintended costs that tend to increase the longer the program stays in operation. First, they tend to require a growing diversion of resources to monitoring program procedures. Second, they tend to deprive a program's intended beneficiaries (who are often less able or less willing to offer implicit interest) from access to program funds. Third, they tend to produce a more corrupt society in general and a more corrupt bureaucracy in particular.

Finally, feeding politically at a donor's trough tends to weaken financial institutions economically and, in particular, to suppress savings mobilization and portfolio diversification. In the precise agricultural regions the development bank is supposed to favor, the diversion of a nation's loan business toward a subsidized agricultural development bank impedes the natural development of efficiently diversified and financially complete financial intermediaries that can take full advantage of scope economies. The "one price" to which the regulation-constrained arbitrage process moves contains wasteful elements of implicit interest that worsen opportunity sets for borrowers and lenders alike. The result is that a socially suboptimal amount of risk bearing takes place, and domestic savings (especially rural savings) are mobilized less effectively than they should be. In the long run, this reduces rather than increases the maximum achievable rate of national economic growth.

Emergence of Re-regulation

Just as regulation calls forth regulatee avoidance, circumvention activity generates political pressure for re-regulation. This third stage in the original process becomes simultaneously the first stage in a fresh cycle of regulation and avoidance.

Re-regulation occurs because external donors and domestic proponents of subsidies for agricultural credit become aware that poor repayment experience and unintended flows of implicit interest serve increasingly to frustrate the purposes of the credit program. The threatened loss of foreign exchange increases domestic proponents' ability to require politicians to tighten reporting requirements in all stages of the credit-granting process and to expand efforts to monitor borrowers' subsequent use of loan funds. It also leads to demands for stiffer penalties on parties guilty of fraud, misrepresentation, corruption, or even nonrepayment of loan funds. In the process, the agricultural bank is likely to be restaffed, reorganized, and even renamed.

What makes re-regulation necessary is the unpredictability of the precise timing and details of avoidance schemes. Avoidance is inherently a creative and reactive activity. Regulation inevitably consists of rules *plus* loopholes. The art of avoidance is to find and exploit the loopholes. Regulatees pursue avenues of "loophole productivity" that would not have been left open had they been foreseen at the outset by sponsors of the operative regulations.

Moreover, the effectiveness of restrictions on the flow of farm credit is further undermined by differences between regulator and regulatee ability to adapt to changes in opportunity sets caused by exogenous economic forces such as changes in inflation rates and farm technology. To satisfy political restraints, government organizations are often suboptimally organized from an economic point of view. To please regional interests, agencies may be excessively decentralized. This makes it hard to transmit head-office priorities effectively to personnel in field offices, especially—as in efforts to assure program compliance and prompt repayment—where the benefits accrue to the head office and negotiation costs fall almost completely on branch-office personnel. To ensure head-office control, loan officers may have to complete thick bundles of forms to document eligibility, at the expense of timely disbursement of loan funds. In addition, regulatees usually have better-motivated employees and easier access to information about the consequences of change. Finally, agency response to change usually has to clear a maze of internal and external red tape. For all these reasons, private borrowers and lenders should be able to adapt their avoidance activity more quickly and efficiently to exogenous shocks than government agencies can adjust preexisting patterns of regulation.

Over time, trying to close program loopholes tends to transform what may initially have been a simple and narrowly targeted system of regulations into a complex and wide-ranging network of government interference. But expansion in the control network cannot go on forever. Eventually, the social cost of monitoring and enforcing program provisions begins to exceed the value to the recipient government of the external subsidy and the program's domestic potential benefits. The rising budgetary expense, social inconvenience, economic waste, and distributional inequity associated with a growing network of controls feed political demands for new approaches, both in recipient countries and in the board rooms of donor agencies.

Policy Implications

Every attempt to use political power to rechannel financial resources kicks off a cycle of economic adjustment and political counteradjustment. Particularly in financial markets where avoidance costs are negligible in the long run, market reactions tend to neutralize political power. Regulatees short-circuit regulatory intentions by finding and exploiting loopholes and by the simpler expedient of disobeying the law. Regulatory avoidance and evasion absorb productive resources by raising the cost of performing regulatory activities and by requiring government agencies to undertake costlier patterns of enforcement.

Far from promoting financial development in agricultural regions, political schemes that hold down explicit interest rates and focus predominantly on the character of loan recipients and the proposed uses of loan proceeds simultaneously inhibit the growth of efficient techniques for diversifying risk and impede the development of self-regenerating financial institutions. To increase the flow of rural finance permanently and reliably, international donors and governments in developing countries must endeavor to work *with,* rather than *against,* financial-market forces. They must emphasize schemes that improve opportunities for risk-bearing and that realize scope economies that flow from a balanced development of *both sides* of lending-institution balance sheets. Above all, they must avoid interfering with incentives for financial intermediaries to diversify risks, to maintain viable rates of loan repayment, and to reach out to absorb rural savings into the financial flow.

The Political Economy of Foreign Donors

To understand why such programs are not already in place, we must look at the political economy of international assistance. Who seeks to give what to whom and for what purpose? Who accepts what from whom and under what conditions? An international donor agency is an intermediary between economic entities in developed and developing countries. It facilitates a flow of credit mixed with subsidies that moves from governments, firms, and citizens in developed countries to agents in the underdeveloped world. Hence, an international assistance agency combines functions that in the domestic economy of a developed country are performed separately by welfare bureaucracies and financial intermediaries.

As intermediaries, donor agencies are pulled by political and economic interests on both sides of the credit and subsidy flow. Simply because they are located in the middle, intermediaries must strive to serve conflicting masters. This leads them to look for ways to smooth over political and economic conflicts between donor and recipient conceptions of the intended use of agency funds.

Understandably, managers of donor agencies wish to forestall political action against them from either side. In the short run, a donor has weak incentives to document the true effects its policies have on developing countries. Program descriptions and reviews may largely stress donor intentions. This approach may insulate assistance agencies and governments in both developed and developing countries from political criticism. Stress on good intentions may lessen conflicts between the goals of donor and recipient governments and mask effects that, if openly observed, could disturb taxpayers in donor and recipient countries alike.

In developed countries, governments, businesses, and households have different perspectives on the purposes served by international assistance. On the one hand, almost all parties are interested in preserving international civil order. To a greater or lesser extent, they also feel a moral obligation to help individuals and countries whose economic condition is markedly less advantageous than their own. On the other hand, the degree of obligation perceived tends to vary with the extent to which citizens in the donor country feel a sense of community with would-be recipients. For example, U.S. citizens invested much more concern in the Marshall Plan for Europe than they have in contemporary efforts at development assistance. Finally, apart from humanitarian motives, many workers and businesses want developing countries to have better access to foreign exchange as a way to improve export markets for their own products.

Governments in developing countries may see assistance agencies as instruments for collecting from developed countries claims for assistance to which their citizens feel a moral right. Representatives of recipient governments negotiate with assistance agencies for their self-assured "fair share" of donor-initiated redistributions of world resources.

Once assistance funds begin to flow, the financial fruits of these negotiations become merely another input into government policies. Governments use international assistance much as they use domestic resources: to strengthen the economic and political power base of ruling politicians.

From the point of view of a ruling politician, the optimal set of economic policies strikes a balance between opportunities for personal enrichment and benefits from strengthening his or her faction's hold on political power. The choices made involve a tradeoff between directing expansions in government resources to oneself and one's supporters as political patronage and investing these resources in programs that promise to improve the nation's standard of living. The balance struck in any particular country at any particular time varies with the extent of societal sanctions against political corruption and with the political potential of such economic issues as the maintenance of civil order, macroeconomic performance, and inequalities in the distribution of income.

A New Direction for Assistance Agencies

Whenever international funds are channeled initially through an agency responsible to a recipient government, ruling politicians will see that the agency places the government's political needs ahead of uses naively envisaged by citizens in donor countries. Like governments in recipient countries, managers of assistance agencies must operate under a short policy horizon. In the short run, most of these managers perceive their careers as benefiting more from assisting governments to disguise the policy tradeoffs they actually make than from spotlighting how recipient governments may circumvent the priorities of donor countries.

But assistance agencies that are unwilling to blow the whistle on recipient-country subterfuge encourage the production of more subterfuge. In turn, hypocrisy in the design of developing-country credit-allocation programs fosters program-level bureaucratic corruption. Rather than demonstrating for citizens of developing economies the benefits of capitalist freedom, such an attitude increases the overall degree of government interference in a recipient country's economic life.

When hidden, conflicts between the goals of recipient-country governments and donor-country taxpayers spread popular disillusionment concerning the usefulness of continued development assistance. Over time, the failure of aid programs to achieve the goals set for them by citizens of donor countries undermines political support for providing further assistance. As disillusionment leads to cuts in funding, managers of assistance agencies will be forced to pay close attention to donor-country priorities. They will have to direct their staffs to uncover distortions in past programs and to redesign patterns of assistance that evidence an ability to learn from past mistakes. To do this, programs to promote rural finance should be openly experimental in funding strategy and should focus on the self-interest of private players by establishing profit incentives that encourage complete financial intermediaries to develop in rural areas. In particular, assistance agencies should focus on financing promising nongovernmental organizations (NGOs). Moreover, they should be prepared to offer funding in creative ways, not just via direct loans and guarantees but also by packaging NGO securities from developing countries for resale to institutions and households in donor countries. They might even market a mutual fund that specialized in equity investments in developing countries.

Such a radical reorientation of the role played by assistance agencies will raise the level of conflict with recipient-country governments. Local politicians will miss handling the flow of assistance funds, and they will not enjoy having their goals unmasked. In international forums, they will lobby against having their economic policies monitored publicly in terms of standards imposed by foreign donors and lenders. Still, however painful the political infighting may become, recipient governments' pressing short-run need for foreign exchange should keep the discourse civil.

Notes

I am grateful to participants in the April 1981 Workshop on Rural Finance held at Ohio State University for their helpful criticism of my discussion. Special thanks go to Dale W Adams, Richard L. Meyer, Edward J. Ray, Edward Shaw, and J. D. Von Pischke.

1. Analytically, the explanation offered by Von Pischke (1980) closely resembles the slightly more general dialectical theory presented here. Chapter 3 by Bourne and Graham and Chapter 7 by Gonzalez-Vega also fit comfortably into the dialectical approach.

2. In Chapter 16 Ray summarizes the economic explanation of how and why financial intermediaries typically combine these particular functions. Khatkhate and Riechel (1980) describe institutional similarities across countries.

References

Downs, Anthony. *An Economic Theory of Democracy.* New York: Harper Brothers, 1957.

Kane, Edward J. "Good Intentions and Unintended Evil: The Case Against Selective Credit Allocation." *Journal of Money, Credit, and Banking* 9(1977):55–69.

______. "Accelerating Inflation, Technological Innovation, and the Decreasing Effectiveness of Banking Regulation." *Journal of Finance* 36(1981):355–367.

Khatkhate, Deena R., and Klaus-Walter Riechel. "Multipurpose Banking: Its Nature, Scope, and Relevance for Less-Developed Countries." *IMF Staff Papers* 27(1980):478–516.

Ladman, Jerry R., and Ronald L. Tinnermeier. "The Political Economy of Agricultural Credit: The Case of Bolivia." *American Journal of Agricultural Economics* 63(1981):66–72.

Posner, Richard A. "Taxation by Regulation." *Bell Journal of Economics and Management Science* 2(1971):22–50.

Sanchez, N., and A. R. Waters. "Controlling Corruption in Africa and Latin America." In *The Economics of Property Rights,* edited by E. G. Furubotn and S. Pejovich. Cambridge, Mass.: Ballinger, 1974, p. 279–295.

Stigler, George J. "The Theory of Economic Regulation." *Bell Journal of Economics and Management Science* 2(1971):3–21.

Vogel, Robert C. "Rural Financial Market Performance: Implications of Low Delinquency Rates." *American Journal of Agricultural Economics* 63(1981):58–65.

Von Pischke, J. D. "The Political Economy of Specialized Farm Credit Institutions." In *Borrowers and Lenders: Rural Financial Markets and Institutions in Developing Countries,* edited by John Howell. London: Overseas Development Institute, 1980, pp. 81–103.

Von Pischke, J. D., and Dale W Adams. "Fungibility and the Design and Evaluation of Agricultural Credit Projects." *American Journal of Agricultural Economics* 62(1980):719–726.

15
Agricultural Credit, Political Economy, and Patronage

Harry W. Blair

The evidence is now overwhelming that subsidized agricultural credit programs have not been effective in getting credit to the small farmer or in promoting equity over the past two decades. Indeed, the effects of these programs often have been perverse, in that they have tended to further concentrate income away from the rural poor. A growing body of literature, including several chapters in this volume, shows that there is a strong connection between low interest rates and the concentration of income. Earlier country case studies prepared for the Agency for International Development (AID) Spring Review of Small Farmer Credit in 1972–1973 revealed the same pattern (summarized in Donald 1976, chap. 8). Robert's study of South India (1979) in the early decades of this century suggests that, at least in some areas, this process has gone on for a long period.

The Importance of Politics

There are several reasons why subsidized credit programs end up benefiting large farmers. One is the business and bureaucratic interests of the financial intermediary: It costs more per unit of money lent to administer small loans than large ones. Other things being equal, it makes good sense to stress large loans in order to hold down lending costs.

Second, borrowers incur transaction costs for a loan. These include the expenses to get to the lender's place of business, the opportunity costs of work forgone during these visits, bribes, and charges for paperwork. For small borrowers these costs may loom much larger as a proportion of total borrowing cost than for large borrowers. The result is that the latter are more willing to incur the costs and get the loans.

The intermediaries' financial interests and borrowers' transaction costs too often do not attenuate demand sufficiently, however, and further credit rationing is needed. This takes place through the process noted by Kane in Chapter 14. Governments attempt further rationing by regulation rather than by allowing the market to ration by price. But the market circumvents these regulations by adding what Kane calls "implicit interest" in the form of bribes, kickbacks, corruption, and political pressure. Since the wealthier farmers are more able to pay this implicit interest they will get most of the loan money.

If subsidized interest rates direct agricultural loans to the rich, then it should follow that raising those rates to market levels would cut off the differential access enjoyed by the wealthy. In addition to the theoretical argument that such a strategy would work, there is empirical evidence from an experiment in rural finance in Bangladesh that shows small farmers are willing to pay interest rates of up to 30 percent and more on formal loans (Adams 1980). The case for raising interest rates, in a word, is such a good one that one must wonder why governments do not in fact raise rates. Yet subsidized credit programs continue and so do their unfortunate results.

A number of observers feel that politics is the main reason for the persistence of subsidized credit. The large borrowers who gain most from cheap credit want to protect that benefit, and at the same time politicians and bureaucrats want the power and the fruits of corruption that these programs put into their hands. The result is that the programs become politicized, and the economic environment, in the words of Ray (Chapter 16), becomes "multiply distorted"; the problem becomes one of restoring the marketplace and of fostering financial-market solutions to the resource allocation problem.

Both large borrowers and the politicians/bureaucrats are seen as blameworthy in this view, for the former are willing to corrupt and the latter are more than ready to be corrupted. It is the politicians who are most to blame, though; the borrowers are merely doing what is necessary to get their loans, and administrators are just taking advantage of a chance to supplement their meager salaries. Politicians, on the other hand, are building careers on the patronage power that a politicized credit program gives them. Through steering loans in this direction or that, politicians are able to protect and enlarge their constituencies and assemble the necessary support to aspire to higher office.

Credit programs, in this view, must accordingly be "depoliticized." The vested rural interests who use their influence and the government officials who are selling that influence must somehow be neutralized, and credit access must be put on the unbiased footing that the market would provide. The fact is, however, that scarce things of value cannot be depoliticized or removed from the political arena. Any effort to do so is really an attempt to substitute one political solution for another—to change the rules.[1] If interest rates are raised to market levels, the new rules will mean that some will gain (presumably savers and erstwhile nonborrowers) while others will lose (large borrowers and big farmers). That interest rates are not raised is a result in part of the self-serving behavior of officials, politicians, and large borrowers, to be sure, but more fundamentally it results from the nature of the political economy of many countries. It is to this topic that I now turn.

Political Economy of Credit and Patronage

When agricultural credit programs consistently benefit the rural wealthy rather than the intended target populations and when programs run into viability problems, we tend to view them as failures. But it would make more sense to employ Griffin's approach:

> Rather than assume that governments attempt to maximize social or national welfare but fail to do so, it might be more fruitful to assume that governments have quite different objectives and generally succeed in achieving them. Rather than criticizing governments for failing to attain what they did not set out to attain, or offering advice on how to attain a non-goal, it would be instructive if more time were devoted to analyzing what governments actually do and why. (Griffin 1974, 2)

The best way to test this perspective would be to identify the needs of governments and of various strata of the rural population, and then see how agricultural credit policies might answer those needs.

The primary need of a low-income country's government (or, more accurately, of the politicians running it) is to stay in power.[2] This, of course, is a truism, but like so many truisms it is often ignored in explanations of people's actions. The major requirement in meeting that need is stability, and stability in turn is most easily realized by maintaining the support of those groups who could disrupt it. In the cities, where coups d'etat generally take place, maintaining support means dealing with the military, the industrial sector, workers, students/intellectuals, urban consumers, and the bureaucracy itself. A few of these groups are relatively easily coerced into acceptably docile behavior (e.g., industrial workers and lower-level government workers, who even when organized tend to have little real strength), but most of them cannot be dealt with in such cavalier fashion. The military must be given large and increasing budgets; industry its subsidies and import and tax concessions; the students and intellectuals some ideological sops;[3] and urban consumers cheap food.

Coups d'etat do not often take place in the countryside, but insurrections do, and they can be just as dangerous to the regime in power. Understandably, then, governments want to protect their rural flanks. At the same time the larger rural landholders want to retain their positions of wealth, status, and power. Thus an exchange relationship is worked out, in which governments protect property rights and dispense patronage to the rural wealthy, and in return the recipients support the government and use their resources to maintain order in the countryside. That is, they employ their tenancy and sharecropping arrangements, labor-hiring relationships, and money-lending operations (all of which have their customary sanctions such as threats to evict, dismiss, or foreclose, as well as more forceful techniques for collections) to keep things under control. In those relatively few instances when this sort of control begins to break down, the government sends in its police to restore order, but precisely because outbreaks are relatively rare, only a small constabulary is needed. As for the lower strata in the countryside, they generally do not have exchange linkages with the central government, because for the most part they present little threat to it and have little to offer it.

This picture, of course, is a general one. Governments are not monolithic, and all officials do not behave in concert. Some may be genuinely interested in land reform and in rural projects targeted on the poor. Nor is there, necessarily, a conscious connivance between officials and the recipients of their largesse. Rather, some policies succeed in keeping things relatively stable, and these policies tend to be continued over time. Policies like the imposition of low interest rates just seem to be good for everyone who matters—at least in the short run, and the short run is the time frame that those in positions of power tend to be most worried about. But the long-run costs of these policies may be high. As Von Pischke (1981) observes, "It may . . . be argued that the costs of lagging specialized farm credit institution performance are higher, from almost any perspective except political expediency, than those associated with the performance of most development activities undertaken by government." The problem is that for many governments political expediency is the most important perspective.

As Ray points out in Chapter 16, it will not be easy for governments to rationalize rural financial policies. To do so will entail "substantial political risks" and "a painful but necessary transition," in his words.

If the only pain involved in imposing higher interest rates were to be borne by the economically poor and politically weak, we could rest assured that many governments would find the courage to set things right. But as is all too clear, it is the rural rich and powerful who would have to make the sacrifices, and few governments are willing to undermine their main support base in the countryside.

Subsidized credit programs, in sum, tend to succeed all too well in keeping governments in power through political patronage and in maintaining, and even enhancing, the position of rural elites. These programs do so because they are part of a dynamic political economy that serves the interest of both these groups in continuing a status quo that does not include much possibility for either equitable allocation of credit or optimal economic growth.

It should be clear from the discussion thus far that rural financial institutions do not stand outside their economic and political environment but instead are deeply embedded within it. It follows that they cannot be changed without regard for their milieu. Accordingly, it does little good for well-intentioned foreign donors to lecture governments on the need to raise interest rates as if it were possible to do so in a political vacuum. Specifically, a government cannot just raise interest rates to market levels; low interest rates represent a subsidy that (whether originally intended to do so or not) buys the support of constituencies. If a government decides to raise interest rates and thereby to remove the subsidy, then it must also decide to do one of two other things concomitantly. Either it must somehow compensate that constituency for the loss of the subsidy, or it must compensate itself for the loss of that constituency's political support by building up other bases of support.[4]

In other words, a government has three policy choices if it is going to remove interest-rate subsidies: (1) provide some other form of patronage to big farmers, (2) build up some other support group (such as small farmers or landless agricultural workers), or (3) suffer the potential loss of rural support. In view of the risky position almost all regimes perceive themselves to be in, the third option will be rejected if there is any possible way to avoid it, and to all but the most courageous governments even the second course will be fraught with hazards.[5] The second option is seen as risky, despite widespread belief that something has to be done for the other rural constituencies to prevent what amounts to the third option from occurring in the long run. But again, it is the immediate future that governments are most worried about, with the result that intermediate and longer-run needs tend to be deferred.

Donor Options

Against this backdrop, the task of the donor community is twofold. First, donors should help recipient governments devise strategies that would allow them to remove interest-rate subsidies without alienating the rural dominant classes. Second, donors should work at including in these strategies equity-enhancing components that would, even if slowly, improve the position of the rural poor. The point is to try to pursue both options 1 and 2 at the same time.

What might be some of those other strategies that would allow governments to cease subsidizing agricultural credit, yet still nurture their big-farmer constituencies? Deregulating agricultural product prices, increasing government procurement prices, or exchange devaluations might be one answer. This would benefit the larger farmers who produce the most and have the salubrious effect of encouraging them to increase output. But getting prices right would also have undesirable political effects, because—like credit subsidies—low-price policies are there for good reason. Urban consumers tend to react to high food prices by rioting, and most governments are no more eager for urban food riots than for rural insurrections.[6]

Another strategy might be to alter investment patterns that have favored the city over the countryside and industry over agriculture. Having the most (and quite often the best) land, large farmers would presumably benefit the most from new rural investments and thereby be compensated for the loss of subsidized credit. But here again, the policies to be displaced are there for a reason. The industrial constituency has its needs, and if import-substitution strategies are followed in pursuing economic growth, industry will have to be subsidized by the countryside. Even if industrial-growth policies are abandoned or slowed down, the urban sector cannot support the countryside over the long run, for there is just too much of the latter in most developing countries. Agriculture, in sum, will have to support its own investments in the end; the sorts of experimental or pilot project activities that can be undertaken with external aid are by their nature relatively short-term efforts and cannot (except perhaps in a few small and strategic countries on which aid might be lavished) substitute for mobilizing resources within the agricultural sector itself.

A third approach might be to change import controls in order to compensate the larger farmers for the loss of subsidized credit. Most developing countries have restrictions on importing consumer goods. Wealthy farmers would welcome the chance to purchase these high-status items, particularly electronic items and durable goods like automobiles or Jeeps.[7] Again, however, the currency-exchange and import regulations currently in effect have their constituency. The industrialists and importers who have licenses to acquire the scarce foreign exchange to bring foreign goods into the country will be aggrieved if policies are liberalized.

A fourth approach might be to make minor adjustments in a number of policies that would benefit those damaged by higher interest rates. This might include subsidizing the costs of some key investments like small-scale irrigation projects, increasing the price for agricultural commodities slightly, easing currency and import restrictions, and reallocating some of the budget for subsidizing agricultural credit toward subsidizing food for the urban lower and middle classes. There would still be losers (e.g., urban manufacturing entrepreneurs who would face more competition from imported goods), but there would be even more winners if all these changes could be implemented simultaneously. The point here is that a large number of major adjustments would have to be made in a number of key sectors in an economy that its own government sees as being very fragile. Even in a large country like India with its long record of stability, such a multifaceted strategy would be seen as very daring, and in a country where much of the government's thinking centers on whether it will still be in control six months or a year hence, the risks would seem impossibly great.

Making single policy adjustments like raising interest rates affects the equilibrium of political alliances and the way patronage is allocated. Policy planners in low-income countries face much the same constraints of political economy as do policymakers in high-income countries. A large number of special-interest groups representing powerful constituencies greatly constrain the ground for maneuver, particularly for policy planners seeking to help those who are not represented by such groups. But these limitations do not mean that the cause is hopeless or that political leaders, or donors, should stop trying to improve a society's institutional arrangements.

Possible Strategies

Two suggestions might be offered. First, donors and governments should think of agricultural credit more in connection with longer-term strategies for institution building, especially at the local level. In particular there should be more focus on weaving agricultural credit policies and programs into participatory institutions that include those outside the local elite—small farmers, tenants, and the landless. It is only through having a real voice in local institutions that the poor will increase their control over their lives and futures. Emphasis on savings mobilization might be a key element in this strategy.

If donors are successful in convincing governments to raise interest rates up to or near market levels, consequently giving all strata a more equal chance to avail themselves of institutional credit, then it would be fruitful to administer loans through local institutions in which the nondominant classes are allowed some role, such as village councils, cooperatives, and the like. Initially these nondominant groups may well have little voice in running the institutions. But as time goes on, their access to financial services and markets can combine synergistically with the increasing knowledge of political linkages outside the village that comes from participation in the institution itself to give the poor a real place in the system. This may seem a naively optimistic scenario, and to be sure there is considerable evidence indicating that such institutions are difficult to build and are subject to the risks of elite takeover. But there is also evidence, from South Asia (Blair 1982) and elsewhere as well (Korten 1980, 1981), indicating that participatory development institutions at the local level can bring a significant measure of improvement to groups that have not been part of the traditionally dominant strata. Even in a country with developmental prospects as slim as those of Bangladesh appear to be, there is good reason to think that the outlook for such longer-term strategies, especially if combined with credit programs, is a good one (Korten 1980; Chen 1981).

If donors are unsuccessful in eliminating subsidized interest rates but can induce recipient governments to modify credit programs toward longer loan periods and more capital investment in agriculture, a focus on participatory institution building still makes sense. The poor will not benefit as directly or immediately as would be the case if the subsidy were abolished, but they would find more employment and economic security as a result of the capital investments in the agricultural sector. In turn this improved economic position would give the poor a more secure base from which to participate in local institutions and eventually to gain some voice in managing them.

The second suggestion is that donor agencies spend more effort understanding and becoming sensitive to the realities of the political economy of developing countries. In formulating public policy governments face a melange of classes, interest groups, and constituencies, some of them powerful and some less so. There is no guarantee that public policies in the rural development field that take these realities into account will be successful in achieving both growth and equity goals, but it should be clear that strategies that fail to deal with such factors stand little chance of success. The very mixed record of subsidized agricultural credit programs to date offers ample evidence of this.

Conclusions

In the donor community, methods of economic analysis have been developed and honed to a high degree of sophistication, but at the same time little interest has been evidenced in either the political aspects of development or (save for an occasional denunciation of political interference) in political economy. In part, of course, this reluctance reflects the sensitivity of host-country governments to political issues and to even the appearance of foreign political interference with domestic matters. But it also reflects an unwillingness on the part of donors to sully their analysis with the reality of political economy.

This reluctance to enter the thicket of political economy covers an uneasy awareness that dealing with the realities of the development process in most countries is an inelegant and messy business in which choices always seem too constrained from the start and programs can never be implemented as planned without getting compromised, sometimes severely. In trying to modify the big-farmer bias of agricultural credit programs, for example, one may find that it is impossible to substitute other benefits like higher prices because big farmers have already secured these benefits in addition to low interest rates. Or one may find that virtually any program targeted on the rural poor invariably loses over half its impact to corruption. Patterns like this can be discouraging.

In this connection it is worth noting that similar problems are present in the public policy process in the advanced countries as well: Powerful special-interest lobbies block needed changes, and few—if any—policies in the economic sphere ever work out exactly as planned. Yet such difficulties and uncertainties do not mean that there is no point or purpose in trying to improve our policies and systems. On the contrary, the pervasiveness of problems means that there is all the more need to do so. Furthermore, planners and advisers in the developed countries can do a better job if they are sensitive to political realities and weave those realities into their recommendations. Surely the same is true of the low-income countries as well.

It is an old revolutionary saw that one cannot make an omelet without breaking eggs. Perhaps we could change the metaphor to observe that just knowing the proper proportions of economic ingredients is not enough to cook an omelet; one must also understand how much heat is required and how to apply the cooking oil of political economy in order to keep the omelet from sticking to the pan.

Notes

I wish to thank Dale W Adams, Joseph Beausoleil, Robert Firestine, and Charles Sackrey for their suggestions. They are not to blame for any lapses of fact or thought in the paper. The views expressed here do not reflect any official position of the Agency for International Development.

1. For an analysis at a more general level of the impossibility of depoliticization strategies, see Schaffer (1980, 1981).

2. The analysis that follows is traced out in more detail elsewhere for Bangladesh (Blair 1978) and India (Blair 1980). For a somewhat similar analysis of the African situation, see Bates (1981).

3. These are usually leftist in nature, as in empty promises of socialist redistributive policies, but sometimes very conservative, as with groups in India demanding cow protection or communities in Islamic countries demanding prohibition. Sometimes governments wish to appear to support racial claims as well in their efforts to pacify the student/intellectual community—for instance, as in promulgating job quotas excluding ethnic Chinese in Southeast Asia.

4. It could be argued that a government would only be partly alienating its big-farmer support base by removing the credit subsidy, for there are other forms of patronage that could be continued. But given the precarious hold on power that many governments see themselves having, some compensatory action probably still would be necessary.

5. The fact that governments are reluctant to sacrifice their big-farmer constituencies for a chance to build support among landless workers, tenant farmers, or the like does not prevent regimes from pretending to reach out to lower strata with propaganda ploys. The history of failed land-reform efforts in the last decade or two is ample testimony of the appeal of this strategem.

6. Particularly in the smaller states of Africa, discontent over food prices has been an especially sensitive issue (Bates 1981, chap. 2). In some countries, big farmers already have both credit subsidies and high food prices, so the question of trading one benefit for another is not possible.

7. Policies should not be changed to favor big farmers so much that they would be able to import labor-saving machinery like tractors at subsidized prices, thereby using the subsidy to displace agricultural laborers, as happened in Pakistan in the mid-1960s.

References

Adams, Gary D. "Experimental Approaches to Rural Finance in Bangladesh—First Year Findings." Paper for Rural Finance Workshop, April 7–10, 1980, Kathmandu, Nepal, sponsored by Agricultural Development Bank of Nepal and Ohio State University.

Agency for International Development. *AID Spring Review of Small Farmer Credit,* 20 vols. Washington, D.C.: Edited and published by the Agency for International Development, 1973.

Bates, Robert H. *Markets and States in Tropical Africa: The Political Basis of Agricultural Policy.* Berkeley: University of California Press, 1981.

Blair, Harry W. "Rural Development, Class Structure, and Bureaucracy in Bangladesh." *World Development* 6(1978):65–82.

———. "Mrs. Gandhi's Emergency, the Indian Elections of 1977, Pluralism, and Marxism: Problems with Paradigms." *Modern Asian Studies* 14(1980):237–271.

———. *The Political Economy of Participation in Local Development Programs: Short-Term Impasse and Long-term Change in South Asia and the United States from the 1950s to the 1970s.* Ithaca: Cornell University, Center for International Studies, Rural Development Committee, 1982.

Chen, Marty. "Organizing the Poor in Bangladesh: Evolution of an Approach to Rural Development." Unpublished paper presented in Rural Development Seminar at Harvard Institute of International Development, Cambridge, Massachusetts, March 13–14, 1981.

Cohen, John M., and Norman T. Uphoff. "Participation's Place in Rural Development: Seeking Clarity Through Specificity." *World Development* 8(1980):213–235.

Donald, Gordon. *Credit for Small Farmers in Developing Countries.* Boulder, Colo.: Westview Press, 1976.

Griffin, Keith. *The Political Economy of Agrarian Change: An Essay on the Green Revolution.* Cambridge: Harvard University Press, 1974.

Korten, David C. "Community Organization and Rural Development: A Learning Process Approach." *Public Administration Review* 40(1980):480–511.

———. "Management of Social Transformation at National and Sub-National Levels." Unpublished paper, Asian Institute of Management, Makati, Philippines, 1981.

Robert, Bruce L., Jr. "Agricultural Credit Cooperatives, Rural Development, and Agrarian Politics in Madras, 1893–1937." *Indian Economic and Social History Review* 16(1979):163–184.

Schaffer, Bernard. "Insiders and Outsiders: Insideness, Incorporation, and Bureaucratic Politics." *Development and Change* 11(1980):187–210.

———. "To Recapture Public Policy for Politics." Unpublished paper, University of Sussex, England, Institute of Development Studies, 1981.

Von Pischke, J. D. "The Political Economy of Specialized Farm Credit Institutions in Low-Income Countries." World Bank Staff Working Paper no. 446, Washington, D.C., 1981.

Von Pischke, J. D., Dale W Adams, and Gordon Donald, eds. *Rural Financial Markets in Developing Countries: Their Use and Abuse.* Baltimore: Johns Hopkins University Press, 1983.

World Bank. *Agricultural Credit Sector Policy Paper.* Washington, D.C.: World Bank, 1975.

16
Economic Distortions and Financial Reforms

Edward John Ray

This chapter explores the role of finance and financial deepening in the promotion of rural development in low-income countries (LICs). I will argue that it is necessary to understand the general economic setting in order to assess the contribution that can be made by rural financial markets.

Low interest rates are typically a member of a family of economic distortions present in LICs that also include food-price controls, inflation, overvalued exchange rates, trade restrictions, taxes, subsidies, and government investments. These distortions are partly the result of government efforts to speed or redirect development. They also result from political compromises aimed at buying support for the regime or at compensating groups for the adverse effects of other policies.

Distortions in financial markets and other markets are intertwined politically and economically; reforms in one can seriously affect the other. Artificially low food prices, for example, buy urban support for the regime, but they also reduce the incentive for farmers to borrow and reduce farmers' income, capacity to save in financial form, and ability to repay loans. These low food prices have a major effect on the scope, volume, and vitality of financial market activities. Reforms in financial markets can likewise send economic and political reverberations through other segments of the economy. Higher interest rates will cause those who did receive the benefits of cheap credit, generally the politically powerful, to grumble. Such higher rates will also increase the volume of financial savings at the expense of other lower-return activities and consumption.

Financial markets are often repressed because of distortions in other segments of the economy or because of political considerations. Reforming financial markets, therefore, almost always requires other economic or political adjustments. The purpose of this chapter is to discuss the importance of these other economic adjustments.

Policymakers can select one of four paths in making financial market reforms.

1. The most common policy selected is to do little or nothing about distortions in financial markets. Policymakers may employ "second best" arguments to rationalize living with repressed financial markets, or they may endorse financial repression because low interest rates allow them to allocate political patronage efficiently.

2. At the other extreme, policymakers may make a complete switch from an economy with multiple distortions and central directions to an economy that is mainly directed by market forces. This was done in South Korea in the mid-1960s and in Chile in the mid-1970s. In this case reforms in interest-rate policies would be accompanied by major reforms in foreign-exchange rates and in trade, monetary, and fiscal policies.

3. Policymakers could opt to reform policies in financial markets while leaving other distortions in the economy in place. This type of partial reform is almost never carried out. Repressed financial markets concentrate benefits to a relatively small number of borrowers who are often politically powerful, whereas the costs of repression are highly diffused.

4. Policymakers could also opt to reform only a portion of the financial market, a partial version of the partial reform discussed in the preceding paragraph. For example, they might choose to have a reform only in rural financial markets, while not changing policies in other segments of the financial market. If rural financial markets are more severely repressed than other parts of the financial system, partial financial reform may be relatively easy to carry out.

My approach will be to begin with a brief review of the role of financial intermediation with particular emphasis on its potential contribution to rural development. I will stress the role of financial intermediaries in promoting efficient resource use, in providing risk-management services to both savers and investors, in reducing the concentration of both income and wealth, and in making financial markets less susceptible to political manipulation.

Next I will turn to a discussion of real and financial market distortions found in many LICs, including trade restrictions, production taxes and subsidies, capital and labor taxes and subsidies, and controls over financial institutions. Although numerous explanations are given for the existence of such policies, their economic justification is summarized most succinctly in studies of "optimal" intervention analysis, of which Bhagwati (1968) and Magee (1973) are representative. Through the use of a simple model, I will cover economic arguments for systematic government intervention in product and factor markets.

Next I will discuss the deficiencies of optimal intervention analysis. What will emerge will be a real and financial environment with many distortions that is a representative version of the economic realities faced by many LICs. Within that environment, we will be able to ask what role finance can play in promoting growth and development. My fundamental premise is that financial liberalization and fiscal liberalization should be coordinated but almost never are. In part, the discussion of optimal intervention analysis will clarify the extent to which fiscal liberalization and financial-market liberalization are incompatible with central planning and why reforms that do occur are often piecemeal. Shaw wrote that "doing everything almost at once in reform of financial, fiscal and international economic policy seems to be optimal strategy for both faster and steadier growth" (1973, p. 251). If policy recommendations are to be of value there should be a sense of why constraints exist on doing everything at once and of the implications for the development process when only partial reform or partial financial reform is possible.

Financial Intermediation

This section briefly reviews the role of financial intermediation in growth and development when real markets are perfectly competitive and relied upon to allocate resources and income. Assuming that transactions are costly, that information is costly and deteriorates in value as market conditions change, and that the future is uncertain, a demand for financial intermediation will exist. The fact that transactions are costly will create a demand for money and a demand for financial brokers to bring borrowers and lenders together.

Without access to external financing investors would be forced to self-finance. Since there is no reason to expect that access to wealth and investment opportunities are comparably distributed across businesses, a demand for borrowed funds will emerge. Similarly, current income may or may not correspond to current consumption demands of individuals. Individual savers would be willing to lend money to borrowers for some appropriate rate of return. In short, in the presence of nonsynchronization of wealth and investment demand, a demand for borrowed funds exists. With synchronized income receipts and desired consumption expenditures, a supply of loanable funds exists. Transactions costs can be reduced in the real sector through the use of money and in the financial sector through the services of financial brokers.

To the extent that financial brokers are competitive and efficient, the spread between borrowing and lending rates on comparable-term loans will be small. Clearly, financial brokers play a significant role in the economy in signaling the allocation of investable funds.

To explain how brokers become intermediaries, we must recognize that the future is uncertain and that individuals differ both in their assessments of the degree of uncertainty and in their willingness to assume risk. The existence of uncertainty and differences in the appraisal and willingness to bear risk create a potential market for financial intermediaries. Intermediaries profit by providing short-term, highly secure liabilities to savers in exchange for money that in turn can be lent to investors for longer periods of time for a higher, risk-adjusted rate of interest. In addition to the services provided by financial brokers, financial intermediaries facilitate the undertaking of long-term and risky investments that would not have taken place without their services. Financial intermediaries broaden the ability of the economy to allocate resources, particularly in the direction of longer-term and riskier projects at a minimum cost to society.[1]

In competitive markets there is little justification for political manipulation of investment funds. Financial and real markets are efficient. Where competition exists, political attempts to manipulate who gets loans and who does not through subsidized credit programs must reduce the efficiency of the allocative process and reduce society's growth and development potential. In most LICs, however, many markets are not competitive, externalities exist, and central governments do not view their role in the development process as a passive one. "Optimal" intervention analysis is one way of assessing the interrelationships of distortions in an economy.

Optimal Intervention Analysis

As indicated in the first section, it is necessary to modify the perfectly competitive model in order to clarify how financial reforms are related to other major policy considerations. My objective is to model those characteristics that are critical to an accurate assessment of the potential for policy reforms in LICs and for their subsequent success or failure. There are many reasons why countries impose tariffs and manipulate international trade and capital flows, why certain producers are subsidized while others are taxed, why credit is rationed for some potential borrowers and amply available for others. Optimal intervention analysis has been used to provide justification for systematic government intervention in all areas of economic activity. For that reason, a summary of optimal intervention analysis arguments for trade, product-market, and factor-market intervention can be used to outline the key structural elements of a representative LIC.

By focusing on the deficiencies of optimal intervention analysis we can generate a clearer picture of the kind of multiply distorted and constrained economic environment within which policymakers have to judge the value of financial programs and reforms. From this it is possible to provide preliminary answers to two critical questions facing policymakers in LICs: What financial reforms are worthwhile when "doing everything at once" in reform of financial, fiscal, and international economic policy is not possible? Why are policymakers often constrained to consider piecemeal, as opposed to general, reform?

To begin the discussion of optimal intervention analysis I assume a two-country, two-commodity, two-factor world. Assume unless stated, that the country under study is a price taker in international trade as well as a net exporter of traditional-sector goods (agricultural and primary products and perhaps some light manufactures) and a net importer of modern-sector goods (highly fabricated consumer and producer manufactures and high-technology agricultural products). The two factors of production are capital and labor. Factors of production are assumed to be homogeneous, flexibly priced, and fully employed, and production functions are well defined. A social-welfare function with associated well-defined and -behaved welfare indifference curves is assumed to exist as well. The consequences of relaxing many of these assumptions will be an integral part of later discussion.

I begin with a summary of optimal intervention analysis of deteriorating terms of trade for developing countries in world markets.[2] To the extent that the country experiences growth that is biased in the direction of more rapid expansion of traditional-goods production and the commodity terms of trade deteriorate for the home country, free trade could lead to a reduced level of social welfare. This is an example of welfare-reducing growth. The home country has experienced real economic growth, but the level of social welfare has actually declined. Assuming the home country can influence world prices by manipulating trade, a tariff could be used to shift production in the direction of modern-sector goods (import substitution), to bias consumption in the direction of exportables, and to depress the world price of importables. As a consequence, the level of social welfare can be increased (Bhagwati 1968).

A number of arguments have been advanced to justify government intervention in product markets. A common one is that production of modern-sector goods entails the training and disciplining of workers who will later be able to change jobs and provide subsequent modern-sector employers with skilled and disciplined workers not available to initial employers. In effect, generalized job training represents a positive externality in the production of modern-sector goods.

The implication for the economy of positive externalities is that resources are misallocated from the standpoint of society as a whole. There is too much production of traditional-sector goods and too little production of modern-sector goods. A tariff could shift production to the optimal production point, but it would also create a consumption distortion.

A more desirable policy approach would be to put a domestic tax on production of traditional-sector output that would, in turn, be used to subsidize production of modern-sector goods while maintaining free trade. That policy would be optimal in the sense that while it compensated for the existing distortion by shifting production it would not introduce any new distortions. Free trade would permit consumption at the highest obtainable level of social welfare.

I now turn to my final case, factor-market distortions. It is in the context of this discussion that one can begin to sense the deficiencies of optimal intervention analysis and the fundamental incompatability of government credit controls with the emergence and growth of efficient financial markets. Throughout the discussion in this section, I have referred to the dichotomy between the modern sector and the traditional sector rather than between agriculture and manufacturing. The point is that there exist traditional lines and techniques of production in both agriculture and manufacturing that compete for resources with modern lines and techniques of production.

Where financial markets are highly fragmented, many investments will be largely self-financed. In the absence of efficient financial-market signals regarding investment opportunities, individuals will be forced to rely upon their own judgments regarding expected returns and risks from alternative investments. Under these conditions, it is likely that individuals faced with two investment opportunities with the same frequency distribution of returns, but with one in the traditional sector and one in the modern sector, will not view those investments as comparable. Individual judgments will be biased toward a traditional investment project familiar to the individual and away from a new investment opportunity in the modern sector with which the individual has no experience, even though both investments have identical expected returns. Both investment and production will be

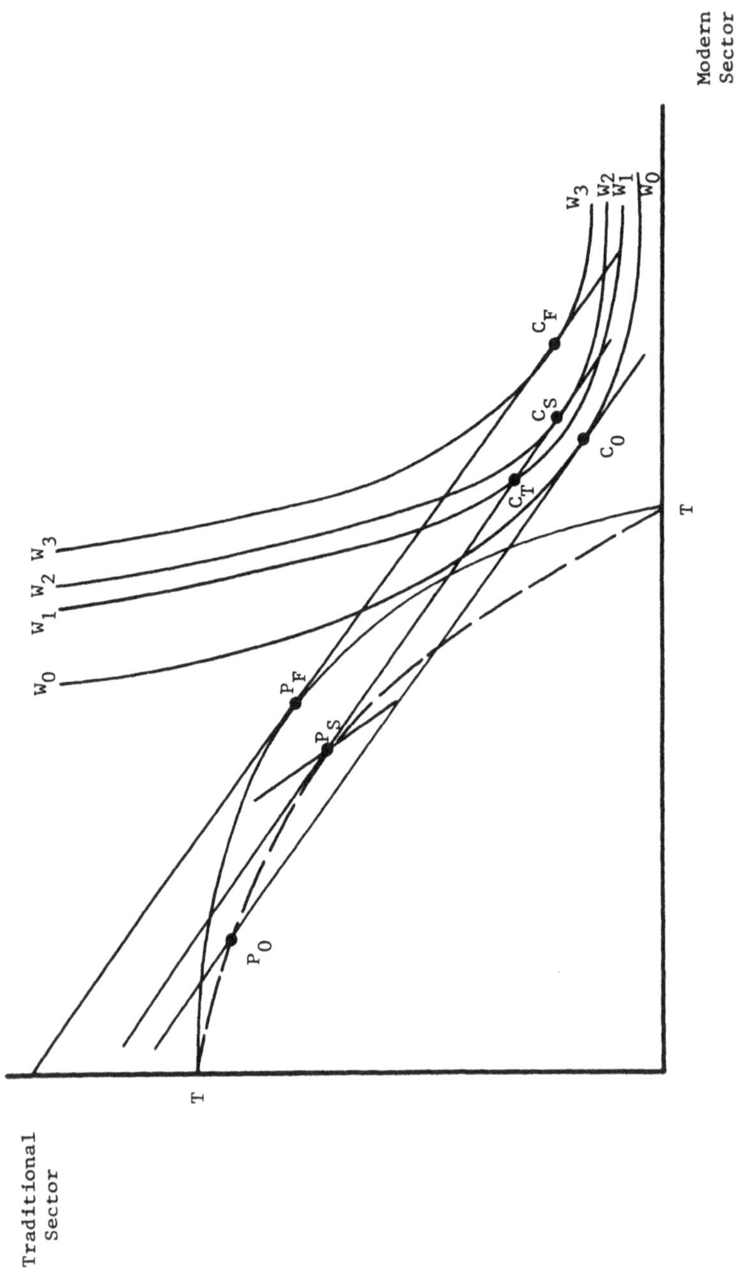

Figure 16.1 Factor-Market Distortions

biased toward the traditional sector. The situation described is illustrated in Figure 16.1, through the use of a production transformation curve labeled *TT*.[3]

If there were no bias in capital allocation toward the traditional sector, production would take place at point P_F, and free-trade exports of traditional-sector goods in exchange for importable modern-sector goods at the fixed world price of imports to exports, reflected by the absolute slope of $P_F C_F$, would lead to consumption at point C_F on the highest obtainable welfare indifference curve, W_3W_3. The bias away from modern-sector investments would result in excess capital going to the traditional sector and in an associated differential in the rate of return on capital, with the rate of return on homogeneous capital higher in the modern sector than in the traditional sector (reflecting an inappropriate risk premium and an underallocation of capital to the modern sector). Production would occur along an operating locus interior to the production possibilities frontier, as indicated by the dashed line production locus, and at a point on the operating locus such as P_0, where the world price line intersects the operating locus from above (Magee 1973). With fixed world prices, production and consumption would be at P_0 and C_0, respectively, and the level of social welfare achieved would be W_0W_0. A tax or subsidy program could favor production in the modern sector and a tariff could shift production to point P_S on the interior locus, but neither could shift production to the production possibilities curve, since the capital-market distortion persists.

At best, a tariff could shift production to point P_S and consumption to point C_T, which would raise the level of social welfare from W_0W_0 to W_1W_1. A tax or subsidy scheme could be used to shift production to point P_S and consumption to point C_S on a higher welfare indifference curve W_2W_2. By contrast, a subsidy on capital use in the modern sector and a tax on capital use in the traditional sector could shift production to point P_F and—through free trade—consumption to point C_F on the highest obtainable welfare indifference curve, W_3W_3.[4]

To this point the simple perfectly competitive model has been amended to include trade restrictions, because domestic producers fail to adapt as quickly to long-run trends in world prices as policymakers could; product taxes and subsidies, because of externalities that can be best perceived and dealt with by policymakers; and taxes and subsidies on capital use, because financial markets either do not exist or are an inferior means for allocating capital compared to government planning. Each form of intervention discussed in this section is already in use. Often policies of intervention are adopted for reasons that have more to do with who has political and economic power than for the reasons discussed here. The concern here is to clarify how such policies work and their consequences for effective financial reform.

One fundamental deficiency is intrinsic in almost all of the literature on optimal intervention analysis. The optimal solution is always biased toward continuous government intervention.[5] That bias is not surprising since the literature itself emerged partly to rationalize extensive government planning. Government planners do not like the uncertainty of the future any more than the rest of us do. They can be expected to have a disinclination to watch passively as rapid and sometimes disastrous economic changes occur within their economies. Their political success or failure turns on an uncertain future that they would rather attempt to control than passively observe, so there is an incentive to look for ways to control or regulate market deficiencies rather than to correct them.[6]

In the example of deteriorating terms of trade, we simply assumed that the government, but not the marketplace, realized that production had to be shifted toward the modern sector. Yet the policy options considered did not include promoting the development of, or deregulation of, already existing financial markets to improve their ability to signal the efficient allocation of resources over time in response to changes in domestic and/or international markets. Even though externalities in production do render market-resource allocation inefficient, many externalities can be internalized by redefining property rights. Even in the case of generalized job training described earlier, consideration is rarely given to government subsidies to producers to cover the costs of noncapturable generalized job training that diminish to zero as the magnitude of the externality decreases with the expansion of the modern sector. However, our third case, involving a subsidy on capital use in the modern sector and a tax on capital use in the traditional sector, is the clearest example of the bias in the analysis away from market solutions.

The inappropriate risk premium on capital use in the modern sector resulted directly from the failure of financial markets to signal efficient capital allocation. Yet the optimal solution, rather than involving the deregulation of existing financial markets or the fostering of financial market development, instead involved more government control in the form of capital-tax and subsidy programs. Such an inherent bias in favor of controls and regulations over market solutions to economic problems, on the part of policymakers themselves, is important to keep in mind.

When government intervention does take place in LICs it differs from the presentation thus far in three important ways: It is not costless, it is not always self-financed, and seldom is it clear how much of which kinds of intervention is called for. I will discuss how each of those points relates to the financing problem.

With respect to the costs of administering a government credit program, it is unlikely that the institutional infrastructure exists in many developing countries to impose a capital subsidy scheme for the modern sector that can be financed by capital-use taxes in the traditional sector. So, even though factor taxes and subsidies seem optimal, the government may find its only or cheapest option is to institute an indirect credit-subsidy scheme financed with production taxes or tariff revenues. In addition, it is quite likely that government revenue from all sources is insufficient to finance government projects including credit programs. In that case, the printing press will be used to produce money to cover government deficits. So the end result is capital credit rationing either mandated without financing or financed by various taxes, including the inflation tax. The consequent lack of fiscal integrity leads to depreciation of the currency, which is often resisted by exchange controls, official foreign loans, and/or additional import restrictions. Domestic private savings and borrowing through financial markets are discouraged by the expectation of accelerating inflation and by interest-rate controls, and private foreign capital inflows are discouraged by unstable monetary and fiscal policy. Upward pressure on the relative price of importables is often dealt with through the imposition of price controls (Ray 1979). The problem facing the planner has compounded itself. Administrative costs of implementing financial support programs, coupled with a lack of revenue-raising infrastructure to finance those programs efficiently and fully, repress both domestic and foreign private financial activity in the country.

The most serious flaw in the analysis, however, is the presumption that the government knows how to allocate claims on resources when financial markets are not providing the "right" signals. When one recognizes that fragmentation in the financial sector implies that potential investors have no systematic information with which to appraise numerous potential investments both within and across sectors of the economy, one realizes the magnitude of the allocative problem facing the policymaker. Yet as long as government credit programs and financial-market regulations obstruct the development of private financial markets, planners will be forced to guess how credit should be allocated.

We have now developed a stylized view of our representative developing country that includes government intervention at every level of economic activity and a bias for regulation and/or intervention over market solutions to economic problems. Differences in administrative costs of alternative forms of government intervention in any given instance may lead to second- or third-best forms of intervention when it does take place. The absence of an efficient tax infrastructure to finance government programs will promote monetary and fiscal mismanagement, overvaluation of the currency, heavy official borrowing abroad, and domestic price and interest-rate controls. Finally, as illustrated in the discussion of government-controlled credit programs, government programs and/or regulations serve as poor substitutes for market solutions to economic problems and play a significant role in preventing market solutions from developing. It is in the context of this multiply distorted environment that I want to consider the role of finance in rural development.

Financial Reform

Earlier I indicated that one question to which I hoped to provide a tentative answer is: Why are we constrained to consider piecemeal, as opposed to general, reform? Beginning with the stylized structure of our representative developing economy, general reform would embody many, if not all, of the following policies: (1) slower monetary growth accompanied by higher taxes and/or reduced government spending to reduce deficits, (2) trade liberalization and currency depreciation along with the removal of domestic price controls, and (3) reduced government regulation and control of production and credit. The respective consequences of these policies would likely be: (1) an increase in short-run unemployment and a redistribution of capital gains in favor of creditors in general and financial asset holders in particular; (2) a general reduction of profits, production, and employment associated with domestic production of importables, an increase in domestic prices of imported consumer goods, and stimulation of export-oriented industries along with some lines of production in the nontradable-goods sector; and (3) a transfer of profits, jobs, and income away from lines of production previously favored by government regulations and subsidies and a redistribution of income away from investors who had previously received subsidized government credit.

In short, general reform, like all economic change, will create economic winners and losers. However, the losers will be those individuals and groups who directly benefit from existing multiple market distortions. They may be able to dictate whether or not current government will remain in power, because economic and political power are highly correlated. Sweeping economic reforms of the kind outlined above are almost never in the economic and/or political self-interest of policymakers currently managing a multiple distorted economic environment. Distortions allow them to allocate "administrative profits" that serve as political patronage.

Even when policymakers are convinced of the desirability of liberalizing trade, stabilizing prices, and deregulating markets, they realize that they might not be around to accept credit for ultimate successes if the lags in the perception of net benefits from such reforms relative to the status quo are very long. In addition, the benefits of reform are often very diffuse and therefore difficult to turn to political profit. As suggested earlier, faced with the fact that the future is uncertain, government behavior is generally biased in the direction of taking action, controlling, and regulating rather than of passively waiting for markets to work their magic. So policy reform is almost always piecemeal.[7]

Against that backdrop we want to know what financial reforms, if any, are possible and desirable and what their consequences would be. Domestic and international planners have the problem of not knowing how to judge the success or failure of a particular reform because its probable consequences were not clear in the first place. For example, both Eckaus (1973) and Tendler (1973) have pointed out that small-farmer credit programs (SFCPs) often have several goals: to promote efficient agricultural production, to redistribute income and wealth to the poor, and/or to develop economically viable financial institutions. Those goals are often incompatible.

There are two obvious reasons why SFCPs fail to function well as equity programs. First, any wealth-transfer program based on discretion rather than competition is subject to manipulation, and wealthier individuals are in the best position to corrupt the system. As Gonzalez-Vega noted in Chapter 10, only 15 percent of all agricultural producers in Latin America have access to formal credit markets and 20 percent of them (only 3 percent of all producers) have gotten 80 percent of the total credit. In an earlier study Eckaus (1973) noted that SFCP loans generally go to middle-class and upper-class borrowers and that high default rates often presumed to redistribute income to the poor are most significant among middle- and upper-income borrowers.

That high default rate among middle- and upper-income borrowers is symptomatic of the second reason for the failure of small-farmer credit programs to redistribute income to the rural poor—government apathy or, perhaps, complicity. Many SFCPs are externally financed. Governments starved for foreign reserves to maintain overvalued currencies borrow to cover trade deficits; they accept loans tied to use in SFCPs with weak intentions of policing them or of allocating scarce domestic resources to make them work. In effect, the loans are viewed as one-time transfers of wealth from abroad, and defaulting on such "loans" is viewed with little concern. If an internal commitment existed to redistribute income to the poor, there would be little chance that SFCPs would emerge as the most economical way of achieving that goal.

An effort can be made to develop viable financial institutions within the rural sector of LICs. To the extent that many developing countries are moving in the direction of deregulating deposit and loan rates in urban areas, allowing rural banks to offer competitive deposit and loan rates would be useful in two important respects. First, rural savers would have a potentially attractive financial form for wealth formation and liquidity balances. In a world of mismanaged monetary and fiscal policy, however, there is a very real possibility that savings mobilization will fail not because the rural poor do not save but because they are wise enough not to trust their savings to unreliable financial institutions.

Second, to the extent that there are legitimate loan opportunities in the rural sector there is a better chance that they will be discovered if there are local banks in the rural area. Commercial bankers generally argue that subsidized credit makes it impossible for them to operate profitably in rural markets and that rural loans are not as profitable as urban loans. They would expect savings mobilized in the rural sector to be invested in the urban sector. Trade restrictions, domestic price controls, a bias in the investment of social overhead capital toward urban centers, production subsidies, and subsidized credit programs do undermine the profitability of investment in the rural sector (Ray 1983). In addition, commercial bankers are faced with distorted information about potential investment opportunities when financial markets are repressed and fragmented, just as individual savers and investors are. Yet money lenders find rural customers for high-interest loans, and they are not in business to give their money away. Even in a multiply distorted environment there will be some profitable investments in the rural sector. If there were increased incentives to compete for savings in rural areas, commercial banks might well find it profitable to hire former informal-market moneylenders as loan officers in their rural branch banks. Although most of the mobilized savings would probably continue to flow to government-nurtured urban centers, some new lending would occur in the rural sector.

If real markets are multiply distorted, SFCPs cannot undo existing resource misallocation. Baker stated the case against SFCPs as a mechanism for improved resource-allocative efficiency when he wrote, "In the absence of reliable input and product markets, transportation and communication systems, and a reasonable flow of dependable information, no SFCP is likely to be wholly or perhaps even tolerably satisfactory. The SFCP may be peculiarly inappropriate as a vehicle for wider infrastructure reform" (1973, p. 44). The peculiarity arises from the fact that efficient financial markets will quickly respond to real market signals regarding resource allocation, but if those signals are distorted, quick financial responses are not too useful.

Again, SFCPs have been developed to achieve several goals that are not always compatible. I would strongly argue that SFCPs are an inappropriate means of achieving any of the goals for which they were designed. Internationally sponsored programs to provide subsidized loans to agriculture in developing countries represent a bad external policy response to bad domestic policies.

What can external funding agencies do? As already suggested, even in the most distorted economic environment savings-mobilization programs offer the possibility of facilitating wealth accumulation and liquidity management in the rural sector. Over time, some loanable funds mobilized in the rural sector are bound to find competitive investment opportunities in the rural area. External funds could be used to subsidize commercial branch banking in the rural sector once SFCPs have been eliminated. What I am advocating here is a subsidy program to accelerate the development of a formerly repressed financial market. The point is to foster a financial-market solution to the resource-allocation problem and not to substitute government programs for a properly functioning financial sector.

What else can external funding agencies do to promote growth and development in LICs? One inappropriate approach that seems to be gaining favor is for external agencies to encourage further distortions in financial as well as other rural markets. Long seems to endorse such a strategy when he observes that "where the conditions of success for a credit program for small farmers are not met, alternative programs—subsidies to the inputs, price supports for the output, more extension work, or even credits to the marketing system rather than the small farmer—may be capable of raising the welfare of small farmers at considerably lower costs than a credit program" (1973, p. 85).

The notion that the appropriate means of escaping the stagnant economic conditions induced by government controls and regulations is the construction of counterweight programs that are comparably heavy-handed and repressive of financial markets is contrary to the spirit of this chapter. Such programs would simply replace the presumption of optimal intervention analysis that domestic planners know what to do with the presumption that external-agency planners know what to do. In addition, if subsidy programs for inputs or output prices supports are specified by external agencies as conditions for making loans to developing countries, one can be certain that they will fail to achieve their goals.

Conclusions

Instead of fostering more market intervention, external agencies should begin by supporting savings-mobilization programs or financial institution building. To the extent that borrowing countries are willing to liberalize trade and rationalize real and financial markets, they are likely to face depressed employment and output conditions and substantial political risks in the short run. External loans could help governments alleviate the worst transition aspects of such a painful but necessary structural adjustment. Again, loans could be used to ease the transition to market liberalization rather than to substitute more controls and regulations for market solutions to resource-allocation problems.

Notes

I am particularly indebted to Dale W Adams, Claudio Gonzalez-Vega, Edward J. Kane, Robert C. Vogel, and other participants in the workshop on Rural Financial Policy, Granville, Ohio, April 16–18, 1981, for direct contributions to the preparation of this paper and to the author's education regarding development problems.

1. To this point, I have at most provided a summary of ideas first and best articulated by Edward S. Shaw (1973) and Ronald I. McKinnon (1973).

2. The necessary and sufficient conditions required to illustrate production frontiers and welfare indifference curves are available from me upon request.

3. The associated algebra is straightforward and available upon request.

4. The algebra associated with this general relationship is available upon request.

5. Two alternative analyses of optimal intervention analysis to deal with labor-market distortions can be found in Lapan (1976) and Ray (1979).

6. In the same sense that Milton Friedman has been heard to describe price controls as a cosmetic approach to inflation, "optimal" intervention

invariably compensates for or covers up a given problem but never solves it.

7. A number of years ago at a workshop on economic development I tried to press Joan Robinson to detail policies that developing countries could pursue to promote more rapid economic progress. She would only respond that first they had to have a revolution. Perhaps that is another, more dramatic, way of saying that general economic reforms in many developing countries would require equally sweeping political changes. As a policy instrument, revolution has been a rather unreliable tool for economic development. Too often it has simply reshuffled political power from one collection of special-interest groups to another.

References

Baker, Chester B. "Role of Credit in the Economic Development of Small Farm Agriculture." In *AID Spring Review of Small Farmer Credit,* vol. 19, edited and published by the Agency for International Development. Washington, D.C., June 1973.

Bhagwati, J. "Distortions and Immiserizing Growth: A Generalization." *Review of Economic Studies* 35(1968):481–485.

Eckaus, Richard S. "Rationalization and Operating Procedures for Small Farmer Credit Programs." In *AID Spring Review of Small Farmer Credit,* vol. 19, edited and published by the Agency for International Development. Washington, D.C., June 1973.

Lapan, Harvey E. "International Trade, Factor Market Distortions and the Optimal Dynamic Subsidy." *American Economic Review* 66(1976):335–346.

Long, Millard. "Conditions for Success of Public Credit Programs for Small Farmers." In *AID Spring Review of Small Farmer Credit,* vol. 19, edited and published by the Agency for International Development. Washington, D.C., June 1973.

McKinnon, Ronald I. *Money and Capital in Economic Development.* Washington, D.C.: Brookings Institution, 1973.

Magee, Stephen P. "Factor Market Distortions, Production, and Trade: A Survey." *Oxford Economic Papers* 25(1973):1–43.

Ray, Edward John. "Factor Market Distortions and Dynamic Optimal Intervention: Comment." *American Economic Review* 69(1979):715–717.

———. "Impact of General Economic Policies on the Performance of Rural Financial Markets." In *Rural Financial Markets in Developing Countries: Their Use and Abuse,* edited by J. D. Von Pischke, Dale W Adams, and Gordon Donald. Baltimore: Johns Hopkins University Press, 1983.

Shaw, Edward S. *Financial Deepening in Economic Development.* New York: Oxford University Press, 1973.

Tendler, Judith. "The Trouble with Goals of Small Farmer Credit Programs (and How To Get Out of It)." In *AID Spring Review of Small Farmer Credit,* vol. 19, edited and published by the Agency for International Development. Washington, D.C., June 1973.

17
Credit and Price Policies in Philippine Agriculture

Cristina C. David

Government economic policies typically undervalue agricultural products in low-income countries (Bale and Lutz 1979). The primary reason for this has been to keep food and materials prices low to promote industrialization. Input price subsidies, public expenditures on irrigation, investments in research and extension, and concessionary credit policies are frequently used in attempts to offset adverse effects of these policies on agriculture production incentives.

Credit policies and programs have stressed expanding the volume of formal agricultural loans at low interest rates and have often been accompanied by supervision and input price subsidies. The underlying premise is that informal sources of funds carry high interest rates that hinder expansion of agricultural output. Officials who favor these types of credit policies often have shown little concern for the negative effects they have on the ability of rural financial markets to perform efficiently and for the effect on savers. They have also ignored the more inequitable loan distribution resulting from such policies.

The performance of credit programs generally has been measured in terms of their impact on agricultural production, investment, and adoption of new technology. A recent evaluation of existing credit research, however, emphasized the serious methodological problems involved (David and Meyer 1980). It concluded that most micro-credit-impact studies are descriptive and are more useful in generating hypotheses than in rigorously measuring loan impact. Only a few studies have used econometric and mathematical programming techniques, and they generally have suffered from conceptual problems arising from the interdependence of production and consumption decision of farm households, the fungibility of credit, and nonprice credit rationing by lenders.

Aggregate credit-impact studies have similar methodological problems, but empirical results are more consistent in showing that little impact on production, investment, and proportion of loans granted to agriculture can be attributed to credit programs and policies (Herdt and Gonzales 1981). These results should not be surprising, because technology and relative prices across commodities and between inputs and outputs are the primary determinants of relative profitability and resource flow directions.

The purpose of this chapter is to analyze how credit policies in the Philippines are related to economic incentives in agriculture and to analyze the extent to which cheap credit is an effective way to offset various "taxes" on agriculture. The first section describes the policies affecting growth of the formal agricultural credit system. The second section presents estimates of the effects of government policies on the relative prices of agricultural products. In the third and final section, it is argued that low interest rates do not alter the incentive structure facing agriculture or resolve equity problems caused by price policies.

Agricultural Credit Policies

Credit has been a major agricultural development instrument in the Philippines. In the early 1950s, the Rural Bank Law was passed to foster rural private banks, and the Agricultural Credit and Cooperative Farmers' Association (ACCFA) was established to promote rural cooperative financial institutions. There are currently more than 1,000 rural banks operating in about 60 percent of the municipalities. They have become the principal distributors of government-sponsored supervised credit. The ACCFA was supposed to develop farm cooperatives providing production and marketing credit. Because of default problems, it has been reorganized and renamed the Agricultural Credit Administration (ACA). It now administers a small supervised-credit program for land-reform beneficiaries.

The government's objective of increasing the credit flow to agriculture has been hampered by low-interest-rates policies. Until the 1981 interest-rate reform, interest rates and other financial charges were regulated by the Monetary Board to conform with the 16 percent ceiling stipulated by the usury law. During the past decade allowable interest rates on formal agricultural credit ranged from 12 to 16 percent and additional loan charges from 2 to 3 percent, depending on the security offered and other terms of the loans. Supervised agricultural credit has carried a lower interest rate of 10 percent with additional charges not exceeding 3 percent. For rural savings deposits, the interest rates were about 6 percent, but higher for time deposits.

Since the late 1960s, official interest rates on agricultural credit have been lower than the scarcity price of loanable funds, with negative consequences on the rate of savings, investments in agriculture, and factor intensities (International Labour Office 1974). Because of rapid inflation, around 20 percent annually during the 1970s, interest rates in recent years have been negative in real terms. This price structure rewarded borrowers and penalized savers. It also created excess loan demand that limited the flow of loans to agricultural projects, especially to small farms, where costs of transactions and risks for lenders were inherently high.

To increase the supply of agricultural credit, the government required that a certain proportion of loan portfolios be allocated to credit for agriculture, much of it through supervised agricultural credit programs. In 1974, the Monetary Board directed all lending institutions to allocate 25 percent of their loanable funds to agriculture, including 10 percent to agrarian-reform beneficiaries. Private commercial banks, however, have strongly resisted this rule. They have responded largely by purchasing qualifying certificates of indebtedness issued by the Central Bank and other "agricultural" government securities, because of the high cost of directly lending to farmers.

Table 17.1 lists total loans granted during the period 1973–1980 by the various special agricultural credit programs (SCPs). Most of these programs linked low-interest, noncollateral loans with extension. Between 1973 and 1975, these programs were also tied to fertilizer price subsidies. Financial institutions were provided preferential rediscount rates, loan guarantees, and assistance in loan administration within these programs. This was financed, in part, by foreign loans.

A major rice-production promotion program, Masagana 99, accounted for almost 80 percent of total loans issued by SCPs during the 1973–1980 period. Since the initial objective of Masagana 99 was to recover from serious crop losses experienced in 1973, priority was given to irrigated areas where the potential for rapid expansion of rice production in the short run was greatest. Programs after Masagana 99, although much smaller in scale, attempted to extend supervised credit to nonrice, rainfed areas.

Problems associated with these programs and policies are now well documented (C. David 1979). Over the past two decades growth in agricultural loans has come mainly from the Central Bank rediscount window rather than from additional equity capital or savings deposits. This is shown by the increase in the share of borrowings from the Central Bank, as a percent of total resources of rural banks, from 8

Table 17.1 Supervised Agricultural Credit Programs in the Philippines, 1973-1980.

Program	Commodity	Loans Issued[a/] (P million)[b/]
1. Masagana 99	Rice	4,554
2. Masaganang Maisan and Masagana 77	Corn	521
3. Gulayan sa Kalusugan	Vegetables	22
4. Cotton Financing Progress	Cotton	71
5. Integrated Agricultural Financing for Virginia Tobacco[c/]	Tobacco	34
6. Rice-Tobacco Supervised Credit Program	Tobacco	3
7. Philippine Tobacco Administration (PTA) Farm Credit Assistance Program	Tobacco	3
8. PTA Facility Loans	Tobacco	1
9. Bakahang Barangay	Cattle	256
10. Biyayang Dagat	Fish	35
Total		P5,500

a/ As of December 31, 1980.
b/ In 1980 U.S. $1.00 was equal to 7.4 pesos.
c/ As of 1979.

Source: Unpublished files, Technical Board For Agricultural Credit.

percent in 1961 to 54 percent in 1975. Low repayment rates have plagued almost all supervised-credit programs. This has undermined the viability of financial intermediaries and further damaged credit discipline among borrowers. The impact of these programs on production at the farm level as well as at an aggregate level has remained unclear. Although Masagana 99 was associated with the rapid increase in Philippine rice production, the growth trend in rice production and adoption of the new rice technology since the late 1960s cannot be attributed to Masagana 99 (Herdt and Gonzales 1981).

Despite these government interventions, Table 17.2 indicates that the real and relative levels of agricultural production loans granted declined after the late 1960s. Since the early 1950s, these loans have grown in real terms, but most of this growth took place in the 1960s. The real value of the loans in 1979 was still far below that of 1969. Agricultural credit as a percent of net value added in agricultural and of total loans granted in the country declined from 27 percent and 20 percent in 1967 to 19 percent and 11 percent in 1979.

These trends are perhaps not surprising since technology and relative prices across sectors and commodities and between inputs

Table 17.2 Selected Indicators of Trends in Loans Issued for Agricultural Production by Bank and Non-Bank Financial Institutions, 1951-1979

Year	Agricultural Loans (P Million in 1972 Prices)[a]	Agricultural Loans as a Percent of Agricultural Value Added	Agricultural Loans as a Percent of Total Loans Issued
1951	376	13	40
1955	534	17	24
1960	2,757	14	20
1961	3,636	19	22
1962	4,022	21	20
1963	4,461	24	20
1964	4,503	25	19
1965	4,420	23	19
1966	4,582	24	19
1967	5,556	27	20
1968	5,665	25	16
1969	5,794	22	16
1970	4,557	22	15
1971	3,943	21	13
1972	3,424	20	12
1973	2,590	19	10
1974	1,725	22	12
1975	1,718	21	9
1976	982	13	--
1977	1,096	16	8
1978	2,534	13	8
1979	3,378	19	11

a/ Refers to loans issued for agricultural production only. In 1979 U.S. $1.00 was equal to 7.4 pesos.

Sources: Unpublished reports by the Technical Board For Agricultural Credit, Central Bank of the Philippines, and the National Economic Development Authority.

and outputs are the most important determinants of relative profitability and hence direction of resource allocation. Larson and Vogel (1980) and others have argued that the use of cheap credit to compensate for the effects of policies that turn terms of trade against food and agricultural exports will have only limited effect on agricultural production. It is too often overlooked that preferential interest rates do not affect relative profitability and that, because credit is fungible, additional liquidity supplied by credit will be allocated to the most profitable enterprise or to consumption, whichever provides the greatest utility.

Price Intervention Policies

The effects of government policies on economic incentives in agriculture have not received adequate attention in the Philippines.

Also, the relationship between these policies and credit activities has not been clarified. The fact that farmers are rational and price responsive has been amply demonstrated by researchers. Price relationships among crops, among agricultural and nonagricultural activities, and between product and input prices have been shown to have important consequences on resource allocation as well as on income distribution. In the Philippines, these price relations have been influenced by interventions intended to achieve several—often conflicting—objectives: food self-sufficiency, low food prices, stable prices, higher farm income, more government revenues, and increased processing of agricultural products. Price controls, export taxes, trade quotas, import tariffs, nationalization of marketing, and the general overvaluation of domestic currency have been important policies affecting relative prices, especially during the past decade. Domestic prices also have been influenced by actions of foreign governments, such as U.S. sugar quotas and the PL 480 program.

The impact of economic policies on agricultural incentives can be measured by the nominal protection rates (NPRs) and implicit tariffs (ITs). Both NPRs and ITs measure the percentage difference between domestic price and border price of products and inputs, respectively.[1] Border prices, usually defined as c.i.f. import prices for importables or f.o.b. export prices of exportables, are converted at official exchange rates and used as bases of comparison because they represent opportunity costs of traded commodities. When border prices are converted at official exchange rates, as in NPR or IT, the difference between domestic and border price is attributed to government price interventions such as trade, fiscal, and price policies. On the other hand, by converting border price at the shadow exchange rate, a measure of net nominal protection rate is obtained. This takes into account all government policies, including the general overvaluation of the exchange rate defended by the protection system.

Table 17.3 presents average NPRs for the Philippines by major commodity groups for two time periods to highlight the impact of increasing government regulation of the agricultural sector.[2] Although government intervention in the later period was part of overall attempts to balance economic growth, many policies were instituted to cushion the impact on consumer prices of the floating of exchange rates in 1970 and the oil and food-grain crises in 1973.

Import-Competing Food Crops

Among the domestically marketed food crops, the food staples rice and corn have historically been the objects of direct price interventions.

Table 17.3 Nominal Protection Rates in Philippine Agriculture, 1955-1980

	1955-1969		1970-1980	
	Proportion of Value Added	Nominal Protection Rate(%)	Proportion of Value Added	Nominal Protection Rate(%)
Food Crops				
Rice	.27	4	.25	-7
Corn	.09	2	.08	1
Other Crops	.13	0	.18	0
Export Crops				
Sugar	.09	60	.09	-23
Copra	.09	- 8	.08	-22
Other Exports	.09	0	.12	- 4
Livestock and Poultry				
Livestock	.11	28	.13	4
Poultry	.07	77	.07	48
Average (Total)	(1.00)	15	(1.00)	- 2

Source: Based on preliminary reports of the project entitled "The Impact of Economic Policies on Philippine Agricultural Development," Philippine Institute For Development Studies and Philippine Council for Agriculture and Resources Research, January, 1982. Basic data were from the Bureau of Agricultural Economics, Central Bank of the Philippines, and National Census and Statistics Office.

Prices of other food crops, such as vegetables, fruits, nuts, roots, and tubers, were less controlled, except potentially through the tariff structure.[3] Domestic prices of rice and corn have been generally close to border prices. In the 1970s average domestic rice prices were below average border prices by 7 percent. In part, this resulted from price interventions in 1973–1975 when the world price of rice and fertilizer rose fourfold.

The National Food Authority is responsible for regulating foodgrain prices to achieve low prices for consumers and adequate price incentives for producers. It buys grains in the domestic market to defend a farm floor price, but the amount of imports or exports that are under government monopoly is the main determinant of grain prices. Previous studies had noted that providing stable and low rice prices for urban consumers tended to dominate the objective of supporting farm price to raise income of small farmers (Mangahas 1972). This was achieved through imports during years of production shortfalls. After 1975, the domestic rice prices became internationally competitive. Some commercial rice exports have occurred since 1978 as a result of the new rice technology and irrigation expansion. Price policy for corn, an important upland crop that is the staple food for about 20 percent of the population, also has the same bias. Moreover, the policy of keeping the price of meat low for urban consumers is another reason for maintaining low corn prices, because of the importance of corn as an animal feedstock.

Price comparisons were not done for the other food crops, such as fruits, vegetables, roots, and tubers, because of the great heterogeneity of products within each commodity group and the fact that many of these crops are not significantly traded. Legal tariff rates are relatively high, up to 100 percent for some crops, but fragmentary evidence indicates that, except for some fruits and vegetables consumed by the very high income families, these relatively high potential protection rates are not fully realized. Domestic prices for other food crops do not seem to be significantly different from prices in other countries, and there are some small exports of fruits, vegetables, and coffee. Thus, it was assumed that, in general, prices of other food crops have not been affected by the protection system; that is, NPR is zero.

Export Crops

Increasing regulation of agricultural exports was significant in the 1970s. Prior to 1970 the government rarely intervened in the production and trade of export crops, except indirectly through the overvaluation of exchange rates and through foreign-exchange regulations. However, sugar quotas that limited exports to 60 percent of production were instituted in 1962 to protect domestic consumers from the increased access of Philippine producers to the highly protected U.S. sugar market. U.S. sugar policy provided an export price for the Philippines much higher than world prices from 1955 to 1969 and resulted in a high nominal protection rate of 60 percent on domestic sugar production.

During the 1970s government policies generally reduced domestic prices of export crops below those that would have otherwise prevailed. Since the floating of the exchange rate in 1970, the value of agricultural crop exports have typically risen and fallen with the world price of copra. In some years, the Coconut Consumers Stabilization Fund (CCSF) levy in *ad valorem* terms has represented a tax of about 20 percent of border price. Although the tax is collected at the miller's level, the incidence of the tax is clearly on the farmer.

About 20 percent of the revenues from the tax supports the direct subsidy on domestic consumption of coconut-oil products. The remainder is supposed to finance development programs in the coconut industry such as replanting, vertical integration, and scholarships. Research shows that only a small segment of the coconut industry actually receives the benefits from these programs (V. David 1977). In addition, the gains from the replanting program are uncertain. It is not known how well hybrid seeds will perform under diverse Philippine conditions. Furthermore, small coconut farmers with few alternative sources of income have been hesitant to face the prospect of waiting for three years to harvest a first crop. At least for the short run, the CCSF levies on coco production may be considered a tax on the industry.

Livestock and Poultry

Livestock appears to offer lower rewards than poultry, but both are more favored than the crop sector. However, incentives seem to have declined for both because of government policy. Average domestic prices of livestock (specifically pork) and poultry were 28 percent and 77 percent higher than their corresponding border prices prior to the 1970s and slightly higher than those predicted by their tariff rates.[4] In the 1970s, percentage price differences declined to levels somewhat lower than the legal tariff rates of 10 percent for livestock and 70 percent for poultry. This may be due to price controls imposed on those products. These controls were accompanied by price controls on mixed feeds and feedgrain and higher imports of corn and other feedgrains to provide a reasonable margin for producers during this period.

Protection of Agriculture and Manufacturing

The direction and rate of resource flows between agriculture and nonagriculture are influenced not only by the nominal rate of protection on product prices but also by policies on agricultural input prices and on incentives in the nonagricultural sector. The effective protection rate (EPR) measures the percentage difference between value added at domestic prices and value added at border prices. It takes the impact of price interventions on inputs into account. Since estimates of EPR for agriculture are not available, Table 17.4 compares the nominal protection rate in agriculture to the implicit tariffs paid by farmers for agricultural inputs and to EPR for manufacturing as estimated by Tan (1979).[5]

Table 17.4 Comparison of Protection Rates in the Agricultural and Manufacturing Sectors, 1970s

	Nominal Protection Rate (%)
Agriculture (Nominal Protection Rates)	- 2
(Net Nominal Protection Rate)	-37
Agricultural Inputs (Implicit Tariffs)	
Fertilizer[a/]	10
Agricultural Chemicals[b/]	28
Hand Tractors[b/]	46
Four-wheel Tractors[b/]	24
Irrigation Pump[b/]	46
Irrigation Gravity (NIA system)[c/]	-55
Mixed Feeds[b/]	33
Manufacturing[d/] (Effective Protection Rate)	44
(Net Effective Protection Rate)	9

a/ Based on prices of urea, ammonium sulphate, mixed fertilizer, and phosphates from 1973 to 1980.

b/ Based on legal tariff rates and sales tax.

c/ Based on comparison of NIA irrigation fees and estimates of annualized cost of irrigation systems by P.F. Moya, L. Small, and S. Bhuiyan, "Cost of Different Types of Irrigation Systems in Central Luzon," Department Paper No. 80-10, Dept. of Agricultural Economics, International Rice Research Institute, Los Banos, Philippines, June 1980.

d/ Based on estimates by N. Tan, "The Structure of Protection and Resource Flows in the Philippines." In Industrial Promotion Policies in the Philippines. Edited by R. Bautista and J. Power. Manila: Philippine Institute of Development Studies, 1979.

As can be noted, government policies have created an incentive structure significantly biased against agriculture. Price intervention policies undermined agricultural profitability during the last decade through lower product prices and higher input prices.

Because the objective of low food prices tends to dominate agricultural-product price policy, it seems reasonable to assume that government interventions in agricultural input markets would try to offset this. However, it is only in gravity irrigation and formal rural credit, as will be discussed later, that there appears to be some government subsidy to producers. Implicit 24 to 46 percent tariffs for agricultural chemicals, agricultural machinery, and feed mixes reduce the effective protection in agriculture created by legal tariffs and indirect sales tax. Despite price controls and direct subsidies on fertilizer, there is still a positive implicit tariff for fertilizer. It appears that the protection of domestic manufacturing of these agricultural inputs, which is also indicated by the level of implicit tariff (but is actually significantly higher for fertilizer because of direct subsidies), has been an important policy consideration.

The overall magnitude of the bias against agriculture is reflected by the measure of net protection rates that includes the impact of the overvaluation of the exchange rate due to the protection system. Although the exchange rate has been allowed to float since 1970, tariffs and other trade restrictions have reduced demand for imports and thus increased the value of domestic currency. For the mid-1970s, Medalla and Power (1979) estimated that the tariff and tax system resulted in a 32 percent overvaluation of the peso relative to a balanced free-trade situation.[6] If this is taken into consideration, penalties on agriculture net of the disincentive effect of an overvalued currency would be even more severe (minus 37 percent), whereas manufacturing still receives a 9 percent net effective protection rate. As a consequence of this general pricing policy, agricultural production is reduced, although for certain commodities such as coconut products and sugar the level of domestic consumption may be somewhat higher than would be expected with no price intervention. The fact that agriculture survives and indeed grows suggests an inherent comparative advantage.

Impact of Credit Policies

The effective subsidy rate (ESR) is estimated to quantify the impact of credit policies. ESR expresses the amount of interest-rate subsidy as a percent of net value added in agriculture at border prices. Subsidy is defined as the difference in the cost of borrowing between agricultural and nonagricultural loans, multiplied by the value of agricultural loans granted. Another method is to estimate the amount of subsidy accruing to the sector as a result of the difference between the nominal interest rate and the rate of inflation.

Differences in interest rates between agricultural and nonagricultural loans from formal financial institutions are small, at most 2 percent. Moreover, interest represents only part of the costs of borrowing. Typically, nonagricultural loans entail lower transactions costs than agricultural loans for borrowers. Even if interest-rate policy results in a cost-of-borrowing differential of 6 percent in favor of agriculture, the effective subsidy rate amounts to only 1 percent. Even if the interest-rate differential is increased by two or three times, it is clear that the interest-rate subsidy will not alter significantly the unfavorable incentive structure in agriculture vis-à-vis nonagriculture created by price policies. On the other hand, a low-interest-rate policy seriously impairs the ability of rural financial markets to efficiently perform financial intermediation. It does not provide incentives for mobilizing financial savings, but does induce an allocation of credit that is based on collateral and wealth rather than on productivity of credit use, failing to improve income distribution while not being necessary to effect technical change.

The impact of the low-interest-rate policy has been generally regressive. The subsidy is shouldered by the lower-income population—that is, holders of currency, bank deposits, and tax payers—through inflation, low interest rates on savings, and direct government outlay. Only about 10 percent of the total implicit interest-rate subsidy is received by agriculture. Within agriculture, credit allocation is also not consistent with employment and equity objectives. Low-cost credit for agricultural machinery shifts the incentive system against use of labor, with little impact on yield. As an example, less than 15 percent of the value of recent loans in the World Bank mechanization program in the Philippines was used for small power tillers. Four-wheel tractors and other large farm equipment were purchased with the bulk of the loans by sugarcane farmers who farmed 50 hectares or more and constituted less than 10 percent of the total number of farmers.

In supervised-credit programs, only farm operators are usually entitled to loans despite the significant numbers of landless households in the rural areas. Rice has been emphasized, but rice farmers are actually better off than average growers of corn, coconuts, tobacco, and other crops. Within the rice sector, priority has been given to irrigated areas close to primary markets, that is, relatively progressive locations with the greatest potential for rapid increases in production in the short run. Loan limits specified on a per hectare basis mean a large loan ceiling for large farms. Perhaps an even more important dimension of inequity in distribution of the implicit subsidies involved in these programs was reported by Esguerra (1981) in a recent analysis of Masagana 99. The study estimated that two-thirds of the implicit subsidies have been received by participating financial institutions as incentives to lend to small farmers and only one-third by the farmer borrowers, mainly from nonrepayment of loans. Furthermore, the distribution of the subsidies accruing to borrowers has been biased in favor of large farmers.

The common belief that extension would be more effective if tied with low-cost credit and vice versa is not clearly verified by empirical evidence. In the case of rice, the modern varieties introduced in 1967 were adopted on 67 percent of irrigated farms and on 45 percent of rainfed farms prior to the Masagana 99 program. The fact that the rate of adoption increased to 85 percent and 71 percent, respectively, in 1977 cannot be attributed to the program, but rather should be viewed as a continuation of the adoption process. In the case of corn, there has been little dissemination of new varieties developed in the early 1970s despite the Maisan 77 and Masaganang Maisan programs, because the new technology apparently did not increase profitability. Extension and development of financial markets are indeed important components of rural development, but the strategy of linking the two has dissipated the efforts of scarce competent technicians in loan administration without improving repayment rates in supervised credit programs.

Concluding Remarks

Interest-rate subsidies have not significantly altered the unfavorable economic incentives in Philippine agriculture caused by government policies. It is not surprising, therefore, that loanable funds to agriculture in real terms have declined despite government credit quotas and special credit programs. Even higher interest-rate subsidies will be ineffective in offsetting penalties from pricing policies because of the fungibility of credit. Additional liquidity will be allocated to activities in which marginal profits or utility is highest. Relative prices as well as yields are the major factors determining rates of return to most enterprises. Cheap credit will not make an unprofitable activity profitable!

It is also clear that credit subsidies through low interest rates worsen income distribution because only a few, typically well-off farmers, receive the bulk of the cheap credit. When interest rates are not allowed to reflect costs of financial intermediation, wealth and political power replace profitability as the basis of allocating credit. In contrast, higher produce prices would benefit more low-income farmers.

The choice of credit to compensate agriculture for other adverse policies reflects administrative ease, availability of external grants and loans, and other short-run considerations. Although easy to carry out, this approach fails to achieve either equity or efficiency objectives. Cheap-credit policies also retard the development of viable formal financial institutions in rural areas. Food self-sufficiency, increasing exports, and improving income distribution require long-run efforts. These include correcting price distortions in real and financial markets and making investments in marketing infrastructure, irrigation, research, and extension. Cheap credit will not overcome production disincentives caused by low prices and/or low yields. Product prices and yields are much more powerful, efficient, and equitable tools for rural development than is cheap credit.

Notes

I wish to acknowledge support for this study from the Rural Financial Market Project of The Ohio State University, the Philippine Institute for Development Studies (PIDS), and the Philippine Council for Agriculture and Resources Research (PCARR). The analyses of price policies draw from the results of a research project entitled "The Impact of Economic Policies on Philippine Agricultural Development," funded by PIDS and PCARR. Dale W Adams, Douglas H. Graham, John Power, and James Roumasset provided valuable comments on earlier drafts of this essay.

1.
$$\text{NPR} = \frac{P_d^m}{P_b} - 1 \times 100; \ \text{IT} = \frac{P_d^u}{P_b} - 1 \times 100 \qquad (17.1)$$

where P_b denotes border price, P_d^u = price paid by the user, and P_d^m = price received by domestic producers and importers. Prices are defined at a comparable point in the marketing chain to ensure that differences between domestic and border prices are due to government interventions rather than to real costs.

2. Annual differences in nominal protection rates were not shown because they would, in general, be related to price fluctuations rather than to policy changes.

3. Tariff protection is redundant for exportable crops and does not apply to food grains in cases in which only the government can import or export. It should also be noted that tariffs are expected to be effective in raising domestic price above border prices only in products that compete with imports. Since most agricultural commodities either are subjected to quantitative trade restrictions or are not significantly traded, price comparisons have been used to measure NPR instead of legal tariff rates.

4. Since international trade in livestock and poultry has been minimal and confined mainly to imports of breeding animals, special cuts of meat for restaurants, or fats for the meat-processing industry, border prices were represented by average c.i.f. import unit values in Hong Kong.

5. NPRs in agriculture are not expected to be substantially different from their EPRs because the proportion of intermediate inputs to value added remains relatively small in Philippine agriculture. Moreover, one can expect

EPRs to be lower than NPRs because of higher protection on agricultural inputs.

6. The situation since the mid-1970s has been one of chronic and growing deficits in current accounts, financed by heavy foreign borrowing. This indicates an even higher percentage of peso overvaluation than that resulting from the tariff and tax system alone.

References

Bale, M., and E. Lutz. "Price Distortions in Agriculture and Their Effects: An International Comparison." World Bank Staff Working Paper no. 359, Washington, D.C., October 1979.

David, C. "Structure and Performance of Rural Financial Markets in the Philippines." Economics and Sociology Occasional Papers no. 598, Department of Agricultural Economics and Rural Sociology, The Ohio State University, May 1979.

David, Cristina C., and Richard L. Meyer. "Measuring the Farm Level Impact of Agricultural Loans." In *Borrowers and Lenders: Rural Financial Markets and Institutions in Developing Countries,* edited by John Howell. London: Overseas Development Institute, 1980.

David, V. "The Barriers in the Development of the Philippine Coconut Industry." MBA thesis, Ateneo de Manila University, Manila, 1977.

Esguerra, E. "The Redistributive Potential of the Masagana 99 Credit Subsidy." MA thesis, School of Economics, University of the Philippines, Manila, August 1981.

Herdt, R., and L. A. Gonzales. "A Reaction to the Study on the Benefits and Costs of Masagana 99 Program." Paper presented at the Fifth National Agricultural Credit Workshop, Zamboanga, Philippines, March 1981.

International Labour Office. *Sharing in Development: A Programme of Employment Equity and Growth for the Philippines.* Geneva: International Labour Office, 1974.

Larson, Donald W., and Robert C. Vogel. "Interaction of Price and Credit Policies in Costa Rican Agriculture." Economics and Sociology Occasional Papers no. 813, Department of Agricultural Economics and Rural Sociology, The Ohio State University, November 1980.

Mangahas, M. "Philippine Rice Policy Reconsidered in Terms of Urban Bias." Institute of Economic Development Research Discussion Paper 72-8, School of Economics, University of the Philippines, Quezon, 1972.

Medalla, E., and J. Power. "Estimating Implicit Tariffs and Nominal Rates of Protection." In *Industrial Promotion Policies in the Philippines,* edited by R. Bautista and J. Power. Makati: Philippine Institute for Development Studies, 1979.

Moya, P., and others. "Cost of Different Types of Irrigation Systems in Central Luzon." Paper no. 80–10, Department of Agricultural Economics, International Rice Research Institute, Los Baños, Philippines, June 1980.

Tan, N. "The Structure of Protection and Resource Flows in the Philippines." In *Industrial Promotion Policies in the Philippines,* edited by R. Bautista and J. Power. Makati: Philippine Institute for Development Studies, 1979.

Part 4

New Directions for Rural Financial Markets

18
Overview of New Directions for Rural Financial Markets

Dale W Adams
Douglas H. Graham
J. D. Von Pischke

The authors of the preceding essays are critical of many policies found in rural financial markets in low-income countries. They argue that erroneous assumptions and mistaken policies are responsible for much of the poor performance in these markets over the past several decades. Although it is easy to criticize existing programs because of their demonstrated weaknesses, it is more difficult to prescribe changes that would remedy these problems. Authors of previous chapters have touched on some of these changes. The chapters in Part 4 give more detail on new policy directions that might help to substantially improve financial market performance. Overall, the authors argue for dramatic changes in the way rural financial markets are used to support development. In the past, these markets have been used largely to channel cheap funds from external donors or governments through lenders to farmers. The interest of rural savers, informal lenders, nonfarm rural firms, and the vitality of financial intermediaries have been largely ignored in these efforts.

The five chapters in this part present insights into how rural financial markets might be better used. These new directions require that policymakers place much more emphasis on market forces to allocate services in financial markets, with interest-rate reform as a cornerstone. More positive attitudes toward informal lenders, the possibilities of mobilizing voluntary financial savings, and extending financial services to nonfarm rural firms are also a major part of this new thinking. With more appropriate policies in these markets it is also likely that healthier financial innovation would emerge. More of these innovations would result in intermediation cost decreases, rather than ploys to evade the intent of regulations. It is further argued that international donors ought to change how they intrude into these markets. In too many cases foreign assistance has reinforced incorrect policies, undermined the process of granting sound loans to farmers, and deflected rural financial markets from providing savings services.

Many policymakers in formal financial markets are geared to do battle with informal lenders. The widely savored assumption that most informal forms of finance are evil has caused policymakers to tilt at windmills in their quest to eliminate the "evil" moneylender. Bouman points out in Chapter 19 that informal financial arrangements provide very valuable services to many rural people. Policymakers and formal lenders ought to take a positive view of informal finance and draw information from these activities that will help to improve the quality of formal services. In most cases, informal lenders provide their clients with valuable services at very nominal costs. Many of these services cannot be provided by formal lenders under any circumstances. With appropriate conditions, informal lending should expand with the expansion in the overall economy and growth in formal finance.

Vogel reports on a highly successful rural savings-mobilization program recently carried out in several areas in Peru. He forcefully argues that similar savings-mobilization efforts ought to be initiated in other low-income countries and, further, that much more stress ought to be placed on savings mobilization in general. He points out that many more people typically avail themselves of savings-deposit services than borrow from formal lenders and that lenders who mobilize a large part of their loanable funds through savings deposits develop a large measure of self-discipline. They are less prone to political intrusions, tend to have fewer problems with loan recovery (because they are lending local people's money), and generally enhance the quality of their services.

Through policy directives, many of the formal credit services available in rural areas of low-income countries are restricted to farmers. Nonfarm rural firms have been largely ignored in these efforts. Chapter 21 by Kilby, Liedholm, and Meyer points out that recent research in a number of low-income countries has shown that these nonfarm firms make up a very large part of the rural economy and are often an important source of income, goods, and services for the rural poor. One might argue that, if policymakers want to have a large impact on the incomes of the rural poor, more headway could be made by promoting these nonfarm firms than by trying to work with the small farmers. Generally the poorest of the poor in rural areas have little or no land. Employment in nonfarm firms is often an important part of the income of these households. Even though some liquidity from formal lenders filters out to a few of these firms, more direct contact among formal lenders and managers of nonfarm firms would be beneficial. Many of these firms could use additional credit, most ought to be using formal deposit and checking facilities, and many could use business advice that intermediaries ought to provide.

Most of the agricultural credit systems in low-income countries have received assistance from external donors, who have put considerable time, effort, and money into these systems over the past couple of decades. Von Pischke argues for major adjustments in the way international donors enter into these markets, putting forth the view that basing credit projects on some assumed credit need is a poor project foundation. Rather, he stresses that loans ought to be made on the basis of creditworthiness—that is, on the ability of the borrower to repay. He also argues that much more attention ought to be given to how a credit project affects the vitality of the intermediary. In most cases, donor credit projects have been justified on the basis of the impact they have on borrowers' economic activities. Von Pischke advocates using the performance of the lender and the overall performance of the rural financial markets as the main criteria to judge the worth of a credit project.

Adoption of the changes in policy suggested by the authors in Part 4 and in previous parts would mean a major departure in the way rural financial markets are used to support development. It would mean learning from the informal lender, stressing savings-deposit sevices, downgrading the importance of agricultural credit, opening rural financial markets to nonfarm rural firms, creating a more healthy environment in rural areas for financial innovation, and making major adjustments in the way external donors relate to these markets. Minor adjustments in the way things have been done in the past will not be sufficient to significantly improve the performance of rural financial markets, if the authors in this volume are correct.

19
Informal Saving and Credit Arrangements in Developing Countries: Observations from Sri Lanka

F.J.A. Bouman

A consensus is growing among researchers that the formal financial sector is not effectively serving the rural populace in the Third World. The view that the poor constitute financial basket cases does not inspire policymakers to search for challenging new concepts and procedures to accommodate them (Von Pischke 1980). This raises the question of how the poor manage their financial affairs. Partially, the answer lies in self-help. Through a long tradition people have devised mutual-aid formulas to satisfy their savings and credit objectives. They also turn to pawnbrokers, shopkeepers, and moneylenders. Surprisingly, this much-abused class of informal financial intermediaries appears to play important roles in self-help institutions.

This chapter is about informal saving and credit in developing countries, with special reference to Sri Lanka. It deals mainly with self-help actions. Apart from recording personal observations, the chapter draws on material gathered by four graduate students who each spent six months in Sri Lanka. M. Overheul and B. Burgers studied the *cheetu,* a rotating savings and credit association (ROSCA) that is popular throughout the world under various names. M. Boot and J. Vel lived in a small village in the mountainous Kandy district in the island's center and studied the savings, credit, and investment behavior of individual families. Discussing daily financial worries with women, they provided a female point of view, so often unaccessible to the male observer.

How People Save

Policymakers and development planners cherish the myth that poor people do not have the spirit of thrift. Recent reports from different parts of the globe challenge this, however, and show that poor people can and do save. They deposit money with church groups, dance societies, ROSCAs, and cultural and age groups, as reported by Miracle, Miracle, and Cohen (1980). They save with finance companies, Christmas clubs, tax-payment groups, pilgrimage funds, and death-aid societies, or they entrust their savings to individuals noted for their financial expertise, such as mobile bankers, pawnbrokers, traders, and moneylenders like the Chettiars in Southeast Asia (Weerasoria 1973).

Thrift comes naturally to households with irregular income flows. Rural families in Sri Lanka, particularly in low-income brackets, show an almost passionate desire to save. Boot reported how a family abstained from using curries with rice meals in an effort to save for an urgent, out-of-village trip. Children at the age of seven or less are taught the virtues of frugal living through parents encouraging them to contribute part of their daily ration of school biscuits to a savings fund. At a recent rural-finance seminar for village workers of Sarvodaya—a well-known rural-development movement in Sri Lanka—participants reported remarkably high savings levels. Of the 41 participants, 25 were males and 16 females, and all were in the age group of 21 to 35 years. The average monthly income of the men was 434 rupees (Rps), the equivalent of US$20, with no great variations among salaries. There were only 5 nonsavers among them, of whom 4 were unmarried. The remaining 20 reported average savings of Rps 112 per month, equivalent to 26 percent of their income. *The savings rate varied inversely with salary:* the lower the wages, the higher the relative savings rate. The women averaged a monthly income of Rps 340 (US$17) and recorded an average savings rate of 21 percent. Similar high savings levels have been reported elsewhere in the Third World (Bouman 1979).

Savings may be held in cash, in goods, or in debt claims. Women with little cash earnings have become very adroit at designing savings tactics. They save in foodstuffs, withdrawing spoonfuls of rice or sugar from the daily meal. The weekly treasure may be stored, converted into cash, or contributed to a *cheetu* fund. For example, at the time when jackfruit is plentiful it is cooked, dried, and stored to provide inexpensive meals later in the year. Food is often hoarded for months in preparation for an expensive event such as the Sinhalese

New Year, a wedding ceremony, or the coming of age of a daughter. The mat weavers in Vel's village habitually saved some cane, the material most important to their craft. At a time when savers cannot practice their trade, because of illness or employment elsewhere, they give this cane to another villager on the basis of a share-weaving contract that divides the proceeds of the sale of the mats between them.

An illustration of saving through debt claims is the case of a laborer who asks the employer to postpone payment of wages until some future date, or the farmer who prefers that the produce buyer defer payment until delivery of the last crop. A most telling example is that of the landlady who asked Boot not to pay for board and lodging until the last day of lodging. Every now and then this landlady borrowed a few rupees from her lodger, but she took great pains to repay these loans within a few days, to preserve the debt claim that was gradually building up. In all these instances, income is deferred. Rather than receiving small amounts early, creditors prefer payment of a lump sum at a later date. Debt claims also get around the problem of finding a proper place to deposit cash, a problem that worries many savers.

People save for a variety of reasons. Because agriculture is a seasonal business, rural households generally have irregular income flows, and one of their main concerns is to balance flows of receipts and expenditures. Saving and borrowing are tools in this balancing process. They are also aspects of risk management. People like to have working balances on hand for the sake of convenience, to meet unexpected expenditures, and for protection in times of hardship (Von Pischke 1978). There are households in Sri Lanka where women keep a bit of rice or money handy for beggars. Others even borrow to preserve wealth. This is best demonstrated by the habit of borrowing money to buy rice cheaply now, rather than depleting stores and being forced to buy higher-priced rice later.

Savings are used for productive investment, consumption, and social welfare (e.g., old-age security, expenses connected with rites of passage, religious festivals, and enhancement of status). It is commonly assumed that poor people principally use savings for consumption and social welfare and that high-income earners invest their surplus funds in productive activities to increase income and hence future consumption. This implies that the poor are not interested in improving their economic and financial position. Our research in Sri Lanka strongly suggests that the rural poor are very interested in improving their economic lot. Low and irregular incomes, however, make these individuals very sensitive to risk. In many cases individuals living in a tiny community are influenced by that community's norms of what constitutes prudent and wise husbandry and what will be regarded as avarice. Storing food for a social ceremony or a wedding is acceptable. But saving large amounts for an investment and future riches, while others go hungry, causes jealousy and criticism. Indivisibility of investments and commodities presents particular problems for households with low income. To buy a tractor, a cow or a sewing machine or to build a house or dig a well for irrigation requires a considerable outlay of cash, and hence a long savings period. This has consequences for savings behavior. Particularly relevant are the questions of whether to save individually or in groups and whether to keep savings at home or deposit them with a trustee.

Most people start to save individually, at home. But as funds accumulate the temptation to sacrifice part of the savings for pressing daily needs grows. The fear of theft and of the claims of prying relatives also grows. After a time, having too large a treasure in the house is no longer convenient. Savers who want to continue to expand their savings have to change tactics. Several options are open; food, goods, and money may be converted into silver, gold, or ornaments, for example. In the case of women, ornaments are commonly regarded as personal property that cannot lightly be claimed, even by relatives. A villager once remarked to Boot that "a woman without ornaments is like a woman without a background—without a family to protect her." Gold and silver have the additional advantage of hedging against inflation; they can easily be converted back into money, they also enhance status, and they may be pawned as loan security.

The saver may also decide to hold funds in the custody of a trustee. This could be a bank, a cooperative, a post office, or a credit union. However, the rural poor rarely feel inclined to approach and confide in an institution with which they normally have few dealings. Despite attractive interest rates—commercial banks in Sri Lanka offered rural depositors interest rates between 14 and 22 percent in 1980—there is still a preference for traditional custodians: the shopkeeper, pawnbroker, merchant, and moneylender; the village priest; a teacher; or someone of equal status. The cautious saver will spread savings over several trustees. Lele (1971) reported how Punjabi cultivators customarily deposited returns from the sale of farm produce with commission agents as a matter of safety and convenience. In Sri Lanka the Chettiars performed the same role in the past. These deposits seldom carry any interest, but they often do have the function of entitling the depositor to a line of credit. By saving with a group or with persons of a firm financial standing, the saver buys security.

Regular deposits establish a reputation of creditworthiness and loan access in case of an emergency.

Group Arrangements

Savings clubs have a number of advantages over individual saving. The saver sheds awkward liquidity, thus avoiding embarrassing claims by relatives and friends. The club is also a safe depository; the cases where a treasurer absconds with the money are rare. Further, a group enhances discipline through contractual savings, because participants agree to a regular and fixed contribution. Members of a *cheetu* frequently state that they prefer positions toward the end of the rotation cycle simply to be forced to continue the savings process. Miracle, Miracle, and Cohen (1980) reported that informal savings associations in Africa, through joint action, provide members a variety of economic benefits, like a discount on bulk purchases or the exchange of economic and market intelligence when traders and similar business people band together.

Illustrative examples of group saving in Sri Lanka are the commodity *cheetu* and the pilgrimage society. In a commodity or article *cheetu*, members make regular, equal deposits to a fund from which each, in turn, will receive the agreed article. Members may benefit from a price reduction by placing a joint order with a store. Although still popular, commodity *cheetu* have experienced difficulties because of inflation. After the first few rounds prices may go up so much that the fund is no longer sufficient to accommodate the last few participants. Usually the lucky early receivers are reluctant to increase their contribution to compensate late receivers.

Pilgrimage societies are another group form of savings. It is customary for Sri Lankans to visit a holy place during one of the religious festivals. By making the journey together, members of a pilgrimage society can bring down the costs of lodgings and bus fare. But inflation can catch participants by surprise. In one case that I came across, 42 members of a club tried to raise Rps 135 each by depositing Rps 15 monthly for nine months with the female organizer, who acted as tour operator. This woman meanwhile used the accumulated savings to finance her private business. At the end of the nine months, however, she refunded each member's deposit, stating that the tour was canceled because bus fares had gone up because of rising fuel prices.

Mutual aid is at the core of numerous group-savings schemes. In Asia the village rice bank is a common example. Participating households contribute rice to a common stock from which loans in kind are made to needy members. After harvest, stocks are replenished. Rice banks are found in Indonesia, India (Bailey 1964), and Korea (Kennedy 1977). In Sri Lanka the rice *cheetu* is a modified form of the rice bank. Mutual aid frequently becomes the equivalent of an insurance policy. A protective fund is accumulated to insure members against large expenses connected with rites of passage like a birth, coming of age, and a wedding or funeral. The most common example is the death-aid society, found in even the poorest regions of Sri Lanka. There are two types of such societies: one collects funds only when a death occurs; the other solicits regular contributions. The latter type is more interesting, because some of these societies do not stop at merely accumulating funds that are left idle between burials. In a community where capital is scarce, this would be a waste of valuable resources. In Poddala, a village in the south of Sri Lanka, the monthly fund of the local society used to be partly utilized to buy ceremonial paraphernalia that were loaned free of charge to members.[1] But assistance was also given for hospitalization, birth, and home improvement, and the society even operated its own home for the aged. Because this welfare–cum–death-aid society had clearly overextended itself financially, it shed most of its welfare functions in 1980 and reverted to a purer form of burial society.

In other villages accumulated funds have been lent. Burgers and Overheul found that burial societies in Kurunegalla and Kengalla lent money to members for short periods. The society in Kengalla had 30 members and maintained strict written rules. Meetings were held weekly and attendance was obligatory. Loans were given against collateral only. Members paid a 10 percent interest rate per month; nonmembers paid 12 percent for loans. Interest income was added to the fund. This burial society had gradually, possibly unintentionally, taken on an important lending function.

There are in Sri Lanka numerous other, more loosely structured, noncommunity-oriented organizations that have safekeeping and lending as their primary aim. Their existence clearly indicates that many people do have a savings need, apart from the demand for credit that is so often emphasized.

Samagan and *polipettye* are regional names for one and the same thing.[2] The principal arrangement in all these group schemes is that participants turn over their savings at regular intervals to an organizer for safekeeping. After a certain period, usually a year, a lump sum is returned that may or may not include a reward in the form of interest. The organizer often uses the savings as working capital for his or her own business, but is also expected to make loans to members and usually to nonmembers as well. Schemes often end with the Sinhalese New Year when households make extra expenditures for food and clothing.

A *samagan* in Binkome, a settlement colony in the south, has 22 members, each contributing Rps 10 monthly. Members may take out a loan by paying interest, provided repayment is made within one month. For a longer-term loan 10 percent per month is paid, with nonmembers paying 20 percent. At the end of one year all savings are returned and the dividends distributed. Those who took out loans receive half as much dividend as the members who did not borrow. Total loans may never exceed 50 percent of accumulated savings. The organizer admitted that he organized this *samagan* to acquire working capital for his trading business.

In general, people judge their informal insitutions superior to banks; a number of people said that it was impossible to get an immediate loan from banks in times of need. The informal interest rates are not considered excessive. In fact, some members take out a loan at 10 percent per month and lend the funds to nonmembers at 20 percent. Moneylending is a normal part of village life.

The *Cheetu*

The *cheetu* is a rotating savings and credit association, similar to those found under different names in all parts of the world (Bouman 1979). It is by far the most popular type of informal financial institution in the country. The basic formula is very simple: A group of participants make regular contributions to a fund that is given to each member in turn. When 12 individuals contribute Rps 25 each in a monthly *cheetu*, each of them will eventually receive a sum of $12 \times 25 =$ Rps 300. After 12 months each player has had a turn, and the *cheetu* will disband or start a new cycle. There may be more or fewer players next time, shorter intervals (e.g., weekly) instead of monthly, and a different contribution.

The ROSCA is primarily a savings device. Members greatly appreciate the discipline of contractual group savings, by which they gradually accumulate a lump sum via small contributions. An extra attraction is that most participants have access to this sum at an earlier date than when saving individually. Imagine that all participants in the above *cheetu* are saving for a radio that costs Rps 300. Saving in a solitary fashion Rps 25 per month, a person can expect to buy a radio in the 12th month. In this *cheetu*, however, 11 of the 12 participants will realize an earlier purchase. Each one will benefit in this way from the arrangement, except the recipient of the final round.

ROSCAs combine saving with lending. A member saves until he or she receives the fund, after which he or she starts to repay a loan in installments. How the rotation of the fund is regulated affects the respective debtor and creditor positions. The common distribution alternatives are order of enlistment, negotiation, lottery, and auction. The choice is determined by the socioeconomic environment and the needs and aspirations of members. When turns are allotted through negotiation, factors such as seniority, marital status, personal need, or social position may be decisive. Compassionate or "calamity cases" customarily enjoy priority status, whereas persons who are considered bad risks are put near the end of the cycle.

The lottery is the most popular way to determine rotation. Players usually meet only once, at the beginning of a cycle, when lots are drawn. After that the positions are known, and it is left to the organizer to collect contributions and distribute these in accordance with the result of the lottery. Of course, individuals may arrange between themselves to change places or split turns. This usually involves some payment for the privilege of receiving the fund out of turn.

In the auction *cheetu* the players compete with one another for the collective deposit at each meeting and thereby determine the order of rotation. Imagine 20 participants and a weekly contribution of Rps 50. Each week there is a collective deposit of Rps 1,000 for sale. By bidding, a player states the amount he or she is willing to forgo in order to obtain the fund. A bid of Rps 200 means that the bidder is satisfied with collecting only Rps 800 instead of Rps 1,000, leaving Rps 200 to be divided among the other participants. Every player who has not already received the fund may bid. The only exception is the president, who always gets the first fund free of discount. The amounts forgone by bidders to obtain the fund are interest payments and administration charges. Bids may go as high as 50 percent—in this case Rps 500—so that participants in an auction *cheetu* can reap handsome rewards. They do not, however, receive the full amount of the bid because the organizer of an auction ROSCA always deducts a commission before the rebate is distributed.

Cheetu rules vary from place to place and are decided at the first meeting. A successful bidder early in the cycle may share in the rebates in subsequent auctions; under other rules the rebate will be shared only by the nonrecipients. A 50 percent bid represents an extreme case, and a sensible president will often limit the bidding, arguing that high discounts increase the potential for default. Combinations of both auctions and lottery are also possible.

Cheetu operations change with the environment. In agricultural zones of poor or limited potential, in stagnant and backward economies, and among low-income groups, the lottery dominates. Auction systems make their appearance in rural areas with growth potential or with a diversified economy, as exemplified in Sri Lanka by the Jaffna peninsula, the southern wet zone, and the booming vegetable-producing areas in Nuera Eliya. They are also popular in towns and cities and among shopkeepers, traders, merchants, and other business people who use the *cheetu* to finance expansion and diversification. Investors—eager for instant capital without much formality—are ready to pay a high price, whereas the patient saver waits until the end, collecting a harvest of interest payments. There is another element in the auction that the lottery lacks. Sri Lankans are notorious gamblers; even in remote areas I have met cultivators who bet on horse races in England! Bidding in an auction introduces the spice of speculation and excitement. An enterprising player may pretend keen interest in the auction when his sole aim is to harass other members. The combination of eagerness for a loan and the fear of loss of prestige can inflate bidding, increasing the discounts that are offered and hence the dividends that can be earned. Naturally this type of game also enhances the probability of default.

Cheetu Membership

One finds traces of *cheetu* in every corner of Sri Lanka, and membership embraces all strata of society. Even the very poor have their clubs with minimal deposits of one or two rupees, a handful of rice and sugar, or government-issued food coupons. There are a few peculiarities, though. One is the general atmosphere of secrecy that surrounds membership. Kennedy (1977), writing about his experience in Korea, attributes this to the dubious official reputation of ROSCAs. Officially, *cheetu* are also suspect in Sri Lanka, and the government has enacted legislation in a vain attempt to control them. In India, national legislation is also pending. The secrecy may have sources other than fear of official disapproval. Individuals appear to make an effort to hide the extent of their involvement in *cheetu* even from their friends and relatives. Members do not want to be constantly harangued to share their savings with others. Even within families, membership is sometimes a closely guarded secret.

Many informants refer to a *cheetu* as a pastime for women. If one judges by numbers alone there are more female than male members. But usually the men pay the greater part of their wives' subscriptions, and women also substitute for their husbands by having two stakes in one *cheetu* or subscribing to two or more clubs. The term "pastime" is hardly appropriate. Gone are the days when ROSCAs, as Geertz

(1962) has put it, had a socializing function. Festive meetings, in which members discuss community and other-than-financial affairs, are now the exception in Sri Lanka. In most lottery societies players meet only once to draw lots and decide the ranking order. In auction *cheetu,* although members still do meet, an atmosphere of business prevails, with members going their own way after the auction is over. The signs of growing individualization in Sri Lankan society are also noticeable in *cheetu.*

Although a *cheetu* may contain more than 40 participants, the ideal group size is judged to be 10 to 20. A small group means a small fund, but faster rotation. A larger group increases the size of the collective savings, but also increases the chances of failure and default. It is difficult for people in an agricultural community, where income is irregular, to make regular subscriptions to a savings club. The availability of off-farm income makes it easier to come up with regular cash deposits. In the rural economy, ROSCAs tend to be small, and their success greatly depends on the skill and financial strength of the organizer.

Commissions and Default

A *cheetu* involves little administration. Organizers carry a small notebook to keep track of both contributions and payouts. Recipients are seldom requested to provide collateral, guarantors, or other forms of security. This makes the *cheetu* vulnerable but keeps costs down. The important cost items in a ROSCA are commissions and default. Although both members and organizers rarely discuss commissions and frequently deny their existence, most presidents receive some payment when a member collects his or her fund. Payments vary between 2 to 5 percent of total contributions. In one instance I came upon a novel way of extracting a commission. In a club at Illawakulam, a village near the west coast, some members paid their contributions partly in eggs. The eggs were arbitrarily valued by the female president below the going market rate, and this enabled her to make a profit on egg sales.

Commissions reward organizers for their troubles and responsibilities. The organizer is responsible for keeping the *cheetu* alive, collecting subscriptions, and pushing slow payers. In cases of default the organizer has the option of accepting the loss, dividing it with other players (with their consent), or dissolving the club and risking his or her reputation. In Sri Lanka regular *cheetu* meetings have become rare, and players may have little inkling of what goes on in their club. This is the cost of the loss of the socializing function of *cheetu*. Because members are willing to leave organizational burdens to the organizers, it is reasonable that organizers get a commission. Default, in principle, is borne by the organizer. Over time, organizers have developed techniques to protect the ROSCA against such mishap. At drawing time they juggle the lots to try to place doubtful cases near the end of the cycle. They also collect contributions in parts, making several rounds instead of one to remind members of their obligations. They defer payment of funds or distribute funds in installments, even when this causes dissatisfaction and grumbling among recipients.

Organizers understandably do not relish talking about default. One female president estimated that in a group of 12 members there is bound to be 1 defaulter. With a certain measure of resignation she volunteered that the defaulter is too often a relative. That would put the loss percentage at about 8, if the defaulter is the first recipient (although this is unlikely, since the president knows her relatives' reputations). If the default takes place halfway through the cycle, the rate comes down to 4 percent. This seems a fair estimate and would explain why commissions seldom exceed 5 percent. The odds do not seem to explain why a person would be willing to take the president's job, although receipt of the first fund free of discount provides additional compensation.

Profile of an Organizer

The profile of the *cheetu* organizer in Sri Lanka has undergone a major face lift. The amiable, social atmosphere of yesterday's ROSCA is rapidly giving way to an impersonal version of a savings and loan society. *Cheetu* membership no longer is confined to the small, communal in-group where the members know each other. Members of a *cheetu* can be drawn from several villages, and the auction system is increasingly popular. This has its implications for *cheetu* strategy, calling for other mechanisms to regulate membership eligibility, group size, rotation of the fund, credit rating, and repayment. The recent high rate of inflation has also had an impact.

The successful organizer nowadays is a businessperson with a solid financial reputation.[3] Only the financially strong can keep a ROSCA afloat by making contributions for members who cannot pay on time. Moneylending has become a logical extension of presiding over a *cheetu,* and many members confirmed in interviews that they regularly borrow from the organizer. One of the attractions of joining a savings club is that it entitles participants to a line of credit in times of need. Who else can offer this security but a person of financial repute?

Business people, for their part, have strong incentives to organize ROSCAs and similar types of savings schemes. It enhances their reputation and creates goodwill. I have seen women in the very popular and competitive catering business who, as a service to clients, were expected to extend credit and organize ROSCAs to stay in business. Another category is the shopkeepers who may have to fall back on *cheetu* to get customers to pay their bills.

Organizers also have a professional interest in savings schemes because of the opportunity these schemes offer for acquiring working capital. They are generally entitled to draw the first fund. Others arrange with players to collect contributions ahead of schedule, perhaps weekly instead of at the end of the month. They may also use members' contributions for short-term lending or to finance private business. A week or a month's respite in capital-scarce economies may mean survival in the extremely competitive short-term lending market. Daily loans, carrying 10 percent interest, delivered in the morning and repaid in the evening, are common in the atomized market trade where a bunch of bananas is resold piecemeal, a pineapple is offered for sale in slices, and a box of sugar is sold in single lumps.

Finally there are commissions. Small payments can become quite attractive when an organizer presides over several clubs at a time, when contributions are substantial, or when the rotation cycle is very short. Managing ROSCAs has become a profession that requires skill. Unmistakably, there is in Sri Lanka a trend toward professionalization of the job. The days when such clubs were viewed as an agreeable pastime are over.

Conclusions

Discussions of the role of informal financial intermediaries in low-income countries are usually colored by emotion, prejudice, and a lack of facts (Barton 1979). Critics often charge that informal financial services are too expensive for the poor. The assumptions of the existence of monopoly profits and the vice-like grip of informal lenders over their borrowers are part of the rationale for cheap formal credit. A fair appraisal of the costs and benefits of informal financial service is, however, impeded by a lack of research. One should not expect monopoly profits to be terribly important, since there are few barriers to entry into informal financial intermediation and competitive forces generally prevail (Ladman and Torrico 1981).

Admittedly, the financial services of informal intermediaries are often costly, but when rural borrowers are presented with a choice between cheap formal and expensive informal credit, they often choose the informal. A survey of consumer finance by Sri Lanka's Central Bank in 1973 estimated that the rural credit market share of the insitutional sector was no more than 21 percent. Some 80 percent of rural households, therefore, depended on informal-sector finance. Since 1977, a severe contraction in formal-sector cultivation loans has increased the relative importance of informal credit.[4] A recent survey in the Philippines described a similar situation (Presidential Committee 1980).

Informal financial arrangements accommodate savers, borrowers, and lenders in the rural economy. Poor rural households have special incentives to save in order to balance uneven flows of income and expenditure and to develop lines of credit. Because of the smallness of actual savings and the indivisibility of prospective investments, it often takes individuals substantial time to save desired amounts. Savers who want to shelter idle funds need to find a safe depository, and they often do this in the informal sector in one of the multitude of individual and group arrangements that exist.

The existence of traditional savings groups in the Third World has been well documented. Less documented is the fact that many such groups are presided over by moneylending entrepreneurs who usually combine several roles: storekeepers, rice millers, landlords, input dealers, and traders. This type of entrepreneur regards the provision of financial services as a necessary cost element in the enterprise. He or she creates goodwill and increases entrepreneurial potential by organizing savings clubs, accepting deposits, and disbursing credit. Savings supplement the working capital and lead to closer personal contact. This allows the entrepreneur intimate knowledge of customers' financial standing and credit rating. Dealing with only a small circle of persons in face-to-face arrangements greatly facilitates his or her lending decisions and reduces both lenders' and borrowers' transaction costs.

To the saver, the attractive part of these arrangements is that a savings deposit creates a line of credit in times of need. Savings purchase security, and the need for security in a survival economy is compelling. The saver-borrower values the quick accessibility and flexibility of the multiple services provided by these entrepreneurs.

But do households in developing economies really have a choice between cheap formal and expensive informal lenders? As Gonzalez-Vega (Chapter 10) and others argue in this volume, low interest rates restrict the access of the poor to formal loans. Lenders, faced with excess loan demand, ration loans to exclude the most costly, the most risky, and the least influential individuals. An additional barrier to access is the cumbersome administrative procedures that accompany formal lending, raising borrowers' transaction costs to levels that are not much different from total costs of borrowing in the informal market.

The repeated demand for small loans, coupled with the risk of lending to agriculture, makes the cost of administering loans to individuals in a penny economy very high. Formal lenders are sensitive to risk and cost and need strong incentives to lend in rural areas. One incentive would be to allow them to raise interest rates on loans to levels similar to their costs of lending (Adams 1980). But to present borrowers with a real alternative, formal lenders should also reduce their elaborate machinery and paper work. More rapid handling of loan applications would make formal lenders more competitive intermediaries.

Speedy handling of loan applications, in turn, requires accurate credit rating of potential borrowers. One way to gauge someone's financial standing is to offer savings-deposit facilities. The informal lender, however, goes several steps further by combining group deposit and lending facilities with a range of services that keep him or her in constant touch with the clientele, thus providing superior information. In contrast to many formal lenders, informal lenders charge differential rates of interest and reduce risk by diversifying into product, input, and processing markets.

The need to assemble accurate information through close personal contact is restrictive. It is revealing that in the Philippines and Bolivia most informal lenders serve only small numbers of borrowers (Presidential Committee 1980; Ladman and Torrico 1981). This is also the case of Sri Lanka, where a moneylender typically serves only 20 to 50 borrowers. Likewise, the organization of informal savings and credit clubs seldom involves more than 20 participants, indicating the managerial limits of group lending.

A reevaluation of the role of informal finance in development is in order. Formal lenders can learn much from informal lenders about the strategies for rural financial intermediation. Informal lenders and organizers of savings and credit groups succeed in providing valuable services at a level where cooperatives, banks, and credit unions often have to discontinue operations because of low repayment rates, mismanagement, and substantial losses. Discontinuity in services undermines peoples' confidence in public financial insitutions.

Rural development planners need to change their views about informal financial intermediaries. This should result in removal of adverse legal restrictions (usury laws, Cheetu Ordinance, Chit Fund Bill) and the discontinuation of campaigns against moneylenders when no reliable data exist on their operations and practices. Instead of attempting to destroy informal intermediaries, innovative approaches that build on their strengths are long overdue.

Notes

I am greatly indebted to the Sarvodaya Research Centre in Colombo for its support and to J. D. Von Pischke and Dale W Adams for their comments and editorial advice.

1. A village may have separate societies for the rich and the poor, and caste differences may also decide membership. Ginimellegaha, a southern village with only 500 families, has three different burial societies.
2. *Samagan* literally means "company," *poli* means "interest," and *pettye* means "box."
3. Other organizers are those who have a regular income. In addition to drawing regular monthly wages, people such as teachers and public servants can fall back on salary advances.
4. Crop-production loans by the Peoples Bank—by far the most important formal financial institution in rural Sri Lanka—fell from an all-time record of Rps 365 million in 1977 to Rps 21.1 million in 1979–1980.

References

Adams, Dale W "Recent Performance of Rural Financial Markets." In *Borrowers and Lenders: Rural Financial Markets and Institutions in Developing Countries,* edited by John Howell. London: Overseas Development Institute, 1980.

Bailey, F. G. "Capital, Savings, and Credit in Highland Orissa, India." In *Capital, Savings, and Credit in Peasant Societies,* edited by R. Firth and B. S. Yamey. London: Allen and Unwin, 1964.

Barton, Clifton G. "Informal Financial Markets and the Design of Rural Credit Programs." In *Problems and Issues of Agricultural Credit and Rural Finance,* edited and published by the Bangladesh Bank. Dacca, 1979.

Bouman, F.J.A. "Indigenous Savings and Credit Societies in the Third World. A Message." *Savings and Development* 1(1977):181–218.

______. "The ROSCA: Financial Technology of an Informal Savings and Credit Institution in Developing Economies." *Savings and Development* 3(1979):253–276.

Central Bank of Ceylon. *Review of the Economy.* Colombo: Central Bank of Ceylon, 1979.

Geertz, Clifford. "The Rotating Credit Association: A 'Middle Rung' in Development." *Economic Development and Cultural Change* 3(1962):241–263.

Kennedy, Gerard F. "The Korean Kye: Maintaining Human Scale in Modernizing Society." *Center for Korean Studies* 3(1977):197–222.

Ladman, Jerry R., and Jose I. Torrico. "Informal Credit Markets in the Valle Alto of Cochabamba, Bolivia." In *1981 Proceedings of the Rocky Mountain*

Council on Latin American Studies Conference, edited by John J. Brasch and Susan R. Rouch. Lincoln: Office of International Programs, College of Business Administration, University of Nebraska, 1981, pp. 83–89.

Lele, Uma. *Food Grain Marketing in India; Private Performance and Public Policy.* Ithaca, N.Y.: Cornell University Press, 1971.

London, Paul A. *Merchants as Promoters of Rural Development: An Indian Case Study.* New York: Praeger, 1975.

Miracle, Marvin P., Diane S. Miracle, and Laurie Cohen. "Informal Savings Mobilization in Africa." *Economic Development and Cultural Change* 4(1980):701–724.

Nayar, C.P.S. *Personal Communication and Finance Corporations: A Study of "Unregulated Banks."* Madras: Institute for Financial Management and Research, 1982.

People's Bank. *Economic Review.* Colombo: People's Bank, January 1978.

Presidential Committee on Agricultural Credit. *A Study on the Informal Rural Financial Markets in Three Selected Provinces of the Philippines.* Manila: Central Bank of the Philippines, 1980.

Von Pischke, J. D. "Towards an Operational Approach to Savings for Rural Developers." *Savings and Development* 2(1978):43–55.

———. "The Political Economy of Specialized Farm Credit Institutions." In *Borrowers and Lenders: Rural Financial Markets and Institutions in Developing Countries,* edited by John Howell. London: Overseas Development Institute, 1980.

Weerasoria, W. S. *The Nattukottai Chettiar Merchant Bankers in Ceylon.* Colombo: Tisara Praasakayo Publishers, 1973.

20
Savings Mobilization: The Forgotten Half of Rural Finance

Robert C. Vogel

Providing loans at low rates of interest is widely believed to be the only essential function of financial institutions in the rural areas of low-income countries. However, the evidence increasingly indicates that policies reflected in low-interest-rate loans are failing to achieve their basic objectives of promoting agricultural output and redistributing income to the rural poor. Because credit is fungible, it is virtually impossible to promote specific agricultural activities with low-interest loans (Von Pischke and Adams 1980), and the main beneficiaries are not the rural poor, because the subsidy implicit in low-interest loans becomes concentrated in large loans to relatively wealthy farmers. Moreover, as Bourne and Graham point out in Chapter 3, financial institutions whose main function is low-interest-rate lending cannot be self-sustaining in the long run. They must instead depend continually on subsidized resources from some external source, typically their government or some international donor.

Ten years ago the *AID Spring Review of Small Farmer Credit* pointed out many of the problems with the subsidized-lending approach to rural finance, and one paper was even devoted to emphasizing the importance of voluntary savings mobilization (Adams 1973). Nonetheless, rural finance projects in low-income countries have continued to stress low-interest loans for agriculture while neglecting savings mobilization in rural areas. This bias toward lending is also reflected in the literature on rural finance; papers on savings generally ignore savings mobilization by financial intermediaries and deal instead with the determinants of the portion of income that is saved rather than consumed. The neglect of savings mobilization by formal financial institutions stands in sharp contrast to the savings activities found in informal finance in rural areas of low-income countries (Bouman 1977).

The neglect of savings mobilization can perhaps be explained in part by the often-heard arguments that savings cannot or should not be mobilized in rural areas of low-income countries. It is said that most of the rural population has no margin for saving over consumption and, in any case, does not respond to incentives such as higher interest rates. It is argued that if financial institutions were encouraged to mobilize savings aggressively, savings would simply be diverted from one institution to another or from rural to urban areas, and higher interest payments to depositors would drive the institutions toward bankruptcy or force them to lend outside of rural areas where higher returns can be obtained. A more basic explanation for the neglect of savings mobilization may be that it is inconsistent with policies of low-interest-rate lending.

This chapter is divided into two main sections. The first outlines four reasons for savings mobilization being an essential part of rural finance policies. The second describes in some detail the successful U.S. Agency for International Development and Banco Nacional para las Cooperativas (AID-BANCOOP) savings-mobilization project that was carried on in Peru during 1979–1981. This project shows that savings can be mobilized in rural areas of low-income countries when the proper incentives are present. The theoretical arguments in favor of savings mobilization together with the success of the AID-BANCOOP project strongly contradict the arguments already cited as to why savings should not, or cannot, be mobilized. Furthermore, the experience with credit unions under the AID-BANCOOP project suggests that the desire to maintain low-interest lending policies, and not the arguments against savings mobilization, are the main reason for the neglect of savings mobilization.

Four Arguments in Favor of Savings Mobilization

Income Redistribution

More equitable income distribution is an important objective of rural finance policies. Policies that improve savings opportunities can do far more to redistribute income toward the rural poor than projects based on low-interest-rate lending. Low interest rates create an excess demand for credit, thereby forcing financial institutions to ration credit away from small borrowers without traditional collateral who are perceived to be risky and costly to serve (Vogel 1979). Such rationing consists not only of loan refusals but also of transactions costs that can easily exceed interest costs for small borrowers (Adams and Nehman 1979). Even without the perverse concentration of credit resulting from low interest rates, an essential function of financial intermediaries—the pooling of resources—brings together relatively small amounts from many savers so that relatively large projects involving economies of scale can be undertaken. Hence, by their nature, financial intermediaries serve more savers than borrowers and have individual deposits that are smaller on the average than loans. Policies that focus on improving services for savers, not for borrowers, are thus the route for helping the rural poor.

There is a myth, already mentioned, that most of the rural population has no savings. If this were true, the rural poor would have become extinct long ago with the onset of the first emergency, and small farmers would have starved while waiting for the next harvest if they failed to save some of the previous harvest. The rural poor, more than anyone else, must have a liquid reserve to meet emergencies. Credit, usually from informal sources, can sometimes supplement this liquid reserve, but credit is available only to those who have actual or potential savings. Even the moneylender will not lend to someone with no accumulated or potential surplus, and friends and relatives, as well as savings and credit societies, usually require the ability to reciprocate (Bouman 1979).

The most important service that financial institutions can provide for rural savers is the opportunity to hold liquid deposits paying interest rates that are positive in real terms. Without this, the rural poor hold a variety of inflation hedges, many of which earn very low rates of return, and pay an inflation tax on any cash and deposits held for current obligations. The rural nonpoor, on the other hand, can often avoid these unfortunate alternatives by investing in trade, industry, or land, possibly in urban areas. There is another myth, also mentioned earlier, that most of the rural population does not respond to interest-rate incentives. This view is often based on response to so-called interest-rate reforms in which interest rates are raised slightly but continue to be negative in real terms. Sometimes interest rates on deposits are raised significantly, but financial institutions are expected to continue lending at low rates of interest. These institutions respond quite logically by discouraging deposits. Instead of convenient locations and hours of operation, rapid service, and a minimum of paper work, they provide the opposite and may impose relatively high minimum transaction size and balance requirements. High transactions costs can affect savers, as well as borrowers, and make the prophecy that the rural poor do not save and do not respond self-fulfilling.

Resource Allocation

Improved resource allocation is the second argument in favor of savings mobilization. Effective savings mobilization by financial intermediaries draws resources away from unproductive investments, especially inflation hedges, as the opportunity is provided to make deposits that earn positive real rates of interest (Vogel and Buser 1976). These resources can be on-lent by financial intermediaries for those activities that promise the highest rate of return (Shaw 1973; McKinnon 1973). Some arguments frequently heard against savings mobilization can actually help to clarify the ways in which effective savings mobilization can improve resource allocation. It is said that aggressive savings mobilization by one institution or one type of institution will only divert deposits from other institutions with no gain to society. However, this neglects the gain to savers, who would not have moved their deposits without being better off, and the fact that the financial institutions earning the highest risk-adjusted returns on funds entrusted to them will be able to compete most effectively for savings.

It is also argued that no additional savings will be generated because the rural population will not save more of their incomes in response to higher interest rates or other improvements in services for depositors. Such arguments confuse the flow of saving with the allocation of a stock of savings among competing assets and raise the question of whether savings allocated to inflation hedges, such as consumer durables, should be counted as saving or as consumption. Regardless of whether more is saved out of income, which is an open question both empirically and theoretically, effective savings mobilization can deploy the stock of assets of the rural population in more productive ways.

Arguments for savings mobilization are sometimes resisted by the assertion that higher interest rates for depositors will force rural financial institutions to lend outside of rural areas and outside priority sectors in order to obtain higher returns. But because credit is fungible, these resources are already flowing toward higher returns, often at a higher cost to society from the circumventing of credit controls. Attempts to control credit allocation not only impose unnecessary costs on society but also rob policymakers of important information. Incentives to misreport credit use mask the flow of resources away from priority sectors, hiding from policymakers the importance of removing the distortions that depress returns in rural areas (Larson and Vogel 1980).

Financial Institutions

The positive effect of savings mobilization on financial institutions is the third argument in favor of savings mobilization. Financial institutions neglecting savings mobilization are incomplete institutions. They not only fail to provide adequate services for rural savers, but they also make themselves less viable, as can be seen most clearly in the high rates of delinquency and default that plague most agricultural development banks (Vogel 1981). When financial institutions deal with clients only as borrowers, they forgo useful information about the savings behavior of these clients that could help to refine estimations of their creditworthiness. Furthermore, borrowers are more likely to repay promptly and lenders to take responsibility for loan recovery when they know that resources come from neighbors rather than from some distant government agency or international donor. Financial institutions that mobilize savings effectively from a variety of sectors are also likely to have a continual flow of resources available for lending, whereas those that neglect savings mobilization are inevitably subject to the feast-or-famine cycle of government and donor projects. Belief in the future availability of loans on a timely basis can be a strong incentive for borrowers to repay promptly.

Incentives

Savings mobilization provides appropriate incentives and discipline not only for rural financial markets and institutions but also for governments and international donors. The fourth argument is that financial institutions are likely to have little interest in savings mobilization or loan recovery when cheap funds are available through government loans, central bank rediscounts, or loans from international donors. It is largely ignored that the volume of resources that can be obtained through effective programs of savings mobilization and loan recovery is potentially far greater than the most optimistic estimates of the amount of subsidized loans and grants available from governments and international donors (Adams 1978). Emphasis on savings mobilization is also incompatible with programs of low-interest-rate lending because financial institutions cannot be expected to mobilize savings and on-lend them at interest rates that cover neither interest payments to depositors nor administrative costs. It has sometimes been alleged that government officials use subsidized lending as a means to distribute patronage (Ladman and Tinnermeier 1981). If true, this provides another reason for imposing the discipline of savings mobilization. International donors who find rural finance projects a convenient way to transfer resources to low-income countries should also find accompanying incentives to encourage rather than retard savings mobilization.

The AID-BANCOOP Savings Mobilization Project

In mid-1979 the U.S. Agency for International Development (AID) initiated a small two-year project in Peru supported by a US$500,000 grant to the Banco Nacional para las Cooperativas (BANCOOP), half for a credit fund and half for technical assistance. The technical assistance included support for opening new BANCOOP offices in the two target areas of Huancayo and Tingo Maria, the creation of a new BANCOOP division to provide technical assistance within BANCOOP and to cooperatives in the target areas, and an adviser to work with BANCOOP. Assistance with savings mobilization was to be directed not only to BANCOOP itself but also through BANCOOP to credit unions in the two target areas. The credit fund and some of the technical assistance were designed to support BANCOOP's rural lending activities, but the following discussion focuses primarily on the experience with savings mobilization.

BANCOOP is not a bank under Peruvian law, but performs most banking functions such as receiving deposits and making loans. BANCOOP is a second-level cooperative. Its directors are elected by the cooperatives that have become members by making capital contributions to BANCOOP. Nevertheless, BANCOOP deals not only with its member cooperatives, but also with nonmember cooperatives, individual members of cooperatives, and the general public. BANCOOP was selected by AID to be the focus of the project for two main reasons: (1) BANCOOP was already following a policy of high interest rates on loans and deposits within the limits imposed by Peruvian regulations, and (2) BANCOOP had been reasonably successful as an urban-based operation and was interested in expanding in rural areas. In order to understand the very adverse environment in which BANCOOP initiated savings-mobilization activities, it is useful to discuss first the recent experience of credit unions in Peru.

After years of impressive growth, Peruvian credit unions began to falter in the mid-1970s, largely as a result of a dramatic upsurge of inflation and the failure of credit unions to adjust their interest rates. From the early 1950s through 1973 the rate of inflation in Peru averaged less than 10 percent per year, but accelerated to over 30 percent per year in 1976 and 1977 and later climbed to over 50 percent. Until mid-1976 interest rates were rigidly controlled by the Peruvian Central Bank at 5 percent on savings deposits, 7 percent on time deposits, and 12 percent on short-term loans. These interest-rate ceilings were raised somewhat in mid-1976 and substantially during 1978. In 1979 and 1980, the main period of concern for this chapter, the ceiling rate on savings deposits was 30.5 percent, and time deposits of one-year duration earned up to 35.5 percent. The stated ceiling rate on loans was 32.5 percent, but effective rates of 60 percent or higher could easily be charged through the use of commissions, compensating balances, and other devices. Early in 1981 interest-rate ceilings were again raised significantly, to 50.5 percent on savings deposits and 54 percent on one-year time deposits, with a stated ceiling rate of 49.5 percent on loans.

When the AID-BANCOOP project was initiated in 1979, none of the five major credit unions in the two target areas had raised their interest rates, continuing the tradition of charging 1 percent per month on loans. With such low rates on loans, they were unable to compete effectively for time and savings deposits because other financial institutions, especially commercial banks, quickly took advantage of the increases in interest-rate ceilings. The credit unions continued to rely almost entirely on members' capital contributions, with dividends limited to 6 percent per year by Central Bank regulations.

Interest-rate policy created perverse incentives and serious problems for the credit unions. On one hand, members have a strong incentive to borrow as much as possible, because when interest rates on loans are far below the rate of inflation, it means that borrowers have to pay back in real terms much less than the amount borrowed. On the other hand, members have little or no incentive to save with their credit unions, because the purchasing power of deposits is rapidly eroded by inflation when adequate interest rates are not paid. Members who make capital contributions to their credit unions do so primarily to secure access to loans; loans can be as much as three times the amount of a member's capital contribution under the regulations of most Peruvian credit unions.

The results of these interest-rate policies can readily be seen in the serious problems experienced by credit unions in the two target areas of the AID-BANCOOP project (Gadway 1979). There were increasing complaints of severe shortages of loanable funds, as members' demands for low-interest loans far exceeded their capital contributions and meager time and savings deposits. Disgruntled members who were told that their approved loans could not be disbursed because of a lack of funds, or that there was no point in even applying for a loan, often ceased making capital contributions and became inactive. For some credit unions the loss of active members created serious repayment problems, as members saw no point in repaying old loans when the prospects for obtaining new loans were bleak. In addition, many credit unions experienced substantial operating deficits as stagnant interest income failed to keep pace with inflating operating costs, and even those that grew in nominal terms saw the purchasing power of their capital dramatically reduced after the mid-1970s.

Savings Mobilization by BANCOOP

BANCOOP initiated its savings-mobilization activities in the two target areas in late 1979 in this adverse economic environment. In addition to having experienced rapid inflation, the Peruvian economy had shown no real growth in several years, and BANCOOP also faced potentially formidable competition from financial institutions, including commercial banks. Nevertheless, as shown in Table 20.1, by mid-1980 each of the BANCOOP target offices had already mobilized far more than the overall mid-1981 goal of US$150,000.[1] The growth in time and savings deposits, whether deflated to real soles or converted to dollars, continued beyond the end of the project and spread to BANCOOP offices outside the target areas. By October 1981, these deposits were equal to more than US$1 million for the Huancayo and Tingo Maria offices and more than US$5 million for all of BANCOOP. The success of savings mobilization, beginning in Huancayo and Tingo Maria, has changed the financial structure of BANCOOP, as time and savings deposits have substantially surpassed demand-deposit balances. Furthermore, according to figures from the superintendent of banks, deposits at BANCOOP grew far more rapidly during 1980 and 1981 than deposits at commercial banks or other financial institutions.

The change in BANCOOP's financial structure has not always been welcomed by BANCOOP officials. Especially in the early stages of the project, BANCOOP officials wanted to mobilize inexpensive resources through demand deposits and capital contributions from member cooperatives, rather than through time and savings deposits, requiring substantial interest payments. However, the hope of mobilizing low-cost resources proved to be illusory. As in the case of credit unions, members make capital contributions to request loans, so BANCOOP found that capital contributions increased loan demand more than the supply of resources available for lending. Demand deposits have not provided a stable source of funds for lending, because inflows and outflows have been large relative to balances, nor have they been low cost, because of the clerical expenses involved. In spite of managers' initial reluctance, time and savings deposits have become the main source of funds for BANCOOP, and the cost of mobilizing these deposits has been far surpassed by the interest earned on the resulting loans.

Table 20.1 BANCOOP's Selected Month-End Deposits Balances (Thousands of Current U.S. Dollars)

	Total BANCOOP			Huancayo Office			Tingo Maria Office		
	Demand Deposits	Savings Deposits	Time Deposits	Demand Deposits	Savings Deposits	Time Deposits	Demand Deposits	Savings Deposits	Time Deposits
1979									
November	625	258	274	60	8	9	58	27	28
December	926	306	329	77	18	9	92	95	47
1980									
January	991	322	358	66	21	22	172	108	63
July	1,583	793	835	219	109	291	135	216	101
December	1,746	1,216	1,113	136	164	286	122	345	106
1981									
January	1,578	1,203	1,129	114	162	254	106	311	122
July	1,627	2,151	1,553	101	252	140	166	487	140
October	2,419	3,314	2,141	89	263	155	314	602	177

Source: BANCOOP unpublished reports.

Analysis of the BANCOOP experience clarifies certain factors that appear to be crucial for successful savings mobilization. First is the payment of high interest rates on time and savings deposits, the maximum permitted under Peruvian regulations, in order to compete with other financial institutions and to draw resources away from inflation hedges and cash hoards. However, regulated interest rates on deposits continued to be negative in real terms throughout 1979 and 1980 and thus were not as effective an incentive as they might have been. The rapid growth of time and savings deposits at BANCOOP during 1981, especially relative to demand deposits, may be related to the substantial increase in interest-rate ceilings at the beginning of 1981.

Confidence of depositors in a financial institution and good service for these depositors are other factors that are crucial for successful savings mobilization. In the quality of service for depositors, BANCOOP has usually, but not always, compared quite favorably to other financial institutions, especially commercial banks. Good service and, to some extent, depositor confidence depend on employee performance, which in turn depends on employee morale and appropriate incentives. BANCOOP's savings campaigns, to be described, have usually involved specific incentives for employees tied to the amount of time and savings deposits mobilized.

BANCOOP's office in Huancayo serves a much more heavily populated area than the office in Tingo Maria opened several months earlier than the latter office. But as shown by the data in Table 20.1, the Tingo Maria office mobilized substantial amounts of time and savings deposits in late 1979 and early 1980, especially during the first savings campaign, whereas the Huancayo office mobilized almost nothing until March 1980. It was found that attempts by a member of BANCOOP's board of directors from Huancayo to intervene in the day-to-day operations of that office had led to a high rate of turnover in managers and other key personnel during most of 1979. This, in turn, harmed employee morale and reduced public confidence in the Huancayo office. In addition, the incentives used in Huancayo during the first savings campaign created serious doubts as to whether any rewards would actually be paid.

Effective savings mobilization campaigns are the final factor to be discussed of those that were crucial to BANCOOP's success. In addition to incentives for employees, the three campaigns run during 1980 had two other important features: effective publicity and attractive prizes. The first campaign, which began in December 1979 and ran through mid-January 1980, involved free instant photographs for those who deposited small amounts, a raffle of cameras, and free cameras for those who made large time deposits. The second campaign, which ran from early February until April, involved a raffle of school supplies and bicycles, free school supplies for small deposits, and free bicycles for large time deposits. The third, which began in July and ran until September, featured raffles of color television sets and other electrical appliances and immediate prizes of these articles for those who made large time deposits. The increases in time and savings deposits at the Huancayo and Tingo Maria offices were unusually large during most of the campaign periods.

The figures in Table 20.1 also reveal that since mid-1980 time and savings deposits have tended to grow faster at the BANCOOP offices outside the target areas. This is not due to shortcomings in the Huancayo and Tingo Maria offices, but rather to the adoption of the same savings-mobilization techniques by other offices. An interesting question is why this took so long. One reason may have been the underpricing of funds for interoffice transfers, which has since been corrected. But the main reason seems to have been the initial belief of most BANCOOP officials that savings-mobilization campaigns were too costly unless paid for with AID funds. This belief proved incorrect, as the costs of the savings campaigns (divided about equally among publicity, prizes, and incentive payments to employees) averaged only about 2 percent of the amounts mobilized, only a small fraction of the interest payments on these deposits.

Analysis of Depositors and Deposits

Preliminary analysis has been made of the more than 3,000 individual savings accounts opened at BANCOOP target offices through August 31, 1981 (Burkett 1981).[2] This analysis indicates more fully the importance of savings-mobilization campaigns, as the number of accounts opened during campaign periods and the balances in these accounts substantially exceed the noncampaign periods. In addition, some interesting differences emerge among the three campaigns. The first campaign tended to be the least successful, perhaps due to the importance of learning by doing. The second campaign, which focused on school supplies, brought more new accounts than the third campaign, which focused on color televisions and other electrical appliances. Not surprisingly, however, the third campaign tended to bring larger deposits. A fear frequently expressed early in the project was that deposits made during campaign periods to obtain prizes would be quickly withdrawn. Ratios of month-end balances to initial deposits show that this did not occur.

Preliminary analysis has also been made of the characteristics of BANCOOP savings-deposit holders with respect to marital status, sex, distance from the relevant BANCOOP office, and occupation (Burkett 1981).[3] Perhaps the most interesting of these characteristics is occupation. According to the 1972 Peruvian census, the population of the provinces served by the Huancayo office is 35 percent rural, and 42 percent of those economically active are engaged in agriculture. For the province served by the Tingo Maria office, the figures are 67 percent rural and 66 percent engaged in agriculture. The occupations of the BANCOOP deposit holders reflect these differences in the underlying population. The Huancayo office serves a broad range of occupations, but relatively few farmers, whereas the Tingo Maria office predominantly serves farmers. In addition, balances in the savings accounts of farmers tend to be larger than those of other occupational groups, so that BANCOOP seems to be reasonably successful in reaching the rural population for which the project was designed. Furthermore, according to figures from the superintendent of banks, the balances in BANCOOP's savings accounts are less highly concentrated in large accounts than is the case for commercial banks.

In addition, interviews were carried out with a random sample of 85 BANCOOP savings-deposit holders at the Huancayo office and a control group of 85 individuals who were not BANCOOP depositors (Poyo 1981).[4] The sample of BANCOOP depositors corresponded quite closely to the universe of BANCOOP depositors in the characteristics mentioned above, and the control group turned out to be quite similar to the BANCOOP sample in economic status and other characteristics. The main reason given for saving by BANCOOP depositors, and by those in the control group who stated that they had savings, was for possible emergencies. Other reasons were much less important but included future investments, the ability to obtain a loan more easily, future consumption, and earning interest, in that order of importance.

When those interviewed were asked why they chose a particular financial institution, the main differences were not between BANCOOP depositors and nondepositors, but rather between individuals who were members of credit unions and those who were not. For credit-union members, the possibility of obtaining a loan was clearly predominant, followed by confidence in the institution, with almost no weight given to any other factor.[5] Those who were not credit-union members placed as much, or more, weight on good service, location, hours, and interest payments. Promotional campaigns were not indicated to be important, but elsewhere BANCOOP depositors stated that radio, television, and newspapers were the primary means through which they came to know of BANCOOP. Such publicity is a key component of savings campaigns. In addition, a substantial majority of BANCOOP depositors and the control group looked favorably on raffles by financial institutions.

The interviews also collected interesting information about sources of savings deposits. From the arguments against savings mobilization and the view that deposits in different financial institutions are close substitutes, it might be expected that transfers from another institution would be the main source. However, only two BANCOOP depositors and none of the control group gave that answer. In addition, when asked what they would have done with funds if they had not been deposited at BANCOOP (or some other institution), both consumption and investment ranked well ahead of deposits at another financial institution. Furthermore, a major reason that those in the control group gave for not being clients of BANCOOP was that they already had an account at another financial institution. Also, the control group often stated that they held savings in the form of cash, inventories, or consumer durables, something depositors almost never did.

Other Project Characteristics

Two other aspects of the AID-BANCOOP project merit brief discussion: BANCOOP's lending performance and the savings mobilization by credit unions. Under the impact of inflation BANCOOP had drastically shortened the maturity of its loan portfolio and had shifted away from cooperatives and toward nonmembers, both businesses and individuals. Successful savings mobilization has allowed BANCOOP to expand its lending to cooperatives and to the agricultural sector in real terms since the beginning of the project. However, uncertainties surrounding the continuing rapid inflation in Peru have kept the maturity structure quite short (Wohanka 1980).[6] In addition, nominal interest rates on BANCOOP loans may still be too low, as reflected in continuing excess demand. With well-known and conveniently located clients demanding all the funds that BANCOOP is mobilizing, there is no incentive for BANCOOP to develop new lending techniques or to search for new clients in more remote rural areas. BANCOOP has also experienced difficulties in lending to some cooperatives that hold the view that BANCOOP, as a bank for cooperatives, should provide cheap funds.

Under the AID-BANCOOP project technical assistance has been available from BANCOOP to help credit unions in the target areas with savings mobilization, but these credit unions have been slow to accept higher-interest-rate policies. By the end of 1979, only two of the five major credit unions in the target areas had raised their interest rates. One of these changed its interest-rate policies only after it had reached the verge of collapse and had received an inordinate proportion of the project's technical assistance in the form of detailed analysis and persistent explanation of the consequences of its low-interest-rate policies (Gadway 1979). The other, however, quickly raised its interest rates to the maximum permitted under Central Bank regulations. These credit unions subsequently received some technical assistance with savings mobilization from BANCOOP and together mobilized approximately the amount of savings that was established as the project goal for all credit unions in the two target areas.

Each of the other three credit unions finally raised its interest rates during 1980, but in each case it was too little and too late to be effective for mobilizing savings under the project. One credit union was convinced to raise interest rates on loans because of operating losses, but the importance of raising interest rates sufficiently to compete with other financial institutions for savings was not recognized. A second raised rates to the maximum permitted on time and savings deposits, but gave so little publicity to these changes that several employees of the credit union were unaware of the change. Both of these credit unions also experienced considerable turmoil in early 1981 resulting in major changes in management. The last credit union did not make any changes in interest rates until almost the end of 1980, and the increases finally made were trivial. Such shortcomings in BANCOOP's lending performance and in savings mobilization by credit unions gave these aspects of the project a mediocre rating in the official evaluation, in contrast to the outstanding grade for savings mobilization by BANCOOP (Adams and Larson 1981).

Conclusions

The AID-BANCOOP project shows clearly that savings can successfully be mobilized in rural areas of low-income countries. Moreover, many of the benefits described under the four arguments in favor of savings mobilization appear to have been achieved. Rural savers were benefited as they deposited their savings at BANCOOP in response to high interest rates and other elements of good service that were provided. Lending by BANCOOP to priority sectors in the target areas also increased, but some of BANCOOP's newly mobilized resources undoubtedly flowed toward higher rates of return in other sectors and areas because of the distortions that have tended to keep returns low in Peruvian agriculture. Successful savings mobilization has made BANCOOP less dependent on governments and international donors for subsidized funds and also appears to have made BANCOOP more financially viable through increased profits and reduced loan delinquency.

The importance of the fourth argument, that savings mobilization provides appropriate incentives and discipline for rural financial markets and institutions, can best be seen by examining more closely the mediocre performance by credit unions. This highlights some of the problems that can be anticipated in projects that emphasize voluntary rural savings mobilization. At least four reasons can be suggested for the reluctance of Peruvian credit unions to change their interest-rate policies, even when such changes were so clearly necessary. First, credit unions may simply be confused by cooperative rhetoric. Members may genuinely believe that raising interest rates on loans would be usurious and that problems can best be dealt with by appeals to altruism, against the economic rationality of individual members. Second, members who are on boards of directors or key policymaking committees may have better access to credit-union loans than most other members and may use the rhetoric of cooperativism to keep interest rates low on loans for their personal benefit. Third, credit-union board members and management change frequently and often have little professional knowledge of economics or finance. They may view as very risky and of little potential benefit any departure from traditional policies. Fourth, credit unions continually hope for some low-cost source of funds through which they can avoid the unpleasantness of raising interest rates to compete for savings. Experience with government agencies or international donors often suggests that such funds may be forthcoming.

The fourth reason for the reluctance of credit unions to raise interest rates appeared to cause some problems for BANCOOP's relationship with credit unions under the project. As indicated above, some cooperatives expected low-interest-rate funds from BANCOOP because it is the bank for cooperatives. Moreover, the fact that BANCOOP had received a grant from AID had been widely publicized throughout the Peruvian cooperative movement. Thus, when BANCOOP officials visited credit unions in target areas, often in the company of AID consultants to the project, the credit unions expected offers of low-interest-rate funds from BANCOOP and were keenly disappointed when all they received were offers of technical assistance with something for which they had no great enthusiasm. In addition, BANCOOP had no specific incentives to provide technical assistance with savings mobilization to the credit unions. It does not appear that BANCOOP feared competition for savings from the credit unions, but rather that the scarce technical-assistance resources that BAN-

COOP might devote to the credit unions would thereby be lost to BANCOOP itself.

In spite of the problems encountered with credit unions under the AID-BANCOOP project, or more generally in Peru and other low-income countries, these institutions appear to have considerable potential to serve the rural poor. They can be seen as a natural outgrowth of indigenous savings and credit societies, and they possess some important advantages in information about their members as both savers and borrowers. Unfortunately, little attention has been paid to understanding the incentives that govern the behavior of such institutions or to incorporating into projects incentives that will encourage effective savings mobilization. The four arguments in favor of savings mobilization and the experience of BANCOOP show that voluntary savings can and should be mobilized in the rural areas of low-income countries. The experience of the credit unions indicates not only some of the difficulties in implementing successful savings-mobilization projects but also what happens to financial institutions that fail to mobilize savings. The challenge for government agencies and international donors is to supplement the resources available in rural areas of low-income countries in ways that take incentives into account and thereby encourage rather than retard effective savings mobilization.

Notes

Financial support from AID Washington and Peru and the collaboration of George Wohanka, Jeffrey Poyo, John Gadway, Paul Burkett, and several BANCOOP and AID officials have been essential for this paper. I am also indebted to many individuals for insights into finance in developing countries, especially to Dale W Adams, F.J.A. Bouman, Claudio Gonzalez-Vega, Edward Shaw, and many of the participants in The Ohio State University rural-finance program. However, none of these individuals or institutions is responsible for the views expressed or errors remaining in this paper.

1. For two reasons this is a conservative measure of the amount of savings mobilized. First, it entirely omits savings deposited but subsequently withdrawn. Second, it is calculated in dollars at the exchange rate for each month, rather than when the savings were mobilized. The exchange rate moved from 250 soles per dollar in late 1979 to almost 500 in late 1981.

2. Time deposits are not yet included in the analysis because data from the Huancayo office were incomplete.

3. It would have been useful to have asked BANCOOP depositors for more information. However, such questioning was kept to a minimum because it could have reduced the effectiveness of savings mobilization by the

imposition of additional transactions costs on individuals opening new accounts.

4. Interviews could not safely be carried out for the Tingo Maria office because of illegal coca production in the area. In Huancayo, the nonresponse rate was quite low. Nonresponses resulted not from refusals to answer, but rather from the inability to locate depositors (of these, almost all had small inactive accounts).

5. Such views are not surprising given the recent history of Peruvian credit unions.

6. Wohanka (1980) also evaluates the impact of successful savings mobilization on BANCOOP's financial viability and finds it to be favorable, although accounting procedures for delinquent loans make BANCOOP's stated profits dubious.

References

Adams, Dale W. "The Case for Voluntary Savings Mobilization: Why Rural Capital Markets Flounder." In *AID Spring Review of Small Farmer Credit*, vol. 19, edited and published by the Agency for International Development. Washington, D.C., June 1973.

______. "Mobilizing Household Savings Through Rural Financial Markets." *Economic Development and Cultural Change* 26(1978):547–560.

Adams, Dale W, and Donald W. Larson. "Evaluation of the BANCOOP Project." Unpublished paper, Agency for International Development, Lima, Peru, May 1981.

Adams, D. W, and G. I. Nehman. "Borrowing Costs and the Demands for Rural Credit." *Journal of Development Studies* 15(1979):165–176.

Bouman, F.J.A. "Indigenous Savings and Credit Societies in the Third World. A Message." *Savings and Development* 1(1977):181–218.

______. "The ROSCA: Financial Technology of an Informal Savings and Credit Institution in Developing Economies." *Savings and Development* 3(1979):253–276.

Burkett, Paul. "Savings Mobilization in the Third World: A Case Study of Peru." Unpublished paper, Syracuse University, August 1981.

Gadway, John. "La Situacion Actual de la Cooperativa de Ahorro y Credito Protectora Ltda. 261." Unpublished paper, Agency for International Development, Lima, Peru, October 1979.

Ladman, Jerry R., and Ronald L. Tinnermeier. "The Political Economy of Agricultural Credit: The Case of Bolivia." *American Journal of Agricultural Economics* 63(1981):66–72.

Larson, Donald W., and Robert C. Vogel. "Interaction of Price and Credit Policies in Costa Rican Agriculture." Economics and Sociology Occasional Papers no. 813, Department of Agricultural Economics and Rural Sociology, The Ohio State University, November 1980.

McKinnon, Ronald I. *Money and Capital in Economic Development*. Washington, D.C.: Brookings Institution, 1973.

Poyo, Jeffrey. "Las Bases de Una Exitosa Movilizacion de Ahorros." Unpublished paper, Economics Department, Syracuse University, August 1981.

Shaw, Edward S. *Financial Deepening in Economic Development.* New York: Oxford University Press, 1973.

Vogel, Robert C. "Subsidized Interest Rates and the Rationing of Agricultural Credit in Developing Countries." In *Problems and Issues of Agricultural Credit and Rural Finance,* edited and published by the Bangladesh Bank. Dacca, 1979.

______. "Rural Financial Market Performance: Implications of Low Delinquency Rates." *American Journal of Agricultural Economics* 63(1981):58–65.

Vogel, Robert C., and Stephen A. Buser. "Inflation, Financial Repression, and Capital Formation in Latin America." In *Money and Finance in Economic Growth and Development,* edited by Ronald I. McKinnon. New York: Marcel Dekker, 1976.

Von Pischke, J. D., and Dale W Adams. "Fungibility and the Design and Evaluation of Agricultural Credit Projects." *American Journal of Agricultural Economics* 62(1980):719–726.

Wohanka, George. "The Impact of Successful Savings Mobilization on BANCOOP's Financial Viability and Lending Behavior." Unpublished paper, Agency for International Development, Lima, Peru, December 1980.

21 Working Capital and Nonfarm Rural Enterprises

Peter Kilby
Carl E. Liedholm
Richard L. Meyer

Research on rural financial markets in developing countries has largely ignored nonfarm rural enterprises. The 1973 *AID Spring Review of Small Farmer Credit* represented an ambitious attempt to summarize theory and empirical evidence about rural finance.[1] Nevertheless, the nonfarm sector is only rarely mentioned in any of the papers presented in this extensive review. Only a few recent articles and reports can be found on some aspects of financing the rural nonfarm sector, and yet this sector accounts for a substantial portion of the work time of from 30 to over 50 percent of the rural population (Chuta and Liedholm 1979; Meyer and Larson 1978). Of this very important segment of the rural economy, only marketing and certain processing industries have received scrutiny from economists. The efficiency of nonfarm firms and the constraints to their development are not long-standing questions. This neglect holds even in the much-researched area of rural financial markets, where the fungibility of finance implies that nonfarm activities are an integral part of household financial analysis; yet, for lack of a comprehensive set of household accounts, these activities are usually ignored by researchers and policymakers.

There are several reasons why the provision of working capital to small nonfarm enterprises in rural areas may be important. First, in a number of surveys a shortage of working capital is reported by entrepreneurs as their first- or second-most pressing problem.[2] Second, private capital markets have generally not served the nonfarm sector because of an absence of collateral and because of the high costs of gathering information. Although public lending programs, concerned with launching relatively large "modern" enterprises, have responded in part by providing long-term capital, there are very few schemes that provide short-term finance. Third, working capital appears to be a relatively larger component of total capital for smaller enterprises than for larger ones.[3] Fourth, the prospects for an efficient lending operation should be better for short-term credit because of short gestation and quick turnover, both of which imply a more rapid learning process for the lender. Finally, lender risks should be lower than those associated with fixed-capital loans inasmuch as working-capital loans are self-liquidating when geared to actual or prospective production orders.

Nonfarm Rural Enterprises

Most microeconomic research deals with a single enterprise or group of enterprises. Typically, specialists in agricultural finance assume that the only commercial activity of the borrower's household is farming. Likewise, researchers and decision makers in the small-industry field assume that industrial borrowers have no commercial commitment other than manufacturing. Failure to consider multiple commercial activities leads to faulty analysis of resource allocation and to development schemes that do not achieve their objectives.

A more realistic modeling of the diversity of rural households is presented in Figure 21.1. A household of Type A is the one most frequently considered in farm management analysis: It is assumed that 100 percent of the productive time is spent in year-round farming activities. Type D is the one assumed by the small-industry specialist: The sole commercial activity is manufacturing. These pure types, however, probably account for less than half of rural households. In Type B the household mixes farm and nonfarm enterprises, such as manufacturing, over the entire year. In Type C households, labor is always 100 percent specialized, but the specialization changes with the season. Types E and F parallel B and C in the simultaneous or sequential mix of commercial enterprises, but here both activities are nonfarm.

A number of studies can be drawn upon to show the proportion of rural households that fall within Types B to F. Census data on nonfarm employment, which exclude those for whom it is a secondary occupation, reveal that for 13 countries from 14 to 49 percent of the rural labor force is engaged in nonfarm activities (Chuta and Liedholm 1979). These activities include manufacturing, processing, repair, construction, trade, transport, and services. If rural towns with up to 20,000 or 30,000 in population are included, the range rises to

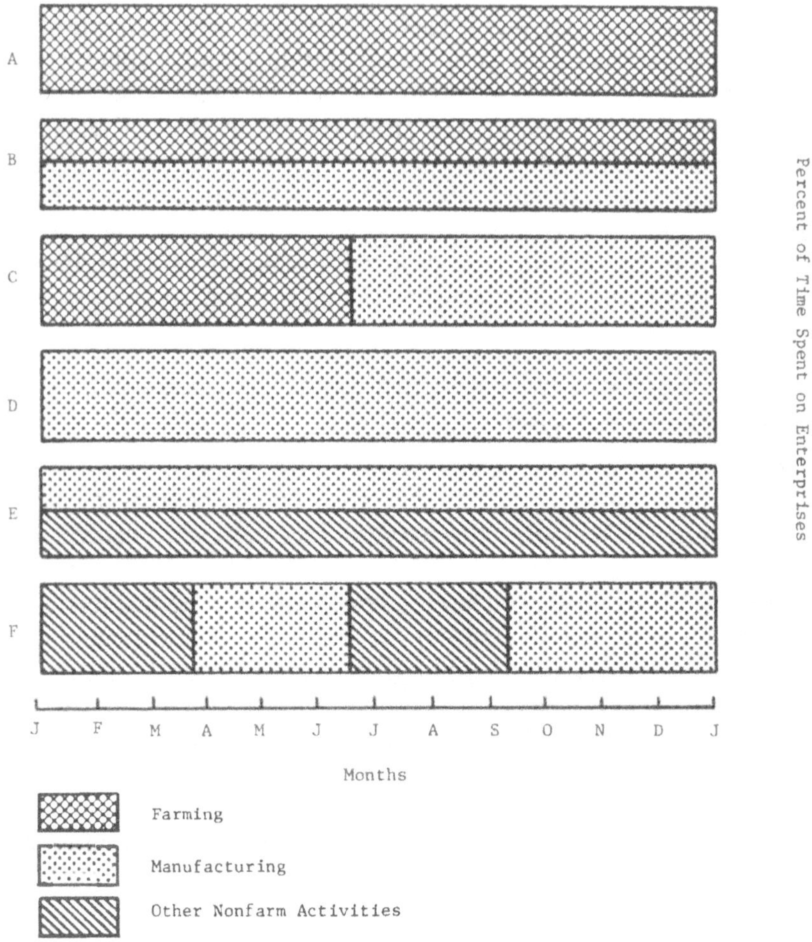

Figure 21.1 Commercial Production and Time Allocation in Rural Households.

24 to 51 percent. And when secondary occupations are brought into the picture, the proportion of rural households that have some of their members engaged in nonfarm commercial activities rises much higher.

Multiple rural household enterprises have far-reaching implications for the allocation of labor and capital. Indeed, in a low-income, high-risk environment the flexibility of the rural household is a major strength vis-à-vis the specialized large-scale producers in the urban sector.[4] With respect to our immediate concern, multiple sources of cash receipts affect the working-capital situation in two ways. First, the demand for external finance associated with an enterprise is affected by its synchronization with the household's other cash-generating activities. In contrast to specialized households (Type A and D), it is virtually certain that two or more simultaneous enterprises (Type B and E) will have nonidentical time patterns of cash flow and hence provide internal cross finance. This complementary effect, which reduces recourse to external borrowing, may or may not hold for Types C and F. Furthermore, with mixed enterprises, households are likely to be subject to less year-to-year income variation and thus be less risky customers when they do borrow.

Rural Industry and Working Capital

Our examination of working capital focuses on a subgroup of nonfarm activities for which there is a reasonable degree of structural homogeneity. This subgroup is rural industry, which includes manufacturing, processing, and repair. As noted earlier, these enterprises, the majority of which are very small, account for a substantial share of rural nonfarm employment.

The sizable literature on small industry by economists,[5] much of which is applicable to rural small-scale industry, covers numerous aspects of small manufacturing ventures; working capital is usually not among these. The explanation of this omission is an orientation by academic economists toward fixed assets, aid donors' interest in lending schemes with high foreign-exchange components, and a paucity of requisite statistics. A recent survey by Kennett (1979) revealed that systematic data on the level and composition of working capital are available only for India and then only for firms engaging 10 or more people.

Working capital is a firm's investment in short-term assets. These consist of cash and short-term securities, accounts receivable, and inventories. Inventories, sometimes referred to as physical working capital, comprise raw materials, work in progress, and finished goods. In accounting terminology the firm's short-term assets are labeled gross working capital or total current assets; this is contrasted with net working capital, which is total current assets less total current liabilities. The concept we employ in this paper is gross working capital, and we pay particular attention to inventories.

The level and composition of working capital is subject to wide variation. Evidence indicates that such variation is related to level of development, to industry group, to type of enterprise within an industry group, and finally, to the individual enterprise. Although inventory appears to be the largest component of working capital in all cases, it is relatively more important in developing countries. In India, for example, inventory represents approximately 60 percent of total working capital of small manufacturing enterprises, whereas in the United States it constitutes only about 40 percent. Further, the relative magnitude of inventory also appears to vary by industry group within a country. In Sierra Leone the inventory-to-sales ratio for small enterprises varies from 1.5 percent for the baking industry to 11.4 percent for carpentry. There are also systematic differences in the inventory-to-sales ratio by major enterprise types within an industry group. In the Sierra Leone tailoring industry, the inventory-to-sales ratio for "factory-type" tailoring enterprises was 10.4 percent, whereas that for "job-shop" tailors, where customers supply the material, was only 2.4 percent. Finally, even within enterprise groupings, there are often wide variations between individual firms. The inventory-to-sales ratios for "job-shop" type tailors in Sierra Leone, for example, range from 0.5 to 5.7 percent.[6]

What accounts for these variations in working-capital composition, particularly inventory? In the next section we examine this issue in terms of the factors affecting the demand for and the supply of working capital.

Demand for Working Capital

The demand for working capital arises because production and sales are not perfectly synchronized: The dates of payment for inputs do not match the dates of corresponding sales receipts. We may divide the factors that are the principal determinants of demand for working capital into seven categories.

1. The quantity of working capital demanded will vary directly with the volume of sales. This follows by definition since the principal use of working capital is to finance labor, raw materials, and other purchased inputs that go into goods produced for sale.

2. The quantity of working capital demanded will vary directly with the degree of uncertainty of market demand and of the flow of production inputs. In Western economies the precautionary element of working capital, particularly its inventory component, is related to the uncertainty of expected sales. In developing countries the situation is very different, with uncertain sales taking a back seat to external environmental risks on the supply side. These include unpredictable events such as failure of the supply of electricity, defective equipment, theft, and breakdown in supply firms that interrupt or reduce sales without causing a compensating reduction in costs. A

second group of unpredictable events is the result of government policies. Shortage of critical spare parts due to import quotas, a flood of duty-free competitive imports owing to issuance of licenses to the politically influential, delayed payment for sales to government agencies, and delays in issuing permits all absorb working capital. Only a small proportion of firms maintain precautionary reserves for these occurrences.

3. The quantity of working capital demanded will vary inversely with the capital intensity of production. The more capital intensive is production, the higher will be fixed capital costs and the lower will be variable costs (assuming fixed assets are owned rather than rented). Variable costs are largely financed by working capital.

4. The quantity of working capital demanded will vary directly with the length of the production period and with the length of the marketing period for raw materials and finished goods. In high-income economies where producers have access to credit, the production and marketing periods are often similar within an industry. In illiquid, low-income economies, substantial working-capital savings are achievable by altering institutional arrangements, particularly with respect to the marketing period.[7]

5. The quantity of working capital demanded will vary directly with economies of large-lot material purchases. Insofar as the transaction cost of placing a raw-material order is fixed irrespective of size and—more importantly—the seller gives price discounts for bulk purchases, it will pay the firm to hold larger raw-material inventories.

6. The quantity of working capital demanded will vary inversely with managerial efficiency. Since gross profits are a major source of cash, anything that reduces profits has the potential to increase demand for working capital. Production inadequacies, such as poor product quality, slow rates of throughput, materials wastage, and machine breakdowns, affect working capital by reducing profits or by lengthening the production period. Financial weaknesses of the entrepreneur, such as nonbusiness cash withdrawals, defaulted customer credit, or clerical thefts, represent a simple leakage of working capital. A manager's marketing shortcomings, such as faulty product-pricing practices, loss of distributors, and transport failures, are reflected in reduced sales revenues. If a firm's search for additional working capital derives from any of these internal causes, then, *ceteris paribus,* receipt of loans or raw materials on credit will undermine the natural pressure for corrective action and result in greater losses.

7. The quantity of working capital demanded will vary inversely with the cost of borrowing. The cost of credit includes the nominal rate of interest charged on the loan, transaction costs incurred by

the borrower, and expected changes in the purchasing power of money over the loan period. As Ladman pointed out in Chapter 9, transaction costs for obtaining a formal loan are surprisingly high and for a small loan proportionately very high.[8] The expected rate of inflation is an offset against the nominal interest charge. Loans in the curb market entail low transaction costs, few complementary services, and higher interest. Informal loans have the great advantage of a short interval between loan request and disbursement.

Supply of Working Capital

There are six sources of finance for firms: two internal and four external. We shall describe the six sources, then examine the factors that determine how much each source is willing to supply.

The original capitalization of rural manufacturing enterprises, including working capital, is overwhelmingly obtained from such internal sources as personal savings, gifts, and informal loans from friends and relatives.[9] The second internal source, the firm's "free cash flow" of depreciation and profit not committed to servicing debt, is the major source of working capital for expanding units. In firms studied in Sierra Leone, 90 percent of funds for expansion were derived from this source, and the figure was 81 percent in sample firms in Haiti. However, although internal cash flow is the most important source of working capital, it should be recalled that because of fungibility there are often substantial "leakages" to other household enterprises, financial investments, or consumption. As with potential managerial inefficiency, the possibility of this type of leakage makes the assessment of creditworthiness difficult.

The four external sources of short-term credit—customers, suppliers, commercial banks, and the curb market—are far less significant. The most important external source is credit from the customer. One form of customer credit is subcontracting in which the customer, typically a much larger firm, supplies the rural enterprises with raw materials required to produce the goods ordered. This usually occurs in firms manufacturing ready-made garments, knitting, furniture, artistic handicrafts, and footwear.[10] More widespread is the practice of having the retail customer supply the producer with either the raw material or a cash down payment to purchase raw materials. Of course, to arrive at the net supply of working capital supplied by customers, we must subtract credit extended to other customers.[11]

Advance payments by customers represent an interesting response to the obstacles faced in a low-income community where financial intermediation is limited. The customer provides resources and receives in return implicit interest in the form of a lower price. The producer avoids the risk inherent in producing for inventory. For communities where income and tastes are stable, it is a very efficient economic innovation.

A second external source of working capital is accounts payable to suppliers. Normally this service is reserved for customers with well-established businesses and good payment records; it is provided without collateral, but the implicit interest rate is high. Supplier credit to large firms in urban areas is quite common. For smaller rural units, typically employing one to three workers, supplier credit is rare.

Commercial banks are a third external source of working capital. Survey data from Sierra Leone, Haiti, and Jamaica indicate that commercial banks provide only 1–2 percent of the initial financing for rural manufacturing units and 0–8 percent for expansion. This very limited participation of commercial banks is due to the collateral requirements and transaction costs facing the borrower and to the high costs and risks associated with such loans, as perceived by the bank.

The final source of external credit is the curb, or informal, financial market. In more than 10 countries of which the authors have personal knowledge, there is no significant use of the curb market by small manufacturing enterprises.[12] Yet the curb market receives a vast amount of attention, unfortunately more exhortatory than investigative in nature. In most cases recourse to moneylenders occurs at infrequent intervals for small loans for a few days in response to emergencies. At interest rates of 50 to 150 percent, reliance on the curb market alone is out of the question given the generally moderate profit rates in manufacturing.

How much working capital each source is willing to provide is determined by its assets and income, the opportunity cost of its funds, the interest rate on working capital, administrative costs, and the risks associated with such loans. In most cases, the cheapest source of working capital is the enterprise's own cash flow. This stems from the absence of administrative costs and an accurate knowledge of risk. On the other hand, the ease of redirecting cash flow from one household enterprise to another means that this internal source of liquidity is far more sensitive to alternative yields among the various household activities than is the case for other sources.

For external sources of funds, on the other hand, transaction costs become more important elements in the cost of funds. Administrative costs of lending to small firms are typically high. Costs of recording and disbursing the loan tend to be fairly constant regardless of the loan size. Information costs required to ascertain risk tend to be high for loans to small firms, owing to the heterogeneity of these enterprises and their general lack of financial records.[13] The risk premium is also likely to be an important ingredient in determining the external supply of working capital to rural, nonfarm enterprises. Although the sector as a whole may well be viable and resilient, failure rates can be quite high. In Sierra Leone the small-enterprise failure rate was approximately 10 percent per year, with the majority failing within the first three years (Chuta and Liedholm 1982).[14]

One of the reasons that "risks" for financial institutions are high in this area is that it is difficult and expensive to obtain the information needed to screen the good borrowers from the "lemons" (Akerlof 1980). Since most formal lenders are not allowed to vary interest rates by risk of borrower and since potentially good borrowers are often indistinguishable from "bad" borrowers, potentially sound borrowers may in some instances be driven out of the market. Commercial banks attempt to reduce the risk premium and the need to gather extensive information by insisting on full collateral and by dealing only with known borrowers. Indeed, in the Philippines, the risks of lending to unknown borrowers were estimated to be 10 times or more the risk of lending to known, creditworthy borrowers (Anderson 1981). Input suppliers and moneylenders, on the other hand, often know more about the borrowers' business than do commercial banks. Yet even they are not immune to high risks. In Sierra Leone, for example, local traders with extensive knowledge of the community found the average 168 percent contractual interest rate on their loans to small rural enterprises yielded an average return of only 43 percent due to delayed payments and default (Linsenmeyer 1976).

Tests of Hypotheses on Working-Capital Demand

What empirical support exists to verify hypotheses about the determinants of demand for working capital? Data are scarce, but some information is available from the Sierra Leone small-enterprise study that enables us to test several propositions with respect to physical working capital. In the 1974 Sierra Leone survey, 250 small-scale manufacturing enterprises were interviewed twice weekly over a 12-month period about their sales, output, costs, profit, inventories, and fixed capital.[15]

The earlier discussion, combined with the data from the Sierra Leone survey, enables us to formulate a demand model. The absence of information on credit supply requires the strong assumption that supply factors are not systematically linked to demand. Of necessity, the dependent variable is the enterprise's total inventory, since data on the firm's other components of working capital are either missing or incomplete. The available variables expected to explain inventory are sales, economic profits, location (rural versus urban), and type of industry group (e.g., carpentry, baking, tailoring). The interest rate, however, is not included as an independent variable since it is assumed that all producers face the same underlying interest-rate structure. Sales would be expected to be positively related to inventory levels. Inventories, following Whitin's (1953) model, are usually believed to be a function of the square root of sales, although alternative specifications have been formulated. Economic profit, defined to reflect the shadow price of all inputs and thus ensure that a marginal firm would have a zero rate of profit, would be expected to have a negative relation to inventory levels. Profits provide a reflection of managerial efficiency. Well-run enterprises would be expected to require less inventory than poorly run ones. Location is also hypothesized to affect inventory levels. Rural enterprises would be expected to carry a higher inventory than those in urban locations because of the more frequent availability of transport and because of the more labor-intensive nature of their production. Finally, the particular characteristics of the specific industry, such as the length of its production and marketing period, will vary from industry to industry and thus lead to differing inventory requirements.

The regression model investigated was specified as

$$\begin{aligned} \mathrm{INV} = {} & \mathrm{a} + \mathrm{b}\sqrt{\mathrm{s}} + \mathrm{c}\,(\mathrm{P}) + \mathrm{d}\,(\mathrm{R}) \\ & + \mathrm{e}\,(\mathrm{C}) + \mathrm{f}\,(\mathrm{B}) + \mathrm{g}\,(\mathrm{T}) + \mathrm{E} \end{aligned} \tag{21.1}$$

where *INV* is inventory level, *a* is a constant, *S* is sales entered in terms of its square root, *P* is economic profits, *R* is a dummy variable equal to one if the enterprise is located in a rural area (i.e., locality size less than 20,000 inhabitants), *C* is a dummy variable equal to one if the enterprise is carpentry, *B* is a dummy variable equal to one if the enterprise is baking, *T* is a dummy variable equal to one if the enterprise is tailoring, and *E* is the error term. The results, based on 138 small-scale manufacturing enterprises that reported the required data, were

$$\begin{aligned} \mathrm{INV} = {} & \underset{(78.2)}{-242.2} + \underset{(1.4)}{10.5\mathrm{S}} - \underset{(.021)}{.095\mathrm{P}} + \underset{(61)}{4.6\mathrm{R}} + \underset{(108)}{256\mathrm{C}} - \underset{(137)}{62\mathrm{B}} - \underset{(64)}{19\mathrm{T}} \end{aligned} \tag{21.2}$$

where $R^2 = .51$; sig $p < .01$. The standard errors are in parentheses.

For a cross-section analysis, the results indicate that the equation provided a reasonably good estimate of the underlying determinants of the demand for inventories. The individual components must now be more fully examined.

Not surprisingly, the level of sales was found to be an important determinant of inventory. The square root of sales coefficient was positive and significant at the 1 percent level. Moreover, the results would seem to provide additional empirical support for the square-root rule, since an alternative linear specification of this relationship provided less powerful statistical results.

Economic profits were also found to be an important determinant. The economic-profits coefficient was negative, as predicted, and significant at the 1 percent level. Thus, our contention seems to be confirmed that managerial shortcomings, for which economic profits is a proxy, would be reflected in larger inventories. The mean inventory-to-sales ratios for different industry groups, arrayed by whether or not the enterprise generated a positive economic profit, are presented in Table 21.1.

The location coefficient, on the other hand, was not found to be statistically significant. Although rural enterprises appeared to possess higher mean inventory-to-sales ratios than their urban counterparts in the industry tabulations reported in Table 21.1, these locational differences are not statistically significant when other variables are taken into account.

Finally, the results of our analysis indicate that there are some significant variations in inventory levels by industry group. Specifically, the carpentry coefficient is positive and statistically significant at the 10 percent level. Indeed, carpentry, which appears to have a longer marketing and production period than other small enterprises, has a significantly higher inventory-to-sales ratio than other enterprises. The bakery and tailoring coefficients, however, were not statistically significant, although in Table 21.1 mean values for the inventory-to-sales ratio appear to vary from one enterprise group to another. Finally, it should be noted that the mean inventory-to-sales ratios for the product groups in Sierra Leone were quite similar to the inventory-to-sales ratios obtained from preliminary analysis of the data for Honduras and Jamaica.

Policy Implications

The heterogeneity of rural nonfarm enterprises within any one country and the variations between countries make it difficult to generalize about the financing of these firms. In some cases, demand

TABLE 21.1

Average Inventory/Annual Sales Ratios for Small-Scale Enterprise Types by Economic Profitability and Location, Sierra Leone, 1974

Industry	Economic Profit		Location		All
	Positive	Negative	Urban	Rural	
Tailoring	.024 (n=34)	.031 (n=31)	.029 (n=38)	.026 (n=27)	.027 (n=65)
Gara Dyeing	.017 (n= 4)	.038 (n= 2)	.022 (n= 5)	.031 (n= 1)	.023 (n=6)
Carpentry	.074 (n=11)	.339 (n= 2)	.099 (n= 9)	.148 (n= 4)	.114 (n=13)
Blacksmith	.030 (n= 6)	.060 (n= 4)	.038 (n= 4)	.045 (n= 6)	.042 (n=10)
Baking	.013 (n= 9)	.020 (n= 4)	.013 (n= 9)	.020 (n= 4)	.015 (n=13)
Other	0 (n= 0)	.203 (n=32)	.116 (n=21)	.312 (n=11)	.203 (n=32)
Total	.036 (n=64)	.114 (n=75)	.056 (n=86)	.114 (n=53)	.078 (n=139)

Source: Computed from survey data collected for the Sierra Leone small scale industry study (Liedholm and Chuta, 1976).

issues predominate; in others, it is supply issues. Nevertheless, several policy recommendations emerge.

Some of the short-run capital problems facing rural enterprises are traceable to demand constraints. Effective demand for working capital may be low because the activity is not economically viable or because particular enterprises may suffer, as our analysis points out, from disabilities such as poor management. Indeed, effective demand is frequently lower than the entrepreneur's perceived demand for working capital because of other problems (e.g., managerial failures, raw-material bottlenecks). These often are misinterpreted as a working-capital shortage.

However, the limited evidence available from countries with adequate profit data, such as Sierra Leone, indicates that a significant fraction of rural nonfarm activities are viable and thus capable of generating a strong effective demand for working capital. An experimental credit program in Bangladesh, designed to provide loans primarily to small farmers, discovered an unexpectedly strong demand for nonfarm loans even at "high" interest rates when the loans were assured (Church and Adams 1979).

In general, constraints on the supply side appear to be more significant in explaining short-run financial problems than those on the demand side. Therefore, most of our policy recommendations refer to supply. Increased flexibility in loan terms, measures to reduce administrative costs and risks of lenders, more experimentation with informal lending sources, removal of imperfections, and better integration of rural financial markets are suggestions that will be examined in greater detail.

Increasing interest rates to enable banks and nonbank intermediaries to more adequately cover their risks and administrative costs emerges as a major policy recommendation. As several authors point out in this volume, controlled interest rates discourage lending to small farmers and nonfarm rural businesses. Several factors may limit formal interest rates, however, from rising to levels that fully reflect risk and cost.[16] First, political considerations may dictate against increasing interest rates for small rural enterprises. Second, higher interest rates may tend to generate adverse selection of borrowers by attracting the riskier and deterring those whose projects have a lower, but far more certain, rate of return (Stiglitz and Weiss 1981). As a result, lenders might still use a credit-rationing system in which good borrowers could be driven out by the improperly screened "lemons."

Consequently, mechanisms are needed to improve the information-gathering and screening procedures of financial intermediaries making short-term loans to rural nonfarm enterprises. In this connection, for example, financial institutions need better procedures to distinguish the true effective demand for working capital from the specious demand that only serves to temporarily sustain a fatally ill enterprise. Norms for inventory and working-capital levels by type of enterprise and sales volume might also be developed for use as rules of thumb in screening as well as in determining loan size.[17] Such improved screening devices should reduce lender risks.

Risks can also be reduced by improving loan-collection procedures. Borrowers able to repay are frequently tempted not to do so, particularly when many borrowers are known to be defaulting. Timely repayment of existing loans should improve if there are prospects of receiving additional loans that are conditioned on the repayment of past debts. Moreover, loan-collection drives, threatened foreclosure, or advertising delinquencies or cases under litigation can have dramatic results. Although it took some time for these procedures to have an effect, they were probably responsible for reducing arrears by half in a Philippine small-scale enterprise project (Anderson 1981).

With lenders' accumulation of experience and improved information, the risks of lending to rural nonfarm enterprises should decline. Loan appraisers' and loan officers' judgments will improve with an increase in knowledge of specific trades and with the experience they gain by lending to this sector. Lending institutions, however, are not going to willingly engage in this "learning by doing" process unless its high cost (principally high default rates) can be reduced. A loan-guarantee scheme is one such cost-absorbing mechanism. Commercial banks would be more willing to provide unsecured short-term loans to rural enterprises if the guaranteed portion of the loan were reasonably high and if all screening costs above those incurred for standard loans could be shifted to the guarantor. To help ensure that the guarantee subsidy is confined to learning, the banks should be given an incentive, such as a declining guarantee over time, to move new borrowers into a normal commercial relationship.[18]

The rural nonfarm sector will benefit from the removal of distortions and constraints in rural financial markets. Because of fungibility, some borrowing supposedly for farm enterprises currently supports nonfarm activities. Constraints placed on the use of rural credit should be removed so that rural households can more easily allocate their financial resources toward uses where they perceive the highest return. Credit controls that attempt to prevent leakage of funds to unapproved uses have only limited success and lower the value of the loan to the borrower while increasing the cost of financial intermediation. Correspondingly, constraints should also be removed that prevent specialized farm lenders from lending to nonfarm enterprises. The heterogeneous nature of rural nonfarm enterprises requires financial services that are flexible and tailored to the local level. Consequently, financial markets that are integrated, decentralized, and relatively unfettered will be needed before many of the financial requirements of these rural nonfarm enterprises can be met. Indeed, rural nonfarm enterprises will derive far greater long-term economic and social benefits from the development of sound rural financial markets than they would from subsidized credit programs and from specialized lending institutions designed to help only a few enterprises.

Notes

We acknowledge the support given by the Agency for International Development to Ohio State University and Michigan State University that made possible writing this paper and conducting some of the surveys and research reported here. We also appreciate the support, encouragement, and criticism of Dennis Anderson, Clifton Barton, Robert Firestine, Donald Mead, and the editors. The usual disclaimers apply.

1. See Donald (1976) for a summary on this review.

2. In Haiti, for example, lack of working capital was the most important problem perceived by the entrepreneurs (Haggblade, Defay, and Pitman 1979). In Jamaica, lack of cash was the second-most-important constraint mentioned by entrepreneurs interviewed in a recent study (Fisseha and Davies 1981).

3. In the United States, for example, data from the 1970s show that the ratio of working capital to fixed capital declined from 2.0 for small to 1.33 for large manufacturing enterprises (Kennett 1979).

4. See Chapter 2 by Meyer and Alicbusan for more detail on the sources and uses of liquidity in rural households.

5. The post–World War II study of small-scale industry in developing economies commenced in India in 1953. During the following decade, research on the "Indian model" was carried out in many Asian and Latin American countries; most of the investigators had connections with the Stanford Research Institute and the Ford Foundation. The focus was on "modern" small industry of relatively large scale, with a policy orientation toward intensive assistance to selected firms. An overview of this tradition can be found in Staley and Morse (1965). After a hiatus of about a decade, interest in small-scale industry reemerged in the garb of appropriate technology and the informal sector. Now the focus is on the lower end of the size distribution, typically with a rural orientation and involving subsidized assistance for a privileged minority. Perhaps reflecting the normal lag between theory and practice, current technical-assistance programs are still virtually all designed on the Indian model.

6. These figures were derived from survey data collected by the 1974 Sierra Leone small-enterprise project (see Liedholm and Chuta 1976 for details).

7. A Kenyan example is illustrative. Producer A, who manufactures common wooden chairs, purchases lumber from a nearby sawmill 4 days before commencing production on a typical order of 20 chairs that take 10 days to produce. The buyer takes delivery upon completion and pays cash. In contrast, Producer B makes high-quality chairs from kiln-dried wood sent from Nairobi, which must be ordered and paid for 56 days prior to its arrival. Production of 20 chairs requires 14 days, and the buyer is given 28 days from delivery to pay. If in each case raw material cost is 40 percent of sales, other variable cost 30 percent, and a 320-day working year is assumed, the working capital ratios (WC) are as follows:

$$\begin{aligned} WC_A &= [.4(4/10) + .70 + (0)] \frac{\text{sales}}{320 \div 10} \\ &= 2.7\% \text{ of annual sales} \end{aligned} \tag{21.3}$$

$$\begin{aligned} WC_B &= [.4(56/14) + .70 + 28/14(.4 + .3)] \frac{\text{sales}}{320 \div 14} \\ &= 16.1\% \text{ of annual sales} \end{aligned} \tag{21.4}$$

8. In Haiti, for example, entrepreneurs reported that more than 50 percent of the formal loans they received took longer than three months to process (Haggblade, Defay, and Pitman 1979).

9. These sources represented 18 percent of the original capitalization of surveyed firms in Sierra Leone (Liedholm and Chuta 1976), 94 percent in Jamaica (Fisseha and Davies 1981), and 91 percent in Haiti (Haggblade, Defay, and Pitman 1979). Further references to these countries are from these sources.

10. In Thailand, Mead (1981) reported that subcontracting can also be found in the production of ready-made garments, silk, wood carvings, furniture, fishnets, knitting, lacquerware, and metal bowls.

11. We have no information on the volume of credit extended to customers, although we know a significant fraction of producers do extend some credit. In Haiti, 70 percent of the sample entrepreneurs reported granting loans, compared to 34 percent in Jamaica.

12. In Haiti 0.9 percent of the firms used moneylenders for the initial purchase of equipment and raw materials; for expansion investment the figure was 1.7 percent. In Sierra Leone initial reliance was 0.9 percent and 3.9 percent for expansion.

13. In the Philippines, for example, administrative costs for a given value of small-enterprise lending were six times those for larger enterprises (Saito and Villanueva 1981). In Jamaica, Wilson (1981) found that it could cost the Small Enterprise Development Corporation as much as J$1,300 to process a J$500 loan application!

14. Moreover, default rates on small-enterprise loans can be quite high. In Jamaica, for example, 40 percent of the loans by the Small Business Loan Board were deemed uncollectable (Wilson 1981); in Kenya up to 45 percent default rates were reported (Kilby 1981). However, low default rates on small-enterprises loan programs have been reported in Ghana (Steel 1977).

15. For more details, see Liedholm and Chuta 1976.

16. This section relies on the discussion in Anderson (1981).

17. The Tandon report (1975) established such norms in India. Data from small rural enterprise surveys, such as reported in Table 21.1, may enable such norms to be established for nonfarm enterprises in other countries.

18. See Kilby (1981) for a more extensive discussion of the mechanism.

References

Akerlof, G. A. "The Markets for 'Lemons': Quality, Uncertainty, and the Market Mechanism." *Quarterly Journal of Economics* 84(1980):488–500.

Anderson, Dennis. "Capital Market, Uncertainties, and the Finance of Small Industry and Agriculture in Developing Countries." Unpublished paper, Oxford University, February 1981.

Church, Philip E., and Gary D. Adams. "Experimental Approaches to Rural Credit in Bangladesh." In *Problems and Issues of Agricultural Credit and*

Rural Finance, edited and published by the Bangladesh Bank. Dacca, 1979.

Chuta, Enyinna, and Carl Liedholm. "Rural Non-Farm Employment: A Review of the State of the Art." MSU Rural Development Paper no. 4. East Lansing: Michigan State University, 1979.

———. "Employment Growth and Change in Sierra Leone Small Scale Industry: 1974–1980." *International Labor Review* 121(1982):101–113.

Donald, Gordon. *Credit for Small Farmers in Developing Countries.* Boulder, Colo.: Westview Press, 1976.

Fisseha, Yacob, and Omar Davies. "The Small-Scale Manufacturing Enterprises in Jamaica: Socioeconomic Characteristics and Constraints." MSU Rural Development Working Paper no. 16. East Lansing: Michigan State University, 1981.

Haggblade, Steve, Jacques Defay, and Bob Pitman. "Small Manufacturing and Repair Enterprises in Haiti: Survey Results." MSU Rural Development Working Paper no. 4. East Lansing: Michigan State University, 1979.

Kennett, David. "The Working Capital Needs of Small Enterprises." Unpublished paper, World Bank, Washington, D.C., 1979.

Kilby, Peter. "Small Scale Industry in Kenya." MSU Rural Development Working Paper no. 20. East Lansing: Michigan State University, 1981.

Liedholm, Carl, and Enyinna Chuta. "The Economics of Rural and Urban Small-Scale Industries in Sierra Leone." African Rural Economy Paper no. 14. East Lansing: Michigan State University, 1976.

Linsenmeyer, Dean. "Economic Analysis of Alternative Strategies for the Development of Sierra Leone Marine Fisheries." African Rural Economy Working Paper no. 18. East Lansing: Michigan State University, 1976.

Mead, Donald C. "Subcontracting in Rural Areas of Thailand." Research Paper no. 5, Rural Off-Farm Employment Assessment Project, Kasetsart University, Bangkok, 1981.

Meyer, Richard L. "Financing Rural Nonfarm Enterprise in Low-Income Countries." *Development Digest* 18(1980):92–100.

Meyer, Richard L., and Donald W. Larson. "Rural Nonfarm Employment: The Recent East Asian Experience." *Journal of Economic Development* 3(1978):91–112.

Saito, Katrine, and Delano Villanueva. "Transactions Costs of Credit to the Small-Scale Sector in the Philippines." *Economic Development and Cultural Change* 29(1981):631–640.

Staley, Eugene, and Richard Morse. *Modern Small Industry for Developing Countries.* New York: McGraw Hill, 1965.

Steel, William. *Small Scale Employment and Production in Developing Countries: Evidence from Ghana.* New York: Praeger, 1977.

Stiglitz, Joseph, and Andrew Weiss. "Credit Rationing in Markets with Imperfect Information." *American Economic Review* 71(1981):393–410.

Tandon Committee. *Report of the Study Group to Frame Guidelines for Followup of Bank Credit.* Bombay: Bombay Reserve Bank of India, 1975.

Whitin, T. M. *The Theory of Inventory Management.* Princeton: Princeton University Press, 1953.

Wilson, Middleton. "Some Problems in Operating a Loan Program for Craft and Emerging Small-Scale Nonfarm Enterprises in Jamaica." MSU Rural Development Working Paper no. 15. East Lansing: Michigan State University, 1981.

22
Improving Donor Intervention in Rural Finance

J. D. Von Pischke

Agricultural credit projects and credit components in rural development projects are an intervention in rural financial markets by development-assistance agencies in many countries. Their popularity is reflected in cumulative commitments by the World Bank for agricultural credit exceeding US$3,500 million by 1981 (World Bank 1981) and by US$209 million in assistance of this type by the Inter-American Development Bank in 1980 alone (Inter-American Development Bank 1981).

Credit projects have provided substantial amounts of liquidity in rural areas and are frequently thought to produce high economic returns. Since the late 1960s, however, critics have argued that the impact of these projects may be considerably more complex than suggested by their design and even that rate-of-return calculations miss or obscure the most important project effects (Adams 1971; David and Meyer 1980; Howse 1974; Kratoska 1975; Penny 1968; Von Pischke and Adams 1980; Von Pischke and others 1981; Youngjohns 1980).

This chapter attempts to explain how rural credit projects are presently designed and why these design techniques often cause serious problems. The discussion goes on to suggest an alternative approach that stresses debt capacity and views credit as part of a financial process. I also examine the extent to which financial and nonfinancial stimulants to rural development may be substitutes or complements.

Current Project Design

Credit-project design includes identification, preparation, and appraisal prior to implementation (Baum 1978). Identification and the early stages of project preparation generally involve two major con-

Table 22.1 Hypothetical Agricultural Budget

	Without Project	With Project	Calcula-tion
1. Produce (tons)	5	10	+
2. Produce consumed on the farm (tons)	2	2	-
3. Marketed produce (tons)	3	8	=
4. Farmgate price per ton ($)	400	400	x
5. Total farm cash receipts ($)	1,200	3,200	=
6. Purchased inputs ($)	200	1,000	-
7. Net Benefit Before Financing[a/] ($)	1,000	2,200	=
8. Loan receipts ($)	-	900	+
9. Debt service ($)	-	1,080	-
10. Net Benefit After Financing[a/] ($)	1,000	2,020	=

a/ "Before financing" refers to the costs and benefits directly related to production. "After financing" includes these costs and benefits and also loan receipts and debt servicing.

siderations dealt with either sequentially or simultaneously: technical objectives and identification of intended project beneficiaries. Technical objectives that are expected to be realized through provision of donor funds may include adoption by farmers of new agricultural technology, such as a technical package of improved seeds, chemical fertilizers, and other purchased inputs (World Bank 1975). Projects are justified in terms of incremental tons of grain or other farm produce, increases in farm income, and rates of return to real resources purchased with loans. Identification of intended project beneficiaries may be done in several ways. Projects may be area-specific or crop-specific or may deal with farmers who are not yet using certain technologies. Another basis for identification is affiliation. Members of a cooperative or some officially organized village unit may be identified as potential loan applicants.

Farm budgets are an important agricultural-credit design tool (Brown 1979; Gittinger [1973] 1981). A highly simplified example is given in Table 22.1, which shows the activities of a representative farm without the credit project and presents estimates of what would occur with the project. (In Table 22.1 only a single "with project" year is shown, in the interest of simplification. The usual analysis incorporates annual figures for each year of the investment's economic life.)

Credit is generally accorded an important role in financing technical packages or innovations provided under projects. The proportion of farm investment cost that is financed by project funds is frequently 80 percent or more. Since farmers are generally assumed to be poor or to have insufficient liquidity, high levels of loan financing are common.

Repayment terms are also derived from the farm budget. In the assumptions used in Table 22.1, for example, loan size ($900 in line 8) is 90 percent of the costs of inputs ($1,000 in line 6). In this simple example the loan is for seasonal inputs, repayable with a 20 percent interest charge at the end of the season ($1,080 is shown as debt service in line 9). There appears to be ample space in this budget for these repayment terms because the incremental (i.e., "with project" less "without project") net benefit before financing is $1,200 (i.e., $2,200−$1,000), which is much greater than the $180 net cost of borrowing (i.e., $1,080−$900).

The most interesting feature of this method of determining loan size and credit terms is the use of the normal-year assumption. Farm or enterprise budgets typically use normal-year assumptions because the sequence of good, normal, and bad years is impossible to predict and because their distribution is not considered important in calculating a representative rate of return. In other words, no allowance is specifically made in conventional farm budgets to accommodate variations in price or yields.

This approach, outlined here in simplified form, is accompanied by problems cited in the critical literature on credit projects. Low levels of repayment performance—a major problem—may reflect high levels of farmer indebtedness, as well as instability in farmers' cash flow (Sanderatne 1978). A complicating factor is that loans from government agencies are often regarded by rural people as grants. Another problem is that specialized farm-credit institutions are often poorly managed (Roberts 1978). This results from emphasis on technological rather than financial factors in project design: Credit projects are typically oriented toward extension of agricultural technologies rather than toward provision of improved financial services. Disappointment has also been expressed with the small number of farmers who gain access to formal loans (Dell'Amore 1976). This may result from technical packages that are not well received by target-group farmers. It may also result from relatively large average loan size, which within the lender's budget limitations obviously restricts the number of borrowers. Also, as Gonzalez-Vega argued in Chapter 10, low interest rates on loans force lenders to restrict credit access, and high levels of overdues limit the amount of energy lenders devote to developing new business (Von Pischke and others 1981). In addition, the costs of institutional credit are considerably greater than suggested by the interest rates charged (Adams and Nehman 1979; Datey 1978), and this discourages lenders from serving new or small borrowers.

An Alternative Approach to Intervention in Rural Finance

The state of the art in credit-project design is primitive. Problems associated with these projects are serious, subtle, generally overlooked, and misunderstood. In view of these problems, how would it be possible to design more effective means of intervening in the operation of rural financial markets? The approach to be outlined can alleviate many of the present problems while stimulating rural financial markets. It consists of three stages. The first is to ascertain the repayment capacity of intended borrowers. The second is to adopt measures that build confidence among borrowers and lenders. The third is to design intervention to create debt capacity. If the reorientation toward these three stages is not feasible, partial application of this approach, applying only one or two of the steps, should still be useful. Improvement in project design could occur incrementally, through a series of small changes.

Determining Repayment Capacity

The repayment capacity of borrowers is vital in the performance of credit projects. Credit-project design should begin with this element, because it reflects a lender's perspective. Focusing on repayment capacity also permits identification of other financial services, such as savings deposits, that would be useful for borrowers and that would also expand the role of finance in development. Three steps may be used to ascertain repayment capacity in the with-project case. The first is to quantify the normal-year uncommitted cash flow of the borrower. The second is to adjust uncommitted cash flow for senior claims on the borrower's liquidity. The third is to quantify the impact of possible adversity on the borrower's cash flow.

Normal-year uncommitted cash flow may be quantified as indicated in Table 22.2, which incorporates the normal year with- and without-project data found in Table 22.1. Uncommitted cash flow is defined as minimum repayment capacity, which is the net benefit before financing adjusted for senior claims on the borrower. Senior claims are financial obligations that the borrower regards as more important than repayment of the prospective loan. Examples of these claims

Table 22.2 Alternative Agricultural Budget

	Without Project	With Project	
		Normal Year	Bad Year
A. Produce (tons)	5	10	5
B. Produce consumed on the farm (tons)	2	2	2
C. Marketed produce (tons)	3	8	3
D. Farmgate price per ton ($)	400	400	550
E. Total farm cash receipts ($)	1,200	3,200	1,650
F. Purchased inputs ($)	200	1,000	900
G. Net Benefit Before Financing($)	1,000	2,200	750
H. Senior claims ($)	500	600	600
I. Minimum repayment capacity= Uncommitted cash flow ($)	500	1,600	150
J. Loan receipts ($)			125
K. Debt service ($)			150

are purchases of food and fuel, taxes, school fees, expenditures for emergencies, and important social ceremonies. Farmer behavior the world over confirms that claims by informal lenders also often rank ahead of those of formal credit institutions. In the example given in Table 22.2, senior claims are expected to be greater with the project than without the project because the farm family's level of income is higher; consequently its consumption and possibly its obligations to members of the extended family and to the community may be greater.

Determining senior claims requires judgment and imposes additional information costs on lenders. Difficulties involved in quantifying senior claims cannot be lightly dismissed, but are not insurmountable. Estimates of senior claims are essentially no more difficult to make than are estimates of certain other variables currently used in project design. In fact, competent lenders with experience in an area are able to give rough estimates for all of the items contained in the adjusted agricultural budget found in Table 22.2. If the lenders are not competent, project design should address this deficiency or use alternative, nonfinancial means of achieving project objectives.

Adjustment for adversity should reflect reasonable expectations about the risks facing borrowers. Projection of bad-year results is not fundamentally different from estimation of normal-year performance.

Further knowledge is required, however, to identify a range of probable outcomes rather than just the most probable outcome.

There is no scientific way of precisely identifying the normal expected adverse situation, although an obvious starting point is a distribution of expected results. Some may prefer to measure it in terms of standard deviations of yields and prices, whereas others would argue for different measures. In a small-holder dairy credit project, for example, loans might be given to farmers for the purpose of assisting their purchase of two improved cows, plus fencing and watering facilities. In this case, adjustment for adversity could begin with attempts to answer the question: What if one or both cows die? Once the lender has made 100 of these loans and has several years of lending experience, the answer to that question will be fairly obvious. The probabilities will be known in rough terms (e.g., one in six that a cow dies within 12 months of purchase by the borrower), and the characteristics of farmers suffering accidential stock losses can be identified. At this point, lending terms and conditions can be redefined. When the lending institution has accommodated the probability of accidental mortality, it can go on to consider the impacts of calving intervals. Once these are factored into a lender's strategy, availability and use of different stock-feeding regimes, milk prices, or marketing arrangements may become interesting to credit decision makers. Adjustment for adversity can, in fact, be based largely on the extent to which the lender is willing to assume the risks of borrowers' inability to repay, which will determine the prudent credit limits that the lender can offer.

In the example given in Table 22.2, production is expected to fall from 10 to 5 tons, whereas the price is expected to increase from $400 to $550 per ton, reflecting an overall fall in agricultural output. Input cost (line F) is reduced in the adverse situation because the use of labor, bags, and transport is less as a result of a small harvest.

The bottom line in Table 22.2, after adjustments for adversity and senior claims, shows the minimum repayment capacity of the prospective borrower. In all years—good, normal, or bad—the borrower is expected to have not less than $150 available for the repayment of a loan. Based on this observation a loan of $125 could be offered with a 20 percent interest charge. Repayment of this loan would absorb all the borrower's $150 adjusted uncommitted cash flow in the bad year.

This illustration shows that the repayment capacity of the farmer in bad years is greatly reduced. If credit terms are specified using normal-year assumptions and without allowances for senior claims, the farmer may not be able to meet debt-servicing obligations in situations that may reasonably be expected to occur. This can embarrass the farmer and jeopardize the liquidity of the lender. In many cases the adjustments for adversity and senior claims leave only a very small amount of liquidity for debt servicing, as shown in Table 22.2. When the bottom line of the exercise is very small, credit may not be an appropriate way to assist the farmer. This concern leads to consideration of alternative means of assisting farmers, as well as of ways to make the financial arrangements for unsatisfactory project participation by farmers more flexible. From this perspective, the bottom line from the analysis is a starting point for project design.

Building Confidence

Confidence is fundamental to finance. The absence of confidence increases information costs and other transaction costs. Businesslike behavior engenders confidence, reduces risk, and lowers transaction costs. Without confidence, private credit markets could not operate. In donor-supported credit projects, however, the question of confidence among borrowers and lenders using project funds is generally not directly addressed. It is apparently assumed that project components supporting the lender and extension services will produce confidence. Given the performance of many projects, however, where extension services do not appear to be very effective and where lenders' thinly stretched management is swamped by the project, confidence is important. Special attention to how credit projects can create or destroy confidence among the various parties involved is needed when financial markets are force-fed.

Certain arrangements between debtors and creditors in projects may encourage cheating (Von Pischke and others 1981). High levels of financing that burden farmers' debt-servicing capacity tempt borrowers not to repay on time. Low interest rates and lax loan administration may tempt the farmer to obtain more credit than will be used for project purposes. Also, given the technological bias of project design, borrowers may be forced to accept an entire technical package in order to receive a loan, when they use only a portion of the package. Incomplete adoption may be rational risk avoidance by the farmer, but it poses problems for projects founded on optimistic assumptions about farmer adoption rates and yields.

Political fanfare surrounding the introduction of a project may also work against good debtor-credit relationships by drawing politics into credit allocation. Poverty or loyalty to certain factions may be stressed over indicators of repayment capacity in the loan-allocation process. This may tempt farmers to believe that the credit program is transitory and that political changes will cause it to disappear.

This short-run perspective weakens the incentive to establish a good repayment record. The farmer suspects that the government will some time again want to use credit to increase food production or the rate of adoption of an improved technology and that loan default will probably not result in denied access to future loans.

There are several questions that should be asked at the early stages of project design for the purpose of strengthening the integrity of debtor-credit relationships. The first is: What services will produce a continuing series of transactions that will build relationships between borrowers and lenders? In certain credit projects, for example, the farmer is expected to visit the lenders' office once each year to make an annual loan payment. This limited relationship is not conducive to building a good understanding of the borrower's business on the part of the lender or of the lender's expectations on the part of the borrower. Services that are used more frequently offer a stronger potential for building strong relationships. They can also increase the value of a good credit rating.

Transactions on savings accounts, for example, may occur several times a year. Money-transfer services, likewise, may be extremely important in areas where farmers do not usually have checking accounts. Needs for transfers may arise because of the nature of the extended family, with certain members working in towns and other members remaining on the farm. Deposit-account and money-transfer services can be used at any time, whereas most loans have a final due date. A reasonable expectation by a provider of deposit and transfer services is that deposit accounts will remain on their books for a considerable length of time and that these and money-transfer services have a certain volume and frequency of use, providing opportunities for the development of new business.

A second question is: What is the commercial value to the lender of accurate and timely information about borrowers and potential borrowers? Relevant information is required to provide useful financial services. Deposit accounts and transfer services generate such information—histories of transactions provide a financial record for the lender. For example, the level and rate of accumulation of deposits provide some indication of the volume of funds that the lender might tap or the borrower might mobilize for loan repayment. The timing of deposits and withdrawals over the farmer's seasonal production cycle may suggest when loan due dates could conveniently be scheduled. Without a sense of history, credit projects fail to provide the long-term perspective to both borrower and lender that is essential to building confidence.

The third question is: What premium, if any, should voluntarism command over coercion in rural development strategy? Regulations and limitations over farmer behavior can weaken confidence, especially when lenders are part of larger control systems and possibly even are required to enforce or to implement regulations and limitations not of their own making. If development is viewed as a top-down phenomenon, credit constitutes a valuable tool of control and dependence, and regulations are normally required to direct farmer behavior. If development is viewed as a bottom-up process, the role of savings becomes more important, and questions of structure for development programs involving credit require more attention. Supervised credit, for example, would appear less attractive, and lines of credit more appropriate. Credit unions, with opportunities for member participation in management and loan decision making, would be preferred to bureaucratic government credit agencies.

Creating Debt Capacity

Debt capacity is borrowing power. It is created by the estimated future payment capacity of the loan applicant and is equal to the amount of credit this capacity can command in financial markets. Creation of debt capacity is a project objective under the approach recommended here. It is a valid objective because minimum repayment capacity of target-group farmers is typically small when adjusted for adversity and senior claims. Debt capacity may be created by technological measures incorporated in a project's technical packages. Farm innovations that increase the uncommitted cash flow or diminish the impact of adversity increase repayment capacity.

More physical infrastructure can also increase debt capacity. Roads that increase access to markets, for example, reduce transport costs, which may reduce the farmgate costs of inputs and increase farmgate produce prices. Telephone, telegraph, radio, and postal facilities reduce information costs. Storage facilities and improvements in storage techniques permit increased control over the timing and prices at which produce is sold and inputs are purchased.

Likewise, price-policy reforms may create additional debt capacity. Commodity prices kept low to subsidize consumers, for example, keep farm incomes and repayment capacity low. Input price policy is also important. Minimum wage legislation may raise the costs of hiring seasonal farm labor, destroying debt capacity. As various authors in this volume argue, government decontrol of interest rates should increase rural access to credit.

Institutional measures outside financial markets may also affect target-group debt capacity. Nonprice efforts to regulate markets often have an important impact on the minimum repayment capacity of the borrower. Monopsony buyers of produce and monopoly input supply arrangements may work against farmers. In addition, contract law and enforcement are often overlooked in credit-project design. Poor loan repayment by borrowers weakens the effectiveness of contract law in rural areas, raising lending and borrowing costs. Land tenure is also a fundamental determinant of repayment capacity. Security of tenure appears essential to credit relationships for reasons of lender risk aversion and because tenure relationships influence the operator's incentive to invest.

Farmer education, extension services, and training for extension agents can create debt capacity by reducing risk to the borrower as well as by providing reassurance to lenders that the technical basis for a borrower's operation is sound. Collective guarantees and aggregation of repayment capacity through farmer organizations may also enhance debt capacity (von Stockhausen 1979).

Institutional measures within rural financial markets can ultimately increase farmer debt capacity. Better accounting and controls in farm credit institutions should help to increase their efficiency, making them more interested in developing new business. Decentralization of decision making accompanied by increased accountability of loan officers may expand farmer access to credit and make loan terms and conditions more responsive to local situations. Upgrading the skills of people working in financial intermediaries may also create debt capacity. In certain instances increased remuneration for staff of government-owned lenders may be necessary to reduce staff turnover and contribute to efficient operations.

Increasing Farmer Debt Capacity

There are financial measures and innovations that could increase debt capacity. These include lengthening the term structures of financial markets, expanding the services of intermediaries, designing more flexible lending and repayment terms, mobilizing local resources, and providing external assistance to enhance the supply of loanable funds.

Lengthening the term structure of financial markets should be especially beneficial to agriculture. In many countries, uncertainty, high and variable rates of inflation, low-interest-rate policies, and gaps in legal systems and enforcement practices discourage long-term financial contracts. This works against farmers in general, because returns from many investments in agriculture have long gestation periods. Land reclamation, drainage, irrigation, pasture development, tree crops, terracing, and other capital improvements frequently have cash flows that are not capable of quickly reproducing the initial investment. In markets where medium- and long-term loans are unavailable, the lengthening of term structures through the provision of medium- and long-term credit obviously greatly increases farmer debt capacity. The lengthening of term structures in markets can be a very difficult task for government, however, because confidence is the fundamental requirement for long time horizons in financial markets. Donors have been very active in providing medium- and long-term funds to help overcome this problem.

Expanding the services of intermediaries may also expand debt capacity. As Bourne and Graham pointed out in Chapter 3, the agricultural lender who provides only medium- or long-term loans is in the worst possible situation from the standpoint of offering diversified financial services to rural people. Contacts with borrowers are limited to intensive start-up periods while loan applications are being reviewed and funds are being disbursed, but then contact declines markedly as interactions are limited to periodic repayments by borrowers. Such a lender may increase service to clients by offering short-term loans. Experience accumulated through provision of credit on different terms provides information to the lender that makes it possible to have greater confidence in borrowers and more information about their use of credit. The intermediary providing only credit may likewise increase service to the target group by offering money-transfer and deposit-account facilities, which also expand the information available for credit decisions and increase the value of clients' relationships with the institution.

Flexible lending and repayment terms increase the debt capacity of borrowers. To return to the example in Table 22.2, the minimum repayment capacity of the intended borrower was only $150 per year in the with-project situation, adjusted for adversity. A prudent profit-oriented lender would not necessarily restrict the loan size to $125 as indicated in Table 22.2, however, because in normal years the representative farmer's minimum repayment capacity is $1,600, leaving considerable untapped repayment capacity. The lender wishing to tap this unexploited repayment capacity could lend substantially more than $125 with arrangements for rescheduling debt-servicing obligations in bad years. This practice is used by village credit cooperatives in India. When harvests fall below a certain level, loan repayments due in the bad year are automatically rescheduled over the following two years. The amount of money that the lender is prepared to tie up in arrears or rescheduled loans determines how much credit the lender can offer above the limit of minimum repayment capacity.

Flexible lending terms increase farmers' debt capacity, but farm credit is often rationed on a per hectare, a per head, or a per tree basis. These rules of thumb minimize lenders' costs of dealing with large numbers of small farmers. Cost-saving efforts such as these are especially attractive to lenders when interest rates are low, because they reduce the lender's transactions costs. This form of lending, however, is not optimal for development, because it does not distinguish between borrowers on the basis of potential and performance. Farmers with great potential are given the same per-unit credit limits as others, whereas the limits may in fact be too high for certain borrowers to handle adequately.

Obtaining flexibility is often difficult in government credit institutions without systems of decentralized decision making based on loan officers' knowledge of their borrowers' operations. Flexibility may also be difficult in lending agencies that do not mobilize deposits but rely on budgeted funds. Inflexible systems limit borrowers' and local loan officers' participation in credit decisions, consistent with top-down approaches to development.

Local resource mobilization increases the debt capacity of target groups because the lender providing deposit services to rural people has valuable information concerning their financial behavior, permitting responsive lending. The multi-service dimension of the relationship builds incentives for businesslike behavior by both the lender and the borrower. Funds mobilized provide a borrowing base for the depositor and a supply of loanable funds for the lender.

Intervening to Create Debt Capacity

A misplaced concern with "credit needs" rather than with the operation of rural financial markets has led to excessive emphasis on external assistance to increase the supply of loanable funds. The debt-capacity approach outlined here would diminish this emphasis and provide donors with more opportunities to improve the operation of rural financial markets in general. Designing rural financial market projects to create debt capacity would greatly change donor intervention. First, credit would be viewed as one of many means of stimulating investment, but not as a tool for working against the basic economic signals perceived by farmers. Neither would credit be used to promote technologies with attractive normal-year returns but with risks beyond the capacity of average borrowers to manage effectively in bad years.

Second, it would be important to promote institutional viability in rural financial markets because viable institutions are more capable of serving farmers than are moribund intermediaries. Institutional viability in the financial sector is measured in financial terms, and the financial health of intermediaries should be of paramount concern.

This has too often been ignored in traditional credit projects. Under the approach proposed here, efforts would be made at all stages in the project cycle to quantify the extent to which rural financial institutions are, or could be, strengthened financially through donor intervention.

Third, design criteria would view financial intermediation as a process, involving confidence, risk, and relationships as well as resource mobilization and allocation. The objective would be to improve the process. In traditional projects the amount of credit delivered is of primary importance. Under the debt-capacity approach a number of other variables—such as costs of delivery, real interest rates, the service mix of institutions, and the return to investments in the financial sector—would be viewed as indicators of the vitality of the process of financial intermediation.

Finally, the debt-capacity approach views rural financial markets as a sector. The function of this sector is to develop and exploit rural debt capacity. Thus, debt capacity created constitutes a useful proxy for development.

Notes

Views expressed in this chapter are those of the author. They should not be attributed to the World Bank, its affiliated organizations, or any individuals acting on their behalf. I wish to thank Dale W Adams and Jerry R. Ladman for their detailed comments on a draft and the other participants in the Workshop on Rural Financial Markets held in Granville, Ohio, in April 1981 for their reactions to an outline of this paper.

References

Adams, Dale W. "Agricultural Credit in Latin America: A Critical Review of External Funding Policy." *American Journal of Agricultural Economics* 53(1971):163–172.

Adams, D. W, and G. I. Nehman. "Borrowing Costs and the Demand for Rural Credit." *Journal of Development Studies* 15(1979):165–176.

Baum, Warren C. "The Project Cycle." *Finance and Development* 15(1978):10–17.

Brown, Maxwell L. *Farm Budgets: From Farm Income Analysis to Agricultural Project Analysis.* Baltimore and London: Johns Hopkins University Press, 1979.

Datey, C. D. "The Financial Cost of Agricultural Credit: A Case Study of Indian Experience." World Bank Staff Working Paper no. 296, Washington, D.C., 1978.

David, Cristina C., and Richard L. Meyer, "Measuring the Farm Level Impact of Agricultural Loans." In *Borrowers and Lenders: Rural Financial Markets and Institutions in Developing Countries,* edited by John Howell. London: Overseas Development Institute, 1980.

Dell'Amore, Giordano. "Discours d'ouverture—Conference mondiale sur le credit a l'intention des agriculteurs dans les pays en developpement." *Finafrica Bulletin* 3(1976):3–13.

Gittinger, J. Price. *Economic Analysis of Agricultural Projects.* Rev. ed. Course Note 32. Washington, D.C.: Economic Development Institute of the World Bank, 1981. (Originally published by Johns Hopkins University Press, Baltimore and London, 1973.)

Howse, C. J. "Agricultural Development Without Credit." *Agricultural Administration* 1(1974):259–262.

Inter-American Development Bank. *Annual Report 1980.* Washington, D.C.: Inter-American Development Bank, 1981.

Kratoska, P. H. *The Chettiar and the Yeoman.* Occasional Paper no. 32. Singapore: Institute of Southeast Asian Studies, 1975.

Penny, D. H. "Farm Credit Policy in the Early Stages of Agricultural Development." *American Journal of Agricultural Economics* 12(1968):32–45.

Roberts, R.A.J. "Personnel Deficiencies in Agricultural Banking Systems in Developing Countries." *Savings and Development* 2(1978):20–42.

Sanderatne, Nimal. "An Analytical Approach to Small Farmer Loan Defaults." *Savings and Development* 2(1978):290–304.

Von Pischke, J. D. "The Political Economy of Specialized Farm Credit Institutions in Low-Income Countries." World Bank Staff Working Paper no. 446, Washington, D.C., 1981.

Von Pischke, J. D., and Dale W Adams. "Fungibility and the Design and Evaluation of Agricultural Credit Projects." *American Journal of Agricultural Economics* 62(1980):719–726.

von Stockhausen, J. *Credit Guarantees as an Instrument for Self-help in Developing Countries.* Bonn: Friedrich-Ebert-Stiftung, 1979.

World Bank. *Agricultural Credit Sector Policy Paper.* Washington, D.C.: World Bank, 1975.

———. *Annual Report 1981.* Washington, D.C.: World Bank, 1981.

Youngjohns, B. J. "Cooperatives and Credit—A Reexamination." In *Borrowers and Lenders: Rural Financial Markets and Institutions in Developing Countries,* edited by John Howell. London: Overseas Development Institute, 1980.

23
An Agenda for Reform of Rural Financial Markets in Low-Income Countries

Douglas H. Graham
Robert E. Firestine

Authors of the preceding chapters have pointed out a number of problems in rural financial markets (RFMs), and they are critical of the way these markets are used in low-income countries. They argue that the achievements of most agricultural credit programs fall far short of goals set by promoters, that these programs also cause other undesirable and often unanticipated results, and that cheap-credit programs have undermined rural development efforts. It is increasingly apparent that many of the current programs and policies in these markets cause inefficient allocation of resources, concentrate income and assets, and sap the vitality of financial intermediaries. A major conclusion that can be drawn from reading these chapters is that wholesale reforms in traditional agricultural credit policies are needed. We present in the following discussion an agenda of issues that might be considered in carrying out these reforms.

Problem Diagnosis

Before discussing treatment, it is useful to summarize the reasons for the problems that permeate many RFMs. These problems are confusing because the issues involved are complex, subtle, and often extensively masked. As a result, many of these difficulties become highly personalized: An individual or small group of officials is commonly blamed for program deficiencies that are seen as unique to a country or institution. Even though managerial shortcomings do explain some poor performance, RFM problems in most low-income countries have at least seven universal causes. The first of these results from misconceptions about the essential nature of credit: that it is a productive input, and that its use can be tightly controlled by policymakers. Instead, credit should be viewed as a claim on resources. These claims are highly fungible, and it is very difficult to control their use.

Traditional assumptions that form an inappropriate foundation for credit projects and policies are a second cause of problems. Much of the discussion in the preceding chapters has challenged conventional wisdom: Not all farmers can productively use additional formal loans, many new techniques are adopted without loans, new techniques will not be adopted in an adverse product-pricing environment (even with loans), rural people will save if given the incentive and opportunity to do so, small farmers do not need low interest rates to induce them to use loans, many farmers do not need supervision to make wise decisions, and financial intermediaries cannot long survive if their revenues do not cover expenses. It is also apparent that informal lenders usually provide valuable services and that policies aimed at their destruction are wasteful. Erroneous assumptions block efforts to reform RFMs.

Damaging policies in RFMs are the third major source of problems. Ubiquitous concessionary interest rates head the list. Other policies include insufficient emphasis on mobilizing voluntary financial savings, too little lending to nonagricultural rural activities, and too little emphasis on the viability of the financial intermediary. Policies that attempt to help the poor and offset adverse price policies through cheap credit fragment rural financial markets, further concentrate incomes, add to resources-allocation inefficiencies, and undermine the ability of RFMs to contribute to development.

General economic policies also diminish the ability of RFMs to perform their developmental role and are a fourth source of problems. Certain policies keep agricultural prices low. Others may discourage investment in research and infrastructure, keeping yields low. Policies that have these impacts reduce the returns farmers and other entrepreneurs get from rural investments. This reduces the number of potential borrowers who can realize high returns from the use of loans and also reduces rural savings capacities. If returns to agriculture are repressed, agricultural lenders and mobilizers of voluntary savings in rural areas will also be repressed.

A fifth reason for RFM problems can be found in confused research and evaluation. Much research, biased by traditional assumptions, has emphasized the demand for credit and attempted to measure the impact of loans at the farm level. Too little analysis has been done of lender behavior, the overall performance of RFMs, and how various policies affected lender behavior; yet these topics are essential to a clear understanding of RFMs. The preceding chapters reported on new lines of RFM research that embrace these topics and focused on causes of malfunctions in RFMs.

Political intrusions are the sixth source of difficulties. In some cases these include political appointments of intermediary managers, mandates from political leaders to lend to certain individuals, and political statements that undermine the willingness of borrowers to repay loans. Political interference may come at a more general level when a government uses credit as a way of allocating political patronage to its supporters or of deflecting criticism. These intrusions lead to loan defaults and poorly managed financial institutions.

The seventh and final source of RFM problems arises through foreign aid in the form of projects. These projects are often aimed at a target group like small farmers or target inputs like fertilizer. The project typically involves an increase in the amount of funds available to the intermediary to service these targets. It may also include technical assistance and reporting requirements aimed at measuring the progress of the project. These aid activities may lead to a patronal relationship, often through the central bank, between the agricultural lender and the international donor. In this situation, scarce managerial time in these banks is spent cultivating donor and government officials to assure access to loanable funds. This diverts attention from mobilizing savings and encourages managers to think of themselves as retail suppliers of external funds, rather than as mobilizers and allocators of local claims on resources.

This "channeling funds" mentality frequently leads to a planning bias at the expense of utilizing market forces to mobilize and allocate resources. This bias may also incorporate the dubious presumption that managers or technocrats in the capital city have the ability to second-guess hundreds of thousands of rural lenders and borrowers in the allocation of credit and agricultural inputs.

Foreign assistance may reinforce various policies that impede the overall performance of the financial system. For example, a foreign donor may support a credit project in which loans are offered at rates well below commercial rates. The lender may also be required to supply costly loan supervision and to provide reports that are largely useless to managers of the institution. In an agency that has a number of projects with foreign donors, each involving separate accounts and different reporting requirements, the intermediary's information channels may become clogged, increasing lending costs. The required reports often have little effect on the way loans are made. At worst, they seriously limit the ability of bank managers to assemble information that is vital to the operations of the institution, such as lending costs.

Agenda for Reform

The RFM problems pointed out in this volume are so serious, and their causes so deeply rooted, that minor adjustments may not make them perform much more efficiently or equitably. In many countries it will be difficult to realize significant RFM improvements without major reforms: changes in the kinds of information that are collected about RFM activities, changes in policies that affect financial market performance, changes in the makeup of institutions providing financial services in rural areas, and changes in the ways donor agencies interact with these markets.

Reforms will not be possible unless policymakers take a fresh look at the role of financial markets in rural development and carefully test traditional assumptions. Useful reorientation will include a recognition that financial intermediation can have substantial negative, as well as positive, impacts on rural development; that financial intermediaries are mostly decent people; and that most farmers in low-income countries are clever and can quickly learn to benefit from financial intermediation. The present overriding concern over borrower behavior must be redirected to lender behavior, because problems on the supply side of financial transactions are much more pressing than are those on the demand side. Supply problems are also much more susceptible to policy adjustments. Designers of reforms should recognize that financial instruments are highly fungible, that it is very costly to try to control their use, and that market forces have a powerful impact on the allocation of claims on resources, regardless of the policymaker's philosophical orientation or objectives.

Reforms in Information

Information that clearly shows how RFMs work, documents results of policies, and identifies causes of RFM problems is required to alter borrower views. Assembling and distributing appropriate information is an important part of the reform process; in many cases this should be the first step. Better information should lead to better policies and better-managed financial intermediaries.

Four traditional types of information are commonly found in and about RFMs. Three of these are regularly assembled by the intermediary: information to establish the creditworthiness of loan applicants, accounting information about the loan, and data required by the donor or government to show how funds are used. The fourth type of information, often collected by someone other than the intermediary, measures the impact on borrower activities that is attributed to loans. This information is used to justify a credit program, policy, or project.

Several major problems arise with this traditional information. First, there is often too much of it. Large amounts of information are collected via farm plans, lengthy loan applications, and farmer interviews. Little of this information, however, is used in decision making by the borrower, the lender, the government, or the donor agency. Second, much of the traditional information collected cannot be used to adequately address credit-impact or credit-demand issues. For example, it is often assumed that a formal loan is the only source of borrower liquidity, that the loan purpose specified in the application is the only use of liquidity by the household, and that changes in borrower liquidity use are directly correlated with the justification given for the loan in the application. Despite the best of intentions, cause and effect is very difficult to establish with these data.

Third, much of the information that is available is "soft." This results from an emphasis on the quantity of information gathered rather than on its quality. Form filling by officials who do not have direct responsibility for making credit decisions, and who may not feel personally involved in the decision process, can easily produce lax acceptance of approximations and uninformed guesses. Data gathering may also occur without effective quality control. Centralized decision making in many formal lending institutions, complicated by political intrusions, can compromise the integrity of the information process.

Fourth, even though large amounts of relatively weak information about borrowers are collected, there are insufficient data in usable form on the performance of the financial intermediary. Few intermediaries, for example, have information on their costs of servicing various types of clients or have a clear picture of loan-repayment status and data on what costs they impose on those who attempt to use their services. Even fewer intermediaries do benefit-cost analysis on the mounds of information collected, and many are not in a position to produce useful estimates of the costs of a credit program. The operating margins allowed these institutions to service a specified target group are often unrealistically low.

In sum, current practice tends to assemble far too much relatively weak information about borrowers—the demand side—and gives far too little attention to information that is vital to understanding the behavior of intermediaries—the supply side. This distorted information reflects the traditional questions that have been asked about

RFMs. Data describing the overall performance of RFMs are frequently scant and not very useful for addressing issues of policy. Information most useful for policy decisions—often not assembled—includes formal agricultural credit stocks and flows, the term structure of agricultural loans, loan-repayment performance measures, and loan-size distributions. Information is also needed on the nominal and real rates of interest, the amount of voluntary financial savings mobilized by RFMs, and interregional and intersectoral flows of financial claims. Policymakers should also be particularly interested in the changes over time in the ratios of agricultural credit to total credit and the ratios of agricultural credit to the value of agricultural production.

Even the best information does not distribute itself. Most governments need to establish an office in the central bank to assemble and distribute this new information and train professionals to use and interpret these data effectively. Conferences, workshops, and seminars can be very effective ways of introducing more meaningful analysis of RFM performance.

Policy Reforms

Throughout this book it has been argued that incorrect policies, both within and outside rural financial markets, are a major factor in the markets' poor performance. Changing these policies is very high on the reform agenda. The policy change that stands head and shoulders above others in terms of need is interest-rate adjustments. Concessionary interest-rate policies combined with substantial amounts of inflation have resulted in negative real rates of interest in RFMs in most low-income countries over the past decade. Effects of these negative real rates of interest are apparent in these markets. For example, lenders often concentrate cheap loans in the hands of relatively few people, and the rich, not the poor, benefit from cheap credit. Low interest rates also force lenders to rely on government or donor money for loanable funds and make it very difficult for the lender to cover operating costs with interest revenues. Reorganization of agricultural credit agencies has occurred in many cases where their costs exceed revenues.

Maintaining positive real rates of interest on formal loans will be a very important factor in improving the performance of RFMs. Positive real rates of interest also allow the financial intermediary to offer much more attractive incentives for savers. Savings mobilization should be reinforced by changes in rediscount facilities in central banks, as intermediaries cannot be expected to mobilize voluntary savings aggressively if they can get funds at low rates through rediscounts. Adjustments in reserve requirements that discourage banks from promoting savings accounts will also be necessary in some cases.

Changes in policies outside financial markets may also allow RFMs to work better. In many countries pricing policies and public investments are biased against agriculture. Low agricultural prices and yields reduce the expected rates of return on resources bought with loans and reduce the farmers' repayment and savings capacities. This hostile economic environment makes it more difficult to lend, recover loans, and mobilize money. In terms of their relative strength in affecting farmer behavior, product prices rank first, yields second, input prices third, and credit availability and interest rates are a distant fourth. Distortions in product prices or yields cannot be offset by cheap-credit policies, which simply further distort the economic environment. Finally, there is a high opportunity cost to society in using scarce resources for ineffective credit projects. Investment in research and related infrastructure, for example, affects the rate of return to farming in a way that cheap credit cannot.

Reforms in Institutional Development

Many of the specialized agricultural lenders created by governments and donor agencies in the last several decades suffer from poor design. These institutions have been heavily dependent on government and donors for their loanable funds. Put another way, their sources of funds have been highly specialized and subject to political decisions. On the asset side, these institutions have been forced to concentrate their portfolios in very narrow target groups: small farmers, livestock producers, rice farmers, or long-term borrowers. Many of these intermediaries are not allowed to diversify their loan portfolios by having short-, medium-, and long-term loans; by making loans to a broad range of economic activities; or by making some loans outside agriculture. Specialization in both assets and liabilities makes these institutions vulnerable. To get more loanable funds they must subordinate their interests to those of the government or the aid donor. Also their fortunes go up and down dramatically with the profits of the narrow clientele group served. If a strong dose of inflation strikes, lenders with mostly fixed-interest-rate, long-term loans in their portfolios suffer large amounts of erosion in the purchasing power of their assets.

More diversified lenders with multiple sources of loanable funds should be developed. They should also be encouraged to diversify their loan portfolio into long- and short-term loans and to extend loans to entrepreneurs outside narrow target groups. The reform of financial institutions ought to expand access to loan and deposit services in rural areas and make more people creditworthy.

Donor Reforms

Donor activities in RFMs have achieved some objectives. Donor assistance has increased the amounts of formal agricultural credit and the number of institutions providing loans to farmers and of trained people to staff these credit agencies. Donors have also funded much of the research and evaluation done on RFMs, financed a large part of the experimentation that has gone on in these markets over the past 30 years, and helped spread the word about what works, what does not work, and why things do not work better.

Despite these accomplishments, donor activities too often worsen rather than improve the performance of RFMs. Several reforms in the ways donors relate to these markets might lead to substantial improvements. Shifting emphasis from credit projects to RFM sector loans is one possibility for reform. Donors and host countries currently spend too much time and effort preparing credit projects. Any country can increase the amount of local currency available in RFMs by diverting part of any increase in money supply to that use; donor aid in this area is largely balance-of-payment support. Aside from the additional foreign exchange, the main impact of an agricultural credit project is on the policies it reinforces or the policies it helps to change. Policy impact, not volume of funds, is the most important feature of the interaction of donors with agricultural credit systems.

A second reform, closely related to shifts from project to sector lending, is revision of criteria used to measure the performance of credit activities. Traditional credit projects are largely justified by what happens at the borrower level. A shift to a sector focus would require that RFM performance criteria be substituted for farm-level measures. Instead of trying to document how many additional tons of product were produced with loans, attention would be placed on measures of institutional efficiency and savings mobilization. A credit project should not be counted as a success if it undermines the vitality of the lenders, if it is associated with an overall decline in the purchasing power of the RFM loan portfolio, or if it helps to reinforce policies that make the RFM even more dependent on outside funding.

A third reform involves changes in the way donors try to influence policy changes. Policy adjustments should be seen as the outcome of a process rather than merely an event that happens when a loan is negotiated. Changing interest rates and agricultural price policies have implications for the entire economy and may require a good deal of government courage. Those who are damaged by changes advocated by most of the authors in this book are usually well organized and are quick to pressure the government not to make changes. The much larger number who are damaged by not changing policies are in turn usually poorly organized and are those who have a difficult time exerting pressure on decision makers. Donor agencies can be instrumental in helping government officials to ask the right questions, encouraging them to assemble information that will better show the performance of these markets, and providing professional encouragement to government technicians who want to make appropriate policy changes. Critical policy changes require broad support and agreement among government technicians, which takes time to achieve. Donors can help to build that base consensus by supporting detailed RFM sector assessments that involve original research, local technicians, and dissemination of information to local policymakers. Donor agencies have felt it is in their interest to formally train technicians from low-income countries to prepare projects. If policy issues are highly important for the success of donor projects, it might be worthwhile for donors also to emphasize training in policy analysis.

A fourth reform involves the employees of donor agencies. Because most of a donor's activities are expressed in projects, many of the employees in donor agencies are project officers. Although a donor agency may have a number of employees who are qualified to develop and supervise a credit project, it may have very few employees who are capable of assessing the performance of RFMs, diagnosing problems, prescribing treatment, and communicating these analyses to decision makers. Donors will need to hire more technicians who can do policy work to assist implementation of reforms; employee incentives that are currently oriented toward the funding of projects may have to be revised.

Conclusions

We hope that the readers of this volume will conclude that all is not well in rural financial markets in low-income countries, that many of the causes for these problems have been identified, and that treatments for these ills are in hand. Effective reform requires major changes in the way rural financial markets are used in rural development. Dramatic adjustments in the sources of loanable funds used by formal lenders lie at the heart of these changes. RFMs would perform much better if they mobilized a large part of their funds from voluntary rural savers. Money from donors and governments is a very poor substitute for funds that are locally mobilized. Savings mobilization would help reduce repayment problems, help keep politics out of RFM operations, force financial intermediaries to behave in a more businesslike manner, and provide a valuable service to rural savers. The largest contribution of RFMs to rural development ought to be savings mobilization, not the dispensing of large amounts of cheap credit.

Another key element in the new strategy for RFMs is to reduce the costs of financial intermediation for both the lender and borrower. Lender and borrower loan-transaction costs should decline with better incentives to seek more efficient ways of making loans; the imposition of high loan-transaction costs on some borrowers is the result of credit rationing by the lender. Eliminating the chronic, widespread excess demand for cheap credit will be a key element in inducing lenders to innovate and reduce these costs.

How can this excess demand be eliminated and rural households be given inducements to hold a much larger part of their savings in formal financial institutions? We feel that adjustments in interest-rate policies must be the cornerstone of policies aimed at these objectives. Positive real rates of interest would force many large borrowers of formal loans to reduce the amount they use and cause lenders to seek new customers, including small- to medium-sized farmers and nonfarm rural enterprises. Instead of devising ways to discourage people from borrowing, lenders would streamline their procedures so that more clients would want loans. The price of loans, largely represented in interest rates, would ration credit in place of artificially imposed borrower loan-transaction costs. The positive real rates of interest would also give potential savers incentives to hold more of their assets in financial form and give lenders a better chance of covering their costs.

Stimulating voluntary savings, reducing the costs of financial intermediation, and maintaining positive real rates of interest in rural financial markets will not cure all of the ills currently found there. Rural financial market reforms are necessary, but perhaps not both necessary and sufficient, to guarantee effective rural development. Complementary policies that improve the rate of return to farming are also needed. RFM policy changes, however, are critical to set in action forces that will make many problems in rural financial markets much more tractable and that will enhance the prospects for more efficient and equitable rural development.

About the Contributors

Dale W Adams is Professor of Agricultural Economics at The Ohio State University. He was born in Utah and attended Utah State and Michigan State universities. He has been a staff economist with the Agency for International Development and a visiting professor at Stanford University. Since the mid-1960s he has done research on rural financial markets in low-income countries under grants and contracts with the Agency for International Development.

Adelaida P. Alicbusan is a Ph.D. candidate at The Ohio State University. She received a Masters degree in agricultural economics from the University of Delaware and a B.S. in agriculture from the University of the Philippines. She has worked for several years as a senior research assistant at the University of the Philippines, Los Baños.

Harry W. Blair is Associate Professor of Political Science at Bucknell University. Born in Washington, D.C., he was trained at Cornell and Duke universities. During 1981-1982 he was on leave from Bucknell, serving as a social analyst with the Office of Rural Development, Bureau of Science and Technology, Agency for International Development, in Washington, D.C.

Frits J. A. Bouman is lecturer at the Agricultural University of Wageningen in the Netherlands. Born in Indonesia, he took his professional training as a sociologist at the University of Nijmegen, the Netherlands. He lectures on agricultural credit and cooperatives at Wageningen.

Compton Bourne is Professor of Economics at the University of the West Indies. He was born in Guyana and attended the Universities of London, Birmingham, and the West Indies. He has taught at the University of the West Indies in both Jamaica and Trinidad since 1969 and was a visiting professor at The Ohio State University.

Carlos E. Cuevas is a Research Associate with The Ohio State University. He was born in Chile and did his graduate work at the Catholic University of Chile and at The Ohio State University.

Cristina C. David was born in the Philippines and is an economist with the International Rice Research Institute. She did graduate work at the School of Economics in the University of the Philippines and at Stanford University. She has been a visiting scholar at The Ohio State University.

Robert E. Firestine is an economist with the Agency for International Development, Washington, D.C. A native of New York State, he attended Rensselaer Polytechnic Institute and Syracuse University. He has taught economics at the University of Florida, Syracuse University, and the University of Texas at Dallas and as a Fulbright Professor at the American University in Cairo.

Claudio Gonzalez-Vega is Professor of Agricultural Economics at The Ohio State University. He was born in Costa Rica, attended the University of Costa Rica, the University of London, and Stanford University, and was on the economics staff at the University of Costa Rica.

Douglas H. Graham attended Yale, Johns Hopkins, and Harvard universities. From 1966 to 1973 he was associated with the Department of Economics, Vanderbilt University, and was director of their Graduate Economics Program in Brazil. From 1973 to the present he has been director of the Latin American Studies Program and from 1979 onward professor of agricultural economics at The Ohio State University.

Edward J. Kane occupies the Everett D. Reese Chair of Banking and Monetary Economics at The Ohio State University. Previously he taught at Boston College, Princeton University, and Iowa State University and held visiting professorships at Istanbul University and Simon Fraser University. Born in Washington, D.C., he received degrees from Georgetown University and the Massachusetts Institute of Technology.

Peter Kilby was born in Buffalo, New York, and educated at Harvard, Johns Hopkins, and Oxford. He is Professor of Economics at Wesleyan University in Connecticut. He has served as fellow, adviser, or consultant with the Development Centre of the Organisation for Economic Cooperation and Development, the East-West Center, the International Labour Organization, the World Bank, Harvard's Institute of International Development, the Agency for International Development, and the Ciskei Commission.

Jerry R. Ladman is Professor of Economics and Director of the Center for Latin American Studies at Arizona State University. He was born in Iowa and did his graduate work at Iowa State University. He was also a visiting scholar at Stanford University and The Ohio State University.

Donald W. Larson is Professor of Agricultural Economics at The Ohio State University. Born in Minnesota, he received degrees from South Dakota State University and Michigan State University. Before joining The Ohio State University in 1970, he was a faculty member at Michigan State University.

Carl E. Liedholm is a Professor of Economics and Director of the Off-Farm Employment Project at Michigan State University. He was acting director of the Economic Development Institute at the University of Nigeria in the mid-1960s, served as chairman of Michigan State University's Economics Department from 1969 to 1974, and was a visiting fellow at Sussex University's Institute of Development Studies, England, and at Yale's Economic Growth Center.

Richard L. Meyer is Professor of Agricultural Economics and Director of International Programs at The Ohio State University. He received degrees from the University of Minnesota and Cornell University. He worked with the Federal Land Bank Association in Minnesota, was a Peace Corps volunteer in Chile, and a Peace Corps staff member in Washington, D.C.

Edward John Ray is Professor and Chairman of Economics at The Ohio State University. He completed his graduate work at Stanford University and also attended Queens College of the City University of New York.

João Sayad is Professor of Economics at the University of São Paulo, Brazil, where he has taught since 1968. He was born in São Paulo, Brazil, and attended the University of São Paulo and Yale University.

Robert C. Vogel is Professor of Economics at University of Miami and Visiting Professor of Agricultural Economics at The Ohio State University. His degrees are from Amherst College and Stanford University. He has previously been a faculty member at Wesleyan University, Southern Illinois University, the University of Florida, and Syracuse University, and he has also served as a senior staff economist on the President's Council of Economic Advisers.

J. D. Von Pischke is a senior financial analyst in the World Bank. He joined the bank in 1976, following several years of consulting work. He obtained degrees from the University of Glasgow, Columbia University, and the College of Wooster in Ohio. His professional experience also includes lecturing at the College of Business Administration at Haile Sellassie I University in Ethiopia and commercial banking in New York, London, and Monrovia.

Index

www.ingramcontent.com/pod-product-compliance
Lightning Source LLC
LaVergne TN
LVHW011112300926
849160LV00008B/361